THOMAS NORTON'S
ORDINAL OF ALCHEMY

EARLY ENGLISH TEXT SOCIETY

No. 272

1975

British Museum MS. Add. 10302, f. 37.

THOMAS NORTON'S
ORDINAL OF ALCHEMY

EDITED BY

JOHN REIDY

Published for
THE EARLY ENGLISH TEXT SOCIETY
by the
OXFORD UNIVERSITY PRESS
LONDON   NEW YORK   TORONTO
1975

© *Early English Text Society*

*Printed in Great Britain
at the University Press, Oxford
by Vivian Ridler
Printer to the University*

PREFACE

THIS work was originally undertaken at the suggestion of Professor Sherman M. Kuhn, Editor-in-Chief of the Middle English Dictionary, and he, together with the Editor emeritus, Hans Kurath, has consistently encouraged and advised me in my work.

The two main manuscripts of this edition are in the British Museum, and I am indebted to the Trustees for permission to publish, to reproduce the two facsimiles, and to quote from manuscripts in their charge. For permission to quote from other manuscripts I am also obliged to the Marquess of Bath, the authorities of the Bodleian Library, and of the libraries of Edinburgh University, and Trinity College, Cambridge, and the Wellcome Historical Medical Library. The Massachusetts Historical Society kindly allowed me to examine their manuscript of the *Ordinal*, and the Editor of *Ambix* has given permission to use some material originally published in that journal.

I wish to thank Mr. T. C. Skeat, Keeper of Manuscripts at the British Museum, and Mr. R. W. Hunt, Keeper of Western Manuscripts at the Bodleian Library, for help in dating manuscripts and for answering several queries; Mr. N. R. Ker and Dr. Emma Mellencamp for their opinions on the main manuscript; the staffs of the libraries in which I worked, especially the Bodleian and the Students' Room and Manuscript Room at the British Museum, and not least Miss Dorothy Coates, formerly librarian at Longleat House.

I am grateful to members of the council of the Early English Text Society for their many suggested revisions and improvements, especially to Professor Norman Davis and Mr. R. W. Burchfield for their encouragement and Dr. P. O. E. Gradon for her editorial corrections. Finally, I owe a great deal to the help of my wife during the early stages of the research on this project.

The cost of visiting libraries in the United Kingdom, obtaining photographs, and other research expenses has been met in part by grants from the Canada Council and the Rackham Fund of the University of Michigan.

CONTENTS

*These plates are reproduced by kind permission of the Trustees of the
British Museum*

INTRODUCTION

MANUSCRIPTS

THE thirty-one known manuscripts of *The Ordinal of Alchemy* are listed here, the Brown–Robbins *Index* numbers being given in parentheses:

1. (1) Oxford, Bodleian MS. E Mus. 63 (S.C. 3652), ff. 2^r–40^r.
2. (2) ,, ,, MS. Ashmole 57 (S.C. 6938), ff. 1^r–end.
3. (3) ,, ,, ,, ,, 1441 (S.C. 7624), p. 79 (last 12 lines).
4. (4) ,, ,, ,, ,, 1451 (S.C. 7629), ff. 2^v, 9^v–11 (extracts only).
5. (5) ,, ,, ,, ,, 1445 (S.C. 7630), pp. 1–4, 7–96.
6. (6) ,, ,, ,, ,, 1464 (S.C. 7635), ff. 1–3, 4^v–44^v.
7. (8) ,, ,, ,, ,, 1479 (S.C. 7643), ff. 254–98^v.
8. (9) ,, ,, ,, ,, 1490 (S.C. 7655), ff. 277–89.
9. (10) Cambridge, Trinity College MS. 910, ff. 3–75^v.
10. (11) ,, ,, ,, MS. 1119, ff. 1–49^v.
11. (12) ,, ,, ,, MS. 1269, ff. 1^r–end.
12. (13) British Museum MS. Harley 853, ff. 26^v–65^r.
13. (14) ,, ,, MS. Royal 18 B. XXIV, ff. 79^r–138^v.
14. (15) ,, ,, MS. Add. 10302, ff. 1–67 end.
15. ,, ,, MS. Sloane 1198, ff. 1–39^v.
16. ,, ,, ,, ,, 1751, ff. 18–72^v.
17. ,, ,, ,, ,, 1873, ff. 3^r–84^r.
18. ,, ,, ,, ,, 2174, ff. 89–116^v.
19. ,, ,, ,, ,, 2174, ff. 117^r–139^v.
20. ,, ,, ,, ,, 2532, ff. 1–50^r.
21. ,, ,, ,, ,, 3580B, ff. 60^v–118^v.
22. ,, ,, ,, ,, 2036, ff. 30–6^v (extracts from Chapters III, VI, VII).
23. (16) Clifton College Library.
24. (17) Lincoln's Inn MS. Hale 84, f. 1^r–end.
25. (18) Longleat MS. 178, ff. 10^v–49^r.
26. (19) *olim* Petworth MS. 103.
27. Dublin, Trinity College MS. 684, ff. 1^r–end.
28. Edinburgh, University Library MS. Laing III 164, pp. 129–227.
29. Massachusetts Historical Society MS. Winthrop 20C, ff. 29^r–65^v.
30. Wellcome Historical Medical Library MS. 580, pp. 1–end.
31. Finch-Hatton MS. 323, ff. 1^r–63^r.

Apart from the eighteen of these listed in the Brown–Robbins *Index* (item 3772), Robbins lists numbers 15, 17, 18, 20, 21, 27,

29, 30 in his 1966 article.¹ So far as I know numbers 16, 19, 22, and 28 have not been noted before. In the Brown–Robbins *Index* there is one mistake; their item number 7 should be deleted.² In the Robbins article in *Ambix* there is a mistake in connection with number 4, MS. Ashmole 1451; the *Summary Catalogue* number is given as 8343, whereas it should be 7629, as in the *Index*.³ For the purposes of this edition I have based my text on the two earliest manuscripts, namely Add. 10302 and, where that is defective, Sloane 1873. I have given variant readings from five others. These seven appear to be the earliest (all but one are probably of the first half of the sixteenth century or earlier), and the five used for variant readings represent major groupings among the manuscripts. I have examined all the manuscripts with three exceptions: the CliftonCollege Library manuscript, which is missing, the Petworth, which was sold in 1928 and cannot be traced, and the Finch-Hatton. Apart from the seven used for this edition all but two of the rest are late-sixteenth- and seventeenth-century versions, and their complete collation has on only one occasion been helpful in restoring a lost reading. Cambridge, Trinity College MS. 910 appears to be mid-century or a little later, but is so closely linked in text with Bodleian MS. E Mus. 63 that I have rarely used it, and then only to show this close connection. Bodleian MS. Ashmole 1479 is of 1565, copied by Richard Walton; it forms part of a group with MS. Sloane 1198 (S) and has some wildly aberrant readings of its own. Descriptions of the seven early manuscripts follow.

A. *London, B.M. MS. Add. 10302*

A leather-bound vellum manuscript, 67 folios, about $5 \cdot 7$ in. $\times 4 \cdot 4$ in., containing the *Ordinal of Alchemy* to the end of Chapter V

---

¹ Rossell Hope Robbins, 'Alchemical Texts in Middle English Verse: Corrigenda and Addenda', *Ambix*, xiii (June 1966), 62–73.

² The error is due to a confusion of S.C. 7624 (Ashmole 1441) with S.C. 7642 (Ashmole 1478); the former has the last twelve lines on p. 79, and a translation of the Latin Preface on pp. 81–2; the latter has the translation also, f. 90ʳ⁻ᵛ as well as the words of the Angel, Master, and Disciple in the illumination at the beginning of Chapter I, but no part of the text of the poem. The item has been omitted in the *Supplement*.

³ S.C. 8343 refers to MS. Ashmole 1451, i, p. 113 (Recipt); [misprinted in the *Summary Catalogue* as (VIII) (Receipts)]. The error has been repeated in the *Supplement* to Brown–Robbins, which is also wrong in altering the S.C. number for MS. Ashmole 1490 from 7655 to 7010.

(i.e. Preface and 1–2682), except for a gap of 120 lines (2503–2622). An older foliation ignores f. 1 and runs from 1 to 66. The gatherings are: one of 9 folios, seven of 8 folios, and one of 2 folios; f. 1 is stuck to a slip (? vellum on paper) which can just be seen between ff. 9 and 10. The gathering containing ff. 58–65 has been wrongly bound, and should follow f. 41.[1] Presumably the three folios[2] representing the gap of 120 lines were originally the beginning of the last gathering, of which the extant ff. 66–7 (containing 2623–82) formed the central sheet. Since the last two Chapters, VI and VII, contain 420 lines, and would thus require eleven folios, three following f. 67 and a final eight probably completed the original manuscript. This would still allow one side for the picture of furnaces referred to at 2842, 2860, and now stuck to f. 1ʳ.

The text is written within a marked border, measuring about 3·7 in. × 2·7 in., the guiding lines being carefully marked and well observed on the whole. Outside the border the margins are about 0·4 in. (top), 1·6 in. (bottom), 1·3 in. (outer), and 0·3 in. (inner). The space between the end of each written line and the border is filled by two ornamental lines of different colours. The two lines forming each rhyming couplet have the same colour combination, the next couplet a different combination. However, only four colours—green, red, blue, and purple—are used, and only two combinations on any one page, the combinations thus alternating from couplet to couplet. The illuminator must have worked on the unbound sheets, because the combinations are identical on matching folios, e.g. 2ʳ and 9ᵛ, 2ᵛ and 9ʳ, etc.

Except for the Latin Preface of forty lines in double column, each full page of writing contains twenty lines, while on f. 32ᵛ six lines and on f. 37ᵛ two lines have been included inside the gold border at the top of the illuminations. Four important lines in the Latin Preface and the Latin lines 1174 and those following 699 are in gold, with some rubbed off to show a white base beneath. Apart from these and initial capitals the rest of the text is in an ink which has faded mostly to a light brown, though some passages remain dark (e.g. the last four lines of f. 35ᵛ, 1317–20), and some

---

[1] Dorothea Waley Singer, in her *Catalogue of . . . Alchemical Manuscripts . . .* (3 vols. Brussels, 1928–31), ii. 557, gives the correct order of the leaves.

[2] Singer (ibid.) incorrectly states that two leaves are missing between 59 and 60.

lines seem to have been gone over in dark ink (e.g. f. 32^r, l. 7, 1185). The coloured ornamental lines sometimes show through, as do the illuminations and ornamental work. The colours on f. 6^v have blotted on to f. 7^r. These and an occasional 'Nota' in the margin are the only marks on the manuscript, which is consequently very legible.

There are six illuminations, of which five are full page or nearly so. The first, on f. 1^r, shows seven furnaces with stills, and two servants tending them. The second, on f. 6^v facing Chapter I, shows a kneeling pupil—a fair-haired figure with rather distinctive features who reappears in subsequent illuminations and perhaps represents the author, Norton—receiving a sealed book from his master while angels look down and comment from above. The third, at the bottom of f. 19^v, shows a kneeling figure saying the Latin prayer which constitutes the last two lines of the page. The fourth, on f. 32^v opposite Chapter IV, shows two servants pounding with mortar and pestle, a third tending a fire, while in the centre the fair-haired figure previously mentioned stirs a pot; from above four heads, labelled Geberus, Arnaldus, Rasis, and Hermes look down and comment. The fifth is on f. 37^v opposite Chapter V, and shows two servants tending furnaces and the Norton figure seated at a table with a balance. John Read in his *Prelude to Chemistry* says that this 'is possibly the earliest representation of a balance in a case'.[1] The last, on f. 67^v, shows astrological figures suitable for the different stages in the preparation of the Philosophers' Stone. The five full-page illuminations all have gold borders surrounded by a floral design.

In addition to these, the Preface, Proem, and all five chapters begin with illuminated capitals, two, three, or four lines deep, and a floral design along two sides of the page. Chapter headings are in gold, and subsections within the chapters begin with gold capitals.

The lines begin with capital letters, usually distinguishable without difficulty from the corresponding small forms, except for *w*, *v* and *y*. The ȝ appears rarely, the þ frequently and almost never confused with *y*. The *y*, consonantal or vocalic, is sometimes dotted or marked with an oblique line, but quite inconsistently. The usual abbreviations occur frequently, and in addition a raised dot is used—especially after *ll* and *d*—to indicate final *e*, as is also a line

[1] London, 1936, Plate 34, facing p. 179.

after *h* and even above *n* or *m* when there seems little likelihood that a second *n* or *m* is intended. See, e.g., *crowne* (303) where the rhyme word *downe* is spelled out, and cf. *stone, gone* (1075-6). The dot is also used twice to indicate a missing *u* in *multiplicacioun* (402) and *substance* (2146). In expanding suspension marks I have tried to conform the spelling *-er, -ir,* etc. to that common in the spelled-out forms 'growynge faste by'.

There are a number of corrections to the text by another hand (or hands) than that of the original scribe. These are mostly insertions of words or letters above, accompanied by a caret mark. Occasionally there are erasures, e.g. *don* (?) erased in 543, and the last letter and suspension mark of *vnctouus* (2131) have been written over an erasure. Insertions, corrections, and erasures are all listed in the textual notes.

The manuscript is described as fifteenth century in the catalogue, and Mr. T. C. Skeat, Keeper of Manuscripts at the British Museum, concurs that 'late fifteenth century' is probable. The ivy leaves of the ornamentation and the architectural styles in the illuminations support a fifteenth-century date.

Dr. Emma H. Mellencamp, Fine Arts Librarian at the University of Michigan, has very kindly given me her opinion on the date of the illuminations. She places them between 1480 and 1490 on the basis most specifically of the costume fashions, but also of the general impression of the painting techniques and spatial structure, all of which place the manuscript, in her opinion, at least a decade before the end of the fifteenth century. In particular the kneeling figure in f. 6ᵛ and the seated figure in f. 37ᵛ (the author alchemist, it seems, in each case), is wearing a *paltock* or *pourpoint*, visible only in the sleeves and lacing across the chest. The lacings were necessary to hold the garment on properly; it was cut in such a wide V in front that it exposed a great deal of the shirt, and had to be firmly laced across to prevent the sleeves pulling it off the shoulders. This type of *pourpoint* appeared in the early 1480s. Very similar garments may be seen in the Dürer self-portrait in the Louvre, 1493,[1] and especially in the group at the extreme left of the panel 'Arrival of the English ambassadors at the court of Maurus' in the St. Ursula Legend of Vittore Carpaccio, 1491-5. The panel is an early one, so that the fashions are those of the

[1] See E. Panofsky, *The Life and Art of Albrecht Dürer* (Princeton, 4th edn. 1955), p. 25.

late 1480s. Furthermore the puffed sleeve of the assistant to the left in f. 1^r is a fashion of the 1480s; it did not appear in the 1470s, and in the 1490s would have been more exaggerated.

Nothing is known of this manuscript before its being owned by Richard Heber (1773–1833), at the sale of whose library it was purchased for the British Museum in 1836.[1] It seems to have been a presentation copy intended for some important person, possibly a prospective patron. Elias Ashmole, who printed the work in *Theatrum Chemicum Britannicum*, 1652, describes a similar manuscript lent him by a gentleman which he used as a basis for his text. He says it had illuminations 'better work then that which was *Henry the seaventh's* own *Booke* (as I am informed by those that have seene both)'.[2] From these illuminations he had the engravings made for his edition, and they must have been almost identical with those of our present manuscript. A slight difference existed, however, for Ashmole speaks of ornamentation of 'Flowers, Birds and Beasts',[2] and of the Nevilles' coat of arms; the present manuscript has only flowers and no coat of arms. Neither can this manuscript be Henry VII's own book, or we should know more of its history. None the less we have the interesting case of three almost contemporary presentation copies with almost identical illuminations.

B. *Oxford Bodleian MS. E Mus. 63 (S.C. 3652)*

This consists of two paper manuscripts, about 12½ in. × 8½ in., of which the first (i. 69 ff.) contains:

> The Ordinal of Alchemy—ff. 2^r–40^r;
> The Compend of Alchemy—ff. 41^r–65^r;
> Verbum Secretorum Hermetis—f. 66;
> An alchemical poem, 'Of Spayne take the clere light'—ff. 67–9.

The first two items are in the same secretary hand, the third and fourth in another hand. There are nine gatherings as follows: two of 9 (i–17), a 7, two of 8, a 9, two of 8, and a 4. Leaves not included in the foliation are missing, two after f. 2, one after f. 23, one before f. 41, one before f. 66, and three after f. 69.

The text of the *Ordinal* is complete except for sporadic omission of single lines with a blank space left in each case, and two omis-

---

[1] *Bibliotheca Heberiana*, 12 Parts (London, 1834–6) Part 11, Lot 1191.
[2] p. 455.

sions without a gap, of six and two lines respectively. There is no ornamentation and no attempt to reproduce the illuminations; the wording only of that at the end of the Proem is recorded without explanation. The text is written 40 to 44 lines to a page with very few corrections, all but two by the scribe. For chapter headings and certain Latin lines the scribe shifted from secretary to Italian hand. There is much marginal annotation by different readers or owners of the sixteenth century, including John Dee and John Gwynn. The whole effect is one of utility, not beauty.

R. W. Hunt, Keeper of Western Manuscripts at the Bodleian, dates this in the first half of the sixteenth century, perhaps the second quarter. This latter suggestion accords with the water-mark—a glove and star very similar to Heawood 2521 (1544–6) or Heawood 2500 (1537).[1] It cannot, however, be placed much after 1550, for its earliest known owner, W. Typsell, who owned it about 1550 according to the *Summary Catalogue*, recorded on the fly-leaf an event of 15 September 1559. The date of '? *c*. 1500' given in the *M.E.D. Plan and Bibliography* is too early.

E. *Edinburgh, University Library MS. Laing III 164*

A paper manuscript about $8\frac{1}{4}$ in. $\times 5\frac{3}{4}$ in., provided with a parchment sheet for binding, 116 folios paginated 1–232. It contains:

Half an incomplete diagram of an alchemical/astrological scheme, the *Celum Philosophorum*, p. 2;
The Compend of Alchemy, with notes, pp. 3–122;
The second half of the diagram of p. 2, p. 123;
Short treatise on Qualities, pp. 125–8;
The Ordinal of Alchemy, pp. 129–227;
Scattered lines from *The Ordinal*, p. 229;
Arithmetical jottings, pp. 230–2.

The *Compend* appears to be bound within the incomplete diagram in seven gatherings of 8 and one of 4. There follows a single sheet of much older paper folded over to form 4 pp. 125–8. Then four gatherings of 14, 12, 12, and 14 complete the manuscript.

The Ordinal of Alchemy is complete except for a few missing lines and is written in a single hand with no ornamentation and no reference to the illuminations. The Latin Preface is placed at the

[1] Edward Heawood, *Watermarks Mainly of the 17th and 18th centuries*, Hilversum, 1950. (This is vol. i of *Monumenta Chartæ Papyraceæ Historiam Illustrantia*, general editor E.-J. Labarre.)

end on pp. 225 and 227. The scribe seems to have written rapidly
and made a number of corrections, including the writing in the
margin of missed lines. A late-sixteenth- or early-seventeenth-
century corrector added corrections as far as l. 1266, using a
manuscript similar to, but not identical with, Bodleian MS.
Ashmole 1490 (S.C. 7010), copied by Simon Foreman in 1588.
This is one of a group represented in the variants in this edition
by R, but containing unusual and often foolish readings. This
corrector also wrote an English translation of the Latin Preface
after the end of the English text, p. 224, English chapter headings
up to Chapter III, and some side notes. He also rewrote the first
syllables of the first words of the Proem and Chapters I–III, forming the words Tomas Norton, indicating that he knew part of the
anagram formed by the initial syllables. A second, heavy-handed,
corrector altered spellings and expanded suspensions on the first
page only, appearing no more after l. 24 except to write 'of ye
Ordinall of Alchymy' after the first corrector's 'The first chapter',
p. 137, just as he had added 'to ye Ordinall of Alchymy' under
Prohemium, p. 129.

The hand of the text is a rather ugly secretary hand of about the
same date as B. The watermark of pp. 129–232 is a glove and
flower with a 3-like figure in the palm and a fleur-de-lis at the
wrist, similar to Heawood 2497 (1541) or Briquet 11370 (1545).
The earlier part, pp. 1–124, also has a glove and flower, practically
identical with Heawood 2495 (1531). The older sheet, constituting
pp. 125–8, has a crossed cannon watermark very similar to Briquet
5723 (1497–1502); the four of this general type in Briquet, 5721–4,
are from 1486 to 1502.

The manuscript had associations with Suffolk in the sixteenth
century. On the inside of the front cover are written the place-
names Harwych, Walderswyke (Walberswick), Sowold (? South-
wold), Caston Hauen, Keslonde (? Kessingland), Pakefelde,
Kyrkley, Leystofte (Lowestoft), Corton, Gorleston. Also on the
inside front cover is the signature Robert Olyuer; the Olivers of
Sudbury were a Suffolk family, and a Robert Oliver was engaged
in a lawsuit with Elizabeth Quodington in 1569, and either he or
a younger namesake received a grant of land in Onesden in 1606–7.
On p. 104 is the couplet:

> Thys boke in treuthe ys evyn thus
> Longe and perteyne to James Bushe.

The Busshe family was of Mendlesham, but I cannot find a James among them. Two other names, John Someres and John Symson appear on p. 232, but I cannot trace family or other connections among these owners of (or at least writers in) the manuscript.

R. *British Museum MS. Royal 18 B. XXIV*

For description see the *Catalogue*.[1]

A paper manuscript about 12·2 in. × 8·5 in. in a sixteenth-century hand, containing four items of which the *Ordinal* is the third. It is complete except for the Latin Preface, together with descriptions of three of the illuminations, including the master and disciple and the master with a balance, at the appropriate places before Chapters I and V respectively. At the end of the *Ordinal* is a list of 'Authors Recited in this booke' which includes Ripley, presumably on the assumption that he was Norton's master.

The *Ordinal* occupies ff. 79^r–139^r (including the list of Authors), and is headed in the hand of the text 'Thoms nortō of Alchymy'. Another hand has inserted 'Ordinall' above before 'of' with a caret mark. As the *Catalogue* points out, items 2 and 3 are on the same paper in the same hand. Item 2 is the first book of Ascham's *The Scholemaster* which was begun in 1563, and the *Catalogue* adds: 'but the MS. text includes references (e.g. at f. 73, to the Lord Mayor, Sir Thomas Lodge, "even this last yere," viz. 1561–2) which agree with the date named, and this accords roughly with the water mark of the paper.' The watermark is the same as Briquet 2867 (1562). Walter Haddon's verses on Norton are written on f. 79^v; these were not published till 1567, but may have been known before this date.

S. *British Museum MS. Sloane 1198*

A paper manuscript about 11·6 in. × 7·5–8·2 in., containing 131 folios. The first part, ff. 1–39 containing the *Ordinal* was apparently once separate, being an older paper. F. 40^r is numbered 2, and ff. 40–132 contain first some fencing instructions in French (f. 40^r) and then French and Latin alchemical notes of the late sixteenth and seventeenth centuries on paper with different watermarks of contemporary types. On f. 43^r is written 'Liber datus erat Tho: Chaliner militi . . . Anno do: 1597 mense Septembri', and f. 42^v

[1] Sir George F. Warner and Julius P. Gilson, *Catalogue of the Western Manuscripts in the Old Royal and King's Collection* (4 vols. London, 1921), ii. 297.

C 9205 b

contains a recipe attributed to 'Henry Conrath', i.e. Heinrich Khunrath, 1560–1605.

As to the *Ordinal*, ff. 1–7^v, representing ll. 1–522, is in a late-sixteenth-century hand, apparently a sixteenth-century replacement of a lost beginning. The paper of this section has a watermark, a bunch of grapes, very similar to Briquet 13074 (1587) or Heawood 2094 (? *c.* 1590). Moreover, there are six ruled empty lines at the bottom of f. 7^v, and 8^r begins in an earlier hand with l. 519; the later writer overran by four lines before realizing his mistake. The rest of the *Ordinal*, ff. 8–39 is in a mid-sixteenth-century hand, and the hand-and-flower watermark in this section is very similar to Briquet 11383 (1537), less similar to Heawood 2514 (before 1560) or 2541 (after 1547). The character of the writing changes on f. 19^r with the beginning of Chapter V, but my impression is that we have the same scribe as before, but taking more room—thirty-six instead of forty lines to a page—and writing more neatly and carefully. I take the date, therefore, of ff. 8–39 as of the mid-sixteenth century.[1]

The first twelve folios and ff. 37–9 are edged with modern paper for binding, and I cannot see whether ff. 13–14 and 35–6 are so as well. Ff. 15–34 are one gathering. There are no marks on ff. 1–39 which might give evidence of who wrote or owned this manuscript in its original state; the writing of ff. 1–7 is not obviously similar to anything after f. 39.

S$_2$. *British Museum MS. Sloane 2174 (second version)*

This is a paper manuscript of 140 folios, about 11·9–12·1 in. × 7·8 in. It has been extensively rebound on modern paper, and only the following may be original gatherings: ff. 19–32, 50–4, 80–5, 96–109, 120–37.

The first part, ff. 1–116, contains alchemical works including the *Compend* (incomplete), ff. 73^v–85^v, and the *Ordinal*, complete, ff. 89^r–116^v. This is all in seventeenth-century hands on paper with a crowned jug type of watermark common in the late sixteenth and early seventeenth century. The nearest equivalent I can find is Heawood 3584 (1624).

The remainder of the manuscript, ff. 117–40, contains an earlier version of the *Ordinal* lacking the beginning, lines 1–468, and so

[1] Robbins (*Ambix*, xiii (1966), 66) gives this manuscript as seventeenth century; ff. 1–7 may be so late, but not the bulk of the *Ordinal*.

not hitherto recognized. It is headed 'An Ancient book of Alchymy
/ in Verse?' The order of folios is correct except that ff. 128 and
129 are reversed. There is a gap of 394 lines after f. 129, corresponding to lines 1271–1664 of the present edition. Most of f. 140 has
disappeared, but enough is left to see the beginnings of lines 2619
et seq., so that Chapter V must have ended on f. 140ᵛ. Chapters VI
and VII are missing. The top outside corners of the leaves are
worn away, but on f. 125ʳ an old numbering becomes visible;
ff. 125–7 are 16–18, f. 129 is 19 (the correct sequence), and there
follows a gap of six (enough for the 394 missing lines); then follows
f. 130 numbered 27, so that f. 128 must have been 26. The numbering continues visible to f. 139 (36). It is clear from this that the
Ordinal in this version originally began on a f. 1, since seven
folios would have been needed for the missing 468 lines at the
beginning.

This section, ff. 117–39, is in a hand of the first half or middle
of the sixteenth century, on paper with a watermark of the glove
and flower type, IR at the wrist, and a 3 (reversed) at the palm, a
type which runs in Briquet from 1526 on. The closest equivalent,
though not very clear, is Briquet 11376 (1562). The writing is clear
and careful, but there are some corrections and numerous under-
linings and side notes in the same hand; no other hand appears.
The scribe's signature, Thomas Cowtre, appears upside down in
the bottom margin of f. 134ᵛ.

S₃. *British Museum MS. Sloane 1873*

A leather-bound manuscript of 85 folios, the first and last parchment 7 in. × 5 in., the remainder paper, about 7¼ in. × 5 in. except
for three: f. 9, 4⅞ in. × 2⅝ in., f. 35, 5½ in. × 3⅞ in., and f. 41,
5⅝ in. × 3¼ in. This last is pasted along the top to the top of f. 42,
and though the other two odd leaves are bound into their respec-
tive gatherings, they too were probably once pasted to neighbour-
ing leaves. The discoloration along the binding edge of f. 8ᵛ is
consistent with this view, but visual indications are uncertain in
the case of f. 35. The gatherings are: one of 10, three 8s, a 10,
four 8s, and a 9. The outside parchment leaves, which contain
Latin prose in a fifteenth-century book-hand, have been bound in
with the first and tenth gathering, the cut-off edges being visible
after f. 10 and before f. 77 respectively. These were evidently cut
from an old book to serve as covers. F. 9 is bound in extra to the

first gathering, the cut-off edge being visible between ff. 2 and 3; similarly f. 35 is extra to the original fifth gathering, appearing cut off after f. 44. It appears that the original paper manuscript was in ten gatherings of 8.

This conjecture is confirmed by the contents. The *Ordinal*, written neatly in black ink in a book-hand of the first half of the sixteenth century, begins on f. 3ʳ with the Latin Preface, and runs through to f. 84ʳ if we leave out of account the three inserted leaves, ff. 9, 35, and 41. Someone in the latter part of the sixteenth century has written in ink that is now brown some alchemical titles on f. 1ᵛ at the bottom of the Latin, four short pieces of verse on f. 2ʳ, Walter Haddon's verses on Norton—titled 'Gualteri Haddonis carmen in Laudem / Thomae Nortoni'—on f. 84ᵛ, and descriptions of three of the illuminations on the three inserted slips. This writer used mostly a secretary hand, but occasionally an Italian hand, as the Haddon verses and certain passages in the descriptions. In addition a number of marginal notes and drawings of pointing hands throughout appear to be by him; certainly the ink is the same. The last of the four pieces of verse on f. 2, a couplet: 'For Bacon I long whom long I haue sought / Beg borrow or stele hym yf he may not be bought', is on a small piece of parchment stuck to the paper. The indications are that this writer owned the manuscript in an unbound state, provided the parchment covers and accounts of the illuminations, and wrote on the two original fly-leaves, ff. 2ʳ and 84ᵛ.

The *Ordinal* is very clearly and neatly written, twenty lines to a page with no ornament except some not very elaborate capitals; especially in the later chapters these capitals were never put into the vacant spaces left for them. There are very few corrections, and these have been made by the original scribe. The scribe wrote the chapter numbers—viz. Ca.i., Ca.ii., Ca. 3., etc.—at the head of each chapter and on the recto of each folio. He erred at first, calling the Proem Ca.i. until f. 18, the end of Chapter I, but is correct thereafter. The only indication that he knew of illuminations is a note at the end of Chapter V, f. 73ᵛ: 'The figure shuld stonde before ye vj. Chapter folowyng', a reference probably to the astrological figure, f. 67ᵛ in A. It is interesting that twenty misplaced lines are 1179–98, a group of twenty immediately preceding the last six lines of Chapter III, which six lines are contained in A within the border of an illumination; and 1381–2, which are

themselves in A contained within the border of the next illumination, are omitted. The only other missing lines are 1097–1102.
These indications, together with the careful restriction to twenty
lines a page, seem to show that the manuscript may have been copied
from one very like A, despite the almost complete lack of reference
to the illuminations. The text is very close to that of A; the two
even have such idiosyncratic spellings as 'philisopher' in common.
There are, however, sufficient small differences to prevent proof
of direct copying.

The paper has no watermarks at all. Mr. T. C. Skeat, Keeper
of Manuscripts at the British Museum, dates the writing of the
text 'temp. Henry VIII'. At some time the manuscript must have
been damp, for ink from the parchment f. 85^r has blotted onto the
blank sheet, f. 84^v. It has recently been rebound.

EDITORIAL POLICY AND THE RELATIONSHIPS OF THE MANUSCRIPTS

The choice of the base manuscript is easy. A is fifteenth century
and presents the best text despite a sprinkling of errors almost all
easily correctable. Unfortunately it is incomplete, and for the missing sections—2503–622 and the last two chapters—S$_3$ has been
chosen, again an obvious choice. Although it cannot be proved
earlier than others of the manuscripts described, particularly B
and E, it preserves a Middle English type of spelling, and has fewer
errors. It is consistently much closer to A than any other, and
thus by printing these two a single manuscript tradition is presented. In spite of this close general agreement there are very
few agreements between A and S$_3$ against all other manuscripts;
they agree so in error only in: *man* 1145, *his* 2317, and the
spelling *philisophers* 1303, 1941, 2413, 2418; other unique agreements are: *receyving* 863, *on* 935, *Stepneth* 978, *wordis* 1728,
to 1984, *gre* 2135. The only such agreement of any consequence
is *his* 2317 where the error changes the construction and spoils
the sense.

Of disagreements (other than omission of whole lines) between
A and S$_3$ the following are the most noteworthy: *Thogh that,
Trowth if* 59; *causis, clawsis* 72; *lord,* om. 165; *to, do* 222; *convided, convytede* 289; *onyd, vnyd* 420; *nere, more* 425; *gete, purchace*
581; *wastide nye to, fylle to* 672; *Reede, gret* 919; *presence, presentes*

925; *not*, om. 1001; om., *his* 1008; *thei*, om. 1045; *not*, om. 1117; *his aperage, hyr age* 1133; *Mak it onys wel & nevir no more ageyne, He yt makes it ons well nedes neuer more agayne* 1142; *discouerede, dislosyd* 1180; *sore*, om. 1182; *adde, hadd* 1230, *perfeccion, perfect man* 1236; *pure*, om. 1237; *that no þing mishap, yt be no myshappe* 1342; *He ye, ye* 1790; *fuccendid, succendid* 1809; *stynging, stynkynge* 2105; *Also, And so* 2123; *abidinge, bidynge* 2339; *he refluence, her effluence* 2374; *in, with* 2400; *Said, when he said* 2634; *knew, knowith* 2641; *incomplete, a complete* 2651. As may be seen in only nine of these cases does the disagreement cause a change in sense i.e. 72, 222, 1117, 1133, 1230, 1236, 2105, 2374, 2651.

As a result of such correctness and close general agreement between these two manuscripts, emendation has rarely been necessary in A or, where S₃ is the base manuscript, in S₃. In the latter case there are only two of consequence: *laborours* to *labours* 2569, and *contraries* to *contries* 2924; others are merely of spelling: *Micocrosmos* to *Microcosmos* 2510, *virtuous* to *virtues* 2530, *byrge* to *bryge* 3065. Moreover, S₃ serves as a perfect guide to the acceptance or rejection of the corrections in A. I have rarely accepted any of these into the text without the support of S₃.

The textual variants are taken with a few exceptions from the other five early manuscripts described. I have confined these to omissions of words or lines, and additions and alterations of words. Slight variations in word order and spelling variants I have ignored, together with minor word changes, such as changes or omission of the article or in demonstratives and connectives, e.g. *nor* for *ne, or* for *other, therfore* for *wherfore*, and vice versa. Such minor variants cannot without better evidence help in grouping the manuscripts, being probably, as often as not, random. To have recorded them would have made the apparatus unnecessarily bulky. The variants recorded show the main divergencies of the tradition of the text in the sixteenth and seventeenth centuries.

The most widely aberrant tradition is that represented by SS₂. In the following list of the characteristics of this group the spelling is that of S; S₂, where extant, agrees in all but spelling unless otherwise noted.

(i) Frequent omission of lines: 23, 62, 909 (S only), 1283–4, 1309–10, 1432, 1505–6, 1627–8, 1681–2, 1729–30, 1736–8, 1787–8, 1805–6, 1811–12, 1820, 1844 (S only), 1865–8, 1883–90, 1915–16, 1919–22, 1955–1960, 1967–72, 1977–8, 1995–8, 2005–6, 2009–12,

2017–20, 2089–2092, 2097–8, 2103–6, 2129–32, 2141–8, 2165–6, 2207–8, 2255–6, 2267–8, 2287–92, 2297–2300, 2309–12, 2326, 2329–30, 2349–50, 2353–60, 2393–6, 2401–8, 2419–32, 2437–8, 2441–6, 2467–78, 2495–6, 2503–6, 2565–6, 2617–18, 2640 (S only), 2727–8, 2923–4, 2949–50.

(ii) garbled lines: 700, 1114, 1258, 2112, 2113–15, 2258, 2331, 3070, 3094.

(iii) omission of words (a selection of the more noteworthy): *fownde* 48, *so* 73, *made* 117, *seid* 457, *may* 704, *he* 732, *to me* 880, *was* 1039, *your* 1105, *after* 1135, *in* 1321, *not* 1756 (S only), *watirs* 2497, *thyngis* 2725, *new* 2731, *werke* 2764, *nedillis* 2932, *olde* 2953, *egall* 3021.

(iv) frequent change of words, affecting the sense (the text reading, usually A, given first): *loue—knowe* 30, *spede—speake* 43, *vnthryfe—vnthriftie* 46, *myne—mene* 52, *sewe—shewe* 119, *tyme— thinge* 280, *cesyn—do sine* 281, *sewe—showe* 358, *kele—keepe* 408, *onyd—ovie* 420, *a goode mene—of good men* 579, *dowte—thought* 649, *inclyne—declyne* 834, *foialte—seale* 851, *whilome—will(ia)m* 927, *the—by* 1213, *it—I* 1240, *receyve—refrayne* 1315, *make— voide* 1344, *dowte leste—doubtlese* 1363, *dowcet—gentill* 1430, *phisik of mynys—phesick myndes* 1567, *erlye—arthilye* 1651, *prowde appe- tite—proved abetyd* 1893 (S only), *colde—olde* 2029, *sowre—sorowe* (S only) 2149, *pulsis—pylles* 2171, *at—all* 2551, *the fende—thie ffrinde* 2724, *may—myne* 2747, *large—larde* 2801, *fornessis—pic- tures* 2878, *worchinge place—work in plaice* 2920, *mover—mother* 2959, *planet—plaines* 2962, *insufficient—sufficient* 3040, *proieccion —subiecyone* 3060.

(v) A tiresome redundancy: *vnrightfullye—most vnryghteouslye* 82, *he wolde—He thought he wold* 654, *fals—false or faynyd* 688, *iij wisys—thre maner of wayes* 749, *to them—which to them is* 886, *of—medle with* 898, *other—dyuers other* 908, *laborere—great laborer* 1039, *science—noble science* 1043, *mortagon—also mortagon* 1056, *vitrialle—also vitrioll* 1059, *operacions—great operacions* 1062, *daies—good dayes* 1076, *stone—goodly stone* 1155, *wondirful —wonderfull and excellent* 1156, *vertuys—a godly and vertuous* 1188, *entent—mynd and intent* 1207, *grete—very great* 1249, *boylle —also boyle* 1267, *haste—great hast* 1270, *al—all things that be* 1306, *degree—owne degre* 1308, *I hadde auoydide mekille—so I might avoided great & mykyll* 1368, *Bryse—Bryse whose surname* 1383, *strange—verye strange* 1386, *Til—vntyll tyme* 1434, *at his*

nede—ofte at his great nede 1435, *cese —leue & cease* 1437, *reherce—
let vs somthing rehearse* 1438, *vndirstonde—perceive & vnderstond*
1443, *departed—departyd & separatyd* 1447, *can—maie nor cann*
1449, *socowre—comforthe & soccur* 1453, *science—noble science* 1684,
perspicuyte—brightnes & perspycutie 1848, *ambycious—verye ambicyous* 1894, *is—there ys a* 2123, *goode—verie good* 2193, *thikker—
more thicker* 2205, *restore—againe restore* 2293, *werkmen—workmen
nowe* 2696, *well—full well* 2873, *trowe—call I trowe* 2983, *a cercle—
a rounde cyrcle* 3001, *wordly —euery wordlie* 3071, *Is—That ther
is* 3082.

It is noticeable that the text to line 518 shows proportionately
fewer of these characteristics than the remainder of the text. It is
with the text of S where the earlier scribe begins that a close grouping is evident with MSS. Sloane 2174 and 2532, both of the late
sixteenth or seventeenth century. In addition MS. Bodley 7643
(Ashmole 1479) forms a less closely related member of this group,
agreeing only in characteristics (iv) and (v) above, while containing
additional unique aberrations. Since this manuscript was—according to the scribe's own note—copied by Richard Walton in 1565,
I have up to line 468 used its readings to represent this tradition
in place of S, where these readings agree with Sloane 2174 and
2532. It is designated W in the textual notes. From 469 to 518 this
tradition is represented by S₂.

Another closely related group of four manuscripts is represented
by R. Somebody close enough to Ascham to make a copy of *The
Scholemaster* some seven years before publication copied R, and
two other manuscripts of the group are Bodley 6938 (Ashmole 57),
made by Dr. John Dee probably about 1577, and Longleat 178,
made by Francis Thynne in 1573–4. The fourth is Bodley 7655
(Ashmole 1490) and was copied by Dr. Simon Foreman, probably
about 1590; it is probably he who must be held responsible for the
number of unique and eccentric readings which this manuscript
contains. This group represents a tradition of the text apparently
as circulated among men of considerable learning or interest in
learning, and from the point of view of such original users the
tradition is a good one. No lines are omitted; 103 and 104 are
reversed, 845–6 and 3076 are largely rewritten, and 2027–8 is in the
margin. Though all manuscripts except AS₃ modernize the language, in this group the modernization is very consistently carried
out, e.g. *corage—myndes* 19, *Al be it that—althoughe it* 178, *dowte—*

dread 245, *helpe—meane* 261, *tregedie—treacherye* 343, *sewe—folowe* 358, *fawte—lack* 377, *Rayle—range* 619, *can—vse* 882, *medlide—myngled* 912, *costelewe—costly* 1250, *wysis—wayse* 1335, *sparkille—sparck* 1628, *Sethen—Seyng* 1649, *Arismetically—Arithmeticallie* 1655, *felde—fele* 2096, *rewnyng—Runnete* 2312, *planet—planetes* 2962. Moreover the text shows self-confidence in making the meaning clearer and more explicit, and in correcting what were taken as errors, e.g. *hasty—over hastie* 40, *this boke—this hole booke* 174, *it—theyr cunnynge* 348, *destruccion—dissolutyon* 370, *veynes—veynes of ise* 409, *of the newe—agayn of newe* 643, *Haste—ye hurt of hast* 780, *kepte—kepte & vsyd* 992, *canon—chanons yemans* 1163, *magis—om.* 1164, *Shulde—your work shuld* 1300, *Perspicuatly—in perspicuitie* 1863, *appetitis—qualities* 1897, *ne envious—om.* 1937, *resorte—ye most resort* 2168, *yeres—yeres cum* 2478.

There are, of course, a few errors, e.g. *pees—peeres* 240, *sentence—science* 357, *soleyne—soleme* 828, *Alyment—elemente* 1719, *towarde watire more—toward more* 1797, *Evire wone—every wanne* 1828, *virtually—virtuously* 2031, *gleire—clear* 2153, *complect—complet* 2177 (but cf. *complecte—gather vppe* 3079), *wondire—wordes* 2613, *kenne—been* 2695.

E contains a number of variants in common with the SS$_2$ group, and thus shares a common source with it. Examples are: *diligent awayte—diligence & awayte* 325, *the—euery* 786, *proferthe—provith* 813, *know—prove more* 829, *of doctrine—om.* 886, *wel vndirstode—will understond* 1094, *& Ioyne theyme—then & yoyne* E, *theym and done* S, *them and Joyne* S$_2$ 1216, *& symple—in symples* 1222, *ioy—trobyll* 1414, *wolde wynne—purpose to wynne* E, *purpose any thing to wyn* S 1448, *mesure—true mesure* 1580, *Evire wone—Euer one* ES$_2$, *euery mans* S 1828, *paralisie—palysye* E, *paulsye* SS$_2$ 2076, *watir—was* 2235, *om.* 2326, *contrarie—om.* 2517, *om.* 2640, *commendable fassion—commendacion* 2841, *ye lorde of—om.* 2952, *Eye—om.* 3044. In lines 1505-7 the ancestor of E and the SS$_2$ group skipped from the *in* of 1505 to the *in* of 1507. The scribe of E or some intermediary restored the omitted words either from another manuscript, or perhaps from a marginal correction in the source; but the omission was perpetuated in the SS$_2$ group. Other examples of such agreements with members of the SS$_2$ group other than S, before line 518 are: *wynne—fynde* 5, add *hey* 21, add *of* 311, *felonye—vilanye* 350, add *full* 495.

Other errors in E are: lines 59–60, 625, 2606, 2706, 2866 are omitted, and 1978 and 1979 transposed. The following variants affect the sense: *efficient—suffycyent* 393, *maters—metales* 399, *Mynys—myndes* 1331, *can that—cannot* 1459, *phisikis—phisike is* 1485, *withoute—is* 1884, *tastinge—herynge* 1977, *engendre— engendred* 2131, *ovirseyne—euer seene* 2357, *crippynge—cryspyng* 2812, *deerly—dedly* 2846.

B forms a group with T, i.e. Cambridge, Trinity College MS. 910. It is complete with the exception of eighteen missing lines, and has been the 'preferred manuscript' for quotation in the *M.E.D.* The following lines are missing: 255–60, 1173, 1318, 1824, 1952–3, 2089–90, 2207–8, 2298, 2847–8, and also 601–2 are telescoped into one by haplography. A number of single words are omitted of which the following seriously affect the sense: *wrech* 245, *no* 253, *hurt* 952, *dowtid* 1089, *hard* 1394, *ne* 1776, *awnsere* 2605. There are a number of other mistakes, of which the following are the most important since they destroy the sense (the text word given first): *foialte—fryaltee* 139, 851, *convided—counted* 289, *encrece—entreat* 414, *vertually—naturally* 421, *nolde—wold* 618, *refleccion—refection* 664, *his seyntis—this science* 859, *troy tille— Twitill* 986, *owtrage—comtrage* 992, *vnsuspectide—suspected* 1258, *right—light* 1576, *flowe—slowe* 1642, *Alyment—elemente* 1719, *passivis—passibus* 1723, *create—great* 1726, *Azure—aire* 1847, *las—last* 1960, *solide—holy* 2064, *Alimente—elementes* 2194, *congirs—congirers* 2258, *lyme—tyme* 2437, *not—nowe* 2473, *And—to* 2525, *graduacion—generacion* 2630, *seminale—feminale* 2670, *small —finall* 2780, *contries—contraries* 2924, *science as—science is as* 3088.

EDITIONS

The first English edition of the *Ordinal* was Elias Ashmole's '*Theatrvm Chemicvm* Britannicum. *Containing* Severall Poeticall Pieces of our Famous *English Philosophers*, who have written the *Hermettique Mysteries* in their owne Ancient Language. Faithfully Collected into one Volume, with Annotations thereon, *By* Elias Ashmole, *Esq. Qui est Mercuriophilus Anglicus. London.* Printed by *J. Grismond* for Nath: Brooks, at the Angel in *Cornhill.* MDCLII.' The *Ordinal*, together with a translation of the Latin Preface occupies pp. 1–106, with the notes pp. 437–55. The text is good and complete.[1]

[1] The *Theatrum Chemicum* has been reprinted with a new introduction by Allen G. Debus (New York, 1967).

This edition was reprinted in facsimile with an Introduction by
E. J. Holmyard as: '*The Ordinall of Alchimy written by Thomas
Norton of Bristol*, with an Introduction. London, 1928.' This
reprint included Ashmole's notes and prints.

A line-by-line Latin translation had been published by Michael
Maier in Frankfurt, 1618, in his book: '*Tripus Aureus, hoc est,
Tres Tractatus Chymici* Selectissimi, nempe I. Basilii Valentini . . .
Practica . . . ex Germanico; II Thomae Nortoni, Angli Philosophi
Crede Mihi seu Ordinale, ante annos 140. ab authore scriptum,
nunc ex Anglicano manuscripto in Latinum translatum, phrasi
cuiusque authoris vt & sententia retenta; III Cremeri cuiusdam
Abbotis Westmonasteriensis . . . Testamentum . . . Anno.
M.DC.XVIII.' This translation had been promised by Maier in
his *Symbola Aureae Mensae*[1] published in the previous year, where
in Book X, in the section dealing with Roger Bacon, he writes at
some length of other English alchemists. He also records most of
the Preface, and translates into Latin prose the incidents of the
monk, the parson, and Thomas Dalton from Chapter II of *The
Ordinal*, the conversation with Tonsil in Chapter III, the account
of the three alchemists from Chapter V, and a description of
Norton's master from Chapters II and V.[2] Apart from a few minor
misunderstandings of his original, Maier's rendering is accurate
enough to justify Ashmole's commendation, especially if—as it
seems—he knew no English before his visit to this country.
Lamenting the low repute of learned Englishmen in their own
country, Ashmole contrasts their reputation abroad, and speaks of
Maier and others: '*the first of which came out of* Germanie, *to live
in* England; *purposely that he might so understand our* English
Tongue, *as to Translate* Norton's Ordinall *into* Latin *verse,
which most judiciously and learnedly he did: Yet (to our shame
be it spoken) his* Entertainement *was too course for so deserving* a
Scholler.'[3]

The whole of the *Tripus Aureus* was reprinted in the second
(enlarged) edition of the *Musaeum Hermeticum*,[4] a collection of
alchemical works first published in 1625. It is this second edition

---

[1] Frankfurt, 1617, p. 467.

[2] Ibid., pp. 467–80.

[3] *Theatrum Chemicum Britannicum*, 'Prolegomena', A2ᵛ. Maier's version is
not Latin verse, however.

[4] *Musaeum Hermeticum Reformatum et Amplificatum* (Frankfurt, 1677–8),
pp. 433–532.

which has been translated into English by A. E. Waite.[1] In addition, Maier's version of *The Ordinal* was reprinted in Manget's *Bibliotheca Chemica Curiosa*, under the title 'Thomae Nortoni Tractatus. *Crede Michi seu Ordinale*'.[2]

Seven years after the publication of *Tripus Aureus*, *The Ordinal* was translated from it into German verse, under the same title as Maier had given it.[3] Maier's Latin version was no longer than the English original, but the necessity of setting the Latin into German four-stress couplets makes this version long-winded. The seven engravings in this edition are not those reproduced by Ashmole, but typical seventeenth-century symbolic alchemical figures.

THE LANGUAGE OF MS. A

The language of the base manuscript is typical London English of the late fifteenth century, and consequently a complete account of sounds and forms is not necessary. What follows is a description designed to demonstrate the placing of the dialect and to note forms requiring comment.

Spelling and Sounds

OE. *a* + nasal is usually *a*: *man(e* 185, 233, 766 (rhymes with *phisician* 1563–4), *mannys* 510, 1066, 1287, etc., *bigan(ne* 186, 811, 1302, *can* (rhymes with *Ortolane* 1449–50), *than* (rhymes with *man* 1003–4); *from* always. The spelling *wone* 1825, 1828, 1831 appears to represent a WMid. form, or possibly SW. influenced by WMid., cf. the rhyme *mon* : *nōn* quoted by Jordan[4] [268] from *St. Editha*. The apparently long vowel indicated by *woone* 1538 may be due to scribal confusion with *one*, although *one* is not spelt with initial *w* in this text.

[1] *The Hermetic Museum* . . . *Frankfort 1678*, James Elliott and Co., 2 vols. (London, 1893).

[2] Jean Jacques Manget, *Bibliotheca Chemica Curiosa*, etc., 2 vols. (Geneva, 1702), ii. 285–309.

[3] *Chymische Tractat Thomae Nortoni eines Engellanders, Crede Mihi seu Ordinale genandt*, etc., translated from the Latin by Daniel Maisner (Frankfurt, 1625).

[4] The rhyme quoted is probably imperfect, cf. *anoon* : *mon Knyghthode and Bataile*, 1466–7. On the occurrence of long–short rhymes see L. Morsbach, *Mittelenglische Grammatik*, 135 n. 4; also B. Sundby, *Dialect and Provenance of the . . . Owl and the Nightingale* (Lund Studies in English 18, 1950), p. 114.

Before *nd*, usually *o*, *biforehonde* 1300, 2467, *bonde* 958, *bondis* 874, *hond(e* 1025, 1444, 1774, *hondis* 258, 887, *lond(e* 551, 583, 648, etc., *sondyfere* 1059, *stonde* 2273, *vndirstonde* 552, 1299, 1395, etc., *withstonde* 774, but also *hand(e* 1695, 2441, *handis* 1297, *standith* 1786.

OE. *ā*: *oon(e, holi(e, homely, mo, wo*, etc., also from Angl. *-ald*: *bolde, tolde, manifolde*, etc.

OE. *āht* > aht: *taght(e*, 210, 218, 810, *tagthe* 1088, *taught* 695, *tawgthe* 706, 796, *augthe* 824 beside *noght(e, nogthe*, invariably.

OE. *āg*: *owne* 318, 527, 1912, *lowe* (rhymes with *know* 1160), but once *awne* 319, which could be N. or NWMid., but also, and more probably, SE. or London [Jordan, 105 n.].

OE. *ǣ*: spelt *ee, e, del* 33, *dele, somdele* 934, 1118, 1135, *hete* 1455, etc., *leche* 629, *lede, leede* 803, 1018, *leere* 9, 231, 275; *dredful(le* 140, 220, *heere* n. 1057, *mysdede* 88, *reede* n. 1350, *red(ing* 175, 180, *seed* 87, 420, 432, *speche* 1096, *slepyn* 883. Exceptions are *laft(e* pp. (rhymes with *craft* 29–30, 1565–6), beside *left* 47, *late* v. 622, 1003, 1366, etc. *las(se* (rhymes with *brasse* 383–4, *was* 405–6, 413–14, 933–4, 2463–4), *clansith* 1619, 2191, beside *clense* 2286, and *clene* (rhymes with *mene* 1539–40, 2047–8, 2451–2). Reflexes of OE. *ǣ*$_1$ and *ǣ*$_2$ rhyme: *teche : speche* 57–8, 1095–6, 1167–8, *wrech:teche* 245–6; *lede:drede* 803–4. This is not a SW. rhyme on *ę̄*, but on *ę̄* before the dental or palatal consonant [Jordan, 48 n. 2, 81 n. 1, Kökeritz,[1] p. 196; but cf. Dobson,[2] 123, 124]; cf. *nede:drede* 191–2, *dreede:hede* n. [*heed*] 1361–2, also *meete* v.:*secrete* 1469–70, *complete:mete* v. 1585–6.

ME. *e*: occasional instances of *e* > *i* in closed syllables occur [Jordan, 34]; besides the normal S. pt. forms *fille* 1062, *bifille* 899, *befille* 1387 there are: *stynch(e* 2007, 2013, 2018, *ynglond* 1396 beside *englishe* 920, 1400, and the regular *silf(e* 290, 491, 1096, 1111, 1281, beside *self(e* 1140, 2014. For *smyll*, etc. see later in section on rhymes.

ME. *ę̄* is spelt once *ey* in *leys* 66, beside *lesith* 374, *lese* 1654. Asta Kihlbom quotes occasional similar spellings from London

---

[1] H. Kökeritz, *Shakespeare's Pronunciation* (New Haven, 1953).
[2] E. J. Dobson, *English Pronunciation, 1500–1700*, 2 vols. (Oxford, 2nd edn. 1968). References are to paragraphs in volume ii.

correspondents of the fifteenth century, e.g. *treys, heyr, neyd* n., and *seyn* pp.[1]

ME. *i* appears usually as *e* in open syllables: *Eye-ledis* 1953, *mekille* 671, 984, 1368, *seve* (rhymes with *greve*) 314, *wekis* (rhymes with *seekis*) 2462, *wrete* pp. 757 beside *write(n* pp. 689, 1150; *gife* 38, 342, *forgife* 88 are rare beside normal *geve* [? ON. *gefa*] 98, 138, etc., *gevith* 857, 1683, etc., *gefe* 2373. Cf. *besy* 1042, which may possibly represent a SE. form, and *evil(le* 239, 2008, 2015, etc. The later change of ME. *i* to *e* in closed syllables [Jordan, 271] does not appear, cf. *which(e* passim, *bissoppis* 22, *brigge* 633, 640, *swifte* 265.

ME. *i*: the eNE. diphthongization may appear in *vreyne* 1550 beside normal *vrine*; also possibly in *proviyde* 1917, though the *y* probably indicates vowel length.

ME. *o* in *bloke* 1005 is possibly lengthened. M.E.D. records *blōke* see *blok(ke* n. presumably on the basis of the rhyme in *Sir Cleges* 451–2, and perhaps the spellings *bloke* in *Promptorium* and *ploke* in the *Yatton Accounts*. However, long–short rhyme is possible,[2] and the lengthening, if it occurred, is not localized.

OE. *ōht* > *oht*. OE. *oht*: spellings without *u* predominate, as is compatible with London English [Jordan, 124]: *broght* 987, 1902, etc., *brogthe* 1133, *broȝt* 416, *soght(e* 277, 869, 1433, 2329, *besogthe* 1086, *sought* 474, *sowght* 188, 1045, 1680, 2401, *thoght(e* n. 605, 671, 1899, *thoȝt* 257, *thoghtis* 665, *thoght* v. pt. 561, 835, 952, *boght* 187, *wroght* 102, 190, 2086, 2330, etc., *wroȝt* 258, *vnwroȝt* 1679.

OE. *ȳ*: usually spelt *i, y*: *filthi* 461, *fyre* (rhymes with *desire*) 27, 651, etc., *hidde, hydde* 74, 1309, 2288, *kynde* (rhymes with *fynde*) 254 etc., *mankinde* (rhymes with *fynde*) 17, 273, *mynd(e* (rhymes with *behynde, fynde*) 104, 121, 632, 806; *pride* 241, *pryde* (rhymes with *gyde*) 1017; *bild(e* 301, 617, *brigge* 633, 645, *firste* 312, 1198, etc., *fulfille* (rhymes with *wille* n.) 637, *gilte* 641, *hill* 378, *knytt* 2130, 2440 (rhymes with *spirytt*) 2378. The *e*-forms *besy* 1042 and *evil(le* 239 etc., have been mentioned under ME. *i*, and together with the occasional *u*-forms *church* 1898, *cuttynge* 2303, *luste* 3 pt. sg. (which is probably affected by *lust* n.) 2481 beside

---

[1] *A Contribution to the Study of Fifteenth Century English* (Uppsala Universitets Årsskrift, 1926), pp. 56 ff.

[2] In *brok* n. (1), *cok* n. (1), *crokke* n., *flok* n. (1) and (2) the *M.E.D.* does not specify a possible long vowel despite several spellings as *broke(s), coke, ffloke, flokes.*

lyst 1881, *Tewkesburye* 1012, occur not uncommonly in London documents and Caxton [Morsbach, 131 n. 1].[1]

OE. *wyr*: usually appears with *u*, *o*: *worch(e* 12, 722, 1066, etc., *worchyn* 1228, *worching* 710, 2060, etc., *worchingis* 1678, *wors* (rhymes with *curs*) 169, 1036, *worste* 880, beside *werch* 106, *werchith* 1505, and *wirching* 1882, 2282.

OE. *ea*: WS. and K. smoothing to *e* before *hs* appears in *flexe*: *wexe* 1627–8, Anglian *a* in *wax* 1464.

OE. *ēa*, spelt *e*: *dede* adj. 713, and (rhymes with *drede* n.) 656, (with *ledde* n.) 1830, *deth* 2244, *grete* 5, 7, 9, 25, etc., *gret(e)ly* 161, 888, *hedlye* 1229, *lede* n. 465, 467, *ledy* 1825, *lesyng(e* 327, 975, 1388, etc., *re(e)de* adj. 459, 919, 1532, 2069, etc.; shortened in *dedde* 2244, (rhymes with *redde* adj.) 2627–8, (cf. *redde*: *ledde* n. 1537–8), *gretter* 1621, *grettir* 644, *hedde* (rhymes with *bedde* n.) 1012, *ledd* n. 383, *redde* 2644 (rhymes with *bedde*) 1391, *birefte* 906, *cheffare* 340. The rhyme *byleve* n. : *repreve* 2715–16 may be on ME. *ę̄* < *ẹ̄* before the labio-dental (cf. rhymes of *ǣ₁* and *ǣ₂*, *ǣ₁* with *ę̄*), or the stressed vowel of *byleve* may be from the verb *bilę̄ven*.[2] The WS. form appears in *hire* v. 700, *hyre* (rhymes with *desire*) 728, *hyringe* 1978, and perhaps *stiple* 301,[3] but the Anglian *ę̄* is normal, *herd* pt. pp. 1293, 587, *be- bi)leve* v. 687, 900, 1337, 32 (rhymes with *repreve*), *nede* n. 108, 191, 808, etc., *nede* v., *ned(e)ly*, etc.

OE. *eo*: *derk(e* 62, 873, 1779, etc., *derkli* 1673, *derknes* 1521, 1800, *fer(re* 103, 305, 981, etc., *ferforth* 1208, *hert(e* 42, 837, 897, etc., *smerte* v. 41; *werke* n. (rhymes with *clerk* passim) is from the Anglian form with smoothing, beside SW. *worke* n. 255, *workmen* 29. With lengthening *cleve* 2315, 2318, and probably *hevyn(e*, *sevyn(e* 137–8, 271–2.

There is little spelling evidence of early Modern changes. Apart from the slight possibility that *vreyne* 1550 and *proviyde* 1917

---

[1] See also H. Römstedt, *Die englische Schriftsprache bei Caxton* (Göttingen, 1891), p. 14 for *luste*; R. W. Chambers and M. Daunt, *A Book of London English, 1384–1425* (Oxford, 1931), p. 112, line 143 for *besily*; Kihlbom, p. 23.

[2] Dobson, 120, appears to favour the former explanation. If *bileve* 32 is a noun we have another example of this rhyme.

[3] But cf. Dobson, 132 n., and 11, where *stypylle* is explained as quantity variation, shortening of *ę̄* to *i*. On *hyre*, *hyringe*, Dobson, 136 n. 2, allows the possibility of WS. origin, but also suggests the possibility of the rare raising of ME. *ę̄* to *i* before *r*, *s*, *v*, and perhaps *k* (Luick, 481). For *hyre* in London English see Römstedt, p. 17.

represent the diphthongization of ME. *i*, there is evidence for the development of a glide before *r* in *ayer(e* 375, 2438, beside normal *ayre* 390, 1975, 1976, 2224, 2422, etc. [Luick, 505]. Dobson [218] places this 'either during the fifteenth ... or at the beginning of the sixteenth century', and *M.E.D.* has spellings *aier* (? a 1425), *ayer* (? c 1425) *ayere* (c 1440), etc.

Consonants: The development of excrescent *d* after *n* and *l* is a fifteenth-century change, though more fully illustrated in the sixteenth century [Luick, 765. 1. b.d.; Jordan, 262 n. 1; Dobson, 436–7]. Both occur in rhyme, and so in the author's speech: *combynde* v. inf. (rhymes with *kinde*) 1281, the only example in *M.E.D.*, and *feld* (rhymes with *seld*) 1695, *felde* 2096, *feldyng* 432, not in *M.E.D.*

The words *brother*, *other* appear frequently written with medial *d* in rhymes: *brodir(e: odir(e* etc., 1093–4, 1203–4, 1313–14, 1631–2, 2319–20, beside *broder: other* 841–2, *brodire: a nothire* 2033–4. In non-rhyming position only *brodire* 855, *odir(e* 1119, 1396, beside *other* 823, 1609, *othir* 203, 658, 868, *a(n nother* 436, 2233, 2257, 2263, *a nothir(e* 457, etc.

There is no evidence for the later reverse change *d* > *ð* [Jordan, 298; Dobson, 384]: *faders* 144, 263, 1143, 1189, 1961, *modir(e* 1124 and (in rhyme) 1512, *togedire*, 850.

The form *grabbis*, 2144 is not in *M.E.D.* as a variant for *crab(be* n. (2). Luick [*Anglia*, xvi, 488–9] considers the place-name *Grantebryge* > *Cante-* as due to Anglo-Norman pronunciation, with loss of *r* by dissimilation, and Hermann Albert [*Mittelalterlicher englisch-französischer Jargon*, 1922, p. 36] points to voicing of initial *k* to *g* in French works ridiculing English pronunciation of French, e.g. *goiffe* for *coiffe*, *gontre* for *contre*. Sporadic spellings of the error occur in English manuscripts for initial *cr* written *gr* usually in words of French origin, e.g. (from *M.E.D.*) *grampe* for *crampe* n. (1), *grapond* for *crapaude*, *gredence* for *credence*; in words of Germanic origin only *gringle* for *cringle* (place-names only), and *gredil* for *cradel*. This last is surely an error, and the word is really *gridel* n.; *grabbis* therefore remains the only Germanic word apart from the place-name. A number of examples occur of the contrary, *cr* for *gr*: *crace for grace*, *craffe* for *graffe*, *crede* for *grede*, *cret*, *crit* for *gret* n. (3). A similar change is seen in *necligent*, 883.

There is little trace of specifically regional features in the phonology. In addition to the forms commented on above there is the S. and SW. *voole* 2477, *vole* 2478,[1] and the probably SW. form *ire* (rhymes with *desire* v. pr. pl.) 455, *yre* 438, 457,[2] but as isolated examples, these cannot affect the general placing of the dialect. Similarly a few scattered forms suggestive of the NEMid. and N. are not specific: *Askis* 2290 appears in *M.E.D.* frequently from N. and NMid. texts, but also Trevisa, Pecock, and *aske* in the Wycliffe Bible (second version); similarly with *gife* 38, *forgife* 88, where beside the N. and NMid. examples there is *forgif* beside *forgeve* in Paston letters, Trevisa *forgifnes*, and Capgrave *forgifnesse*, while in London documents are *ʒif*, *gif*, *forʒyf*, *foryifnesse*. On *awne* 319, besides the Jordan references (above), see Dobson, 241. The language of manuscript A then, is late-fifteenth-century London English.

Grammatical Features

Pronouns: The possessive and objective plural 3rd pers. are rarely *her*, *hem*; *her* 372, 1314, *hir* 1734; *hem* 422, 507, 859, 1311, 1776, 1794. The originally N. and NEMid. forms *theyre*, *theyme* occur elsewhere. A considerable variation in usage is evident in the incipient standard language of the late fifteenth century.

Verbs: Inf. in rhyme and non-rhyme has no ending except: *seyne* (rhymes with *peyne*) 911; also *sayne* (rhymes with *ageyne*) 3061 in the Sloane MS. section.

The 3 pr. sg. ends in -*i*)*th*(*e*, -*eth*(*e* always, except *Methink* 990, *nede* 1375, and *mett* 2322, which may, however, be pt. The pr. pl. has usually no ending; in non-rhyme 213 examples; in rhyme 37, all but one (*vse* : *refuse* 441–2) with forms other than present plurals. In addition the Mid. -*e*)*n*, -*in* occurs seventeen times, including one rhyme: *moone* : *doone* 2279–80. The others are: *doyn* 149, *cesyn* 281, *perceyuyn* 403, *sechene* 704, *slepyn* 883, *worchyn* 1228, *ben* 1352, *suffren* 1477, *doon* 1592, *cawsen* 1667, *doon* 1685, *eten* 1733, *doon* 1833, *folowyn* 2279, *washen* 2283, *doon* 2326.

The S. ending -*i*)*th* occurs thirty-five times, never in rhyme: *puttith* 4, *doth* 19, *movith* 32, *causith* 64, *restith* 244, *wenyth* 290,

---

[1] For initial voiced fricative in Caxton, however, see Römstedt, p. 30, *valdore*, *vlycche*.

[2] Most of the fifteenth-century examples in *M.E.D.* are from this area, *Piers Plowman C* (Hunterian MS.), and documents from Oxford, Salisbury, Wiltshire, Somerset, Bristol.

makith 320, *causith* 333, *cavsith* 373, *lesith* 374, *hath* 424, *arisith* 693, *hath* 702, *sechithe* 790, *helpithe* 1121, *oppressith* 1780, *drawith* 1799, *levith* 1835, *Causith* 1854, *Makith* 1874, *changith* 1978, 1979, *hath* 1991, *plesith* 1998, *trustith* 2100, *clansith* 2191, *conveith* 2194, *makith* 2201, *tellith* 2229, *makith* 2290, *departith* 2295, *bryngith* 2297, *helpith* 2299, *trustith* 2353, *techith* 2397.

The N. or NMid. *-e)s/-is* occurs six times in rhyme: *says* : *waies* 359–60, *dayes* : *sayes* 499–500, *slevis* : *grevis* 887–8, *affermys* : *termys* 1729–30, *degrees* : *seeis* 1875–6, *seekis* : *wekis* 2461–2. The pp. of strong verbs (including those used adjectivally): with no *-n* ending, twenty-eight examples in non-rhyme position, eighteen in rhyme (with an additional two from the Sloane MS. section); e.g. (non-rhyme): *be* 39, 92, 781, *do* 1367, 1421, etc., *vn)know(e* 14, 974, 1166, 1367, etc., and (rhyme) *fownde, founde* 205, 1220, 2178, 2259, 2301, etc., *forbood* 268 (and in Sloane MS. section *fownde* 2797, *forbodde* 2977), *take* 953.

With *-n* ending, 11 in non-rhyme, 9 in rhyme, e.g. (non-rhyme): *govyn* 189, 262, *born(e* 299, 1396, 1398, *spoken* 2219, and (rhyme) *sayne* 566, *ovir)seyne* 699, 1141, 2357, etc., *go(o)ne* 713, 1037, 1076, etc.

The evidence of grammatical forms confirms that of the phonology. The Midland verb forms predominate, but there is a mingling of S. and N. or NEMid. forms, and the meeting-place for these is presumably London or the SEMid. area. The scribe wrote a fair proportion of S. pr. pl. forms in *-ith*, and pp. forms without *-n* ending in non-rhyming position where change was easy. The unusual forms, the six N. pr. plurals and the inf. with *-ne*, are all in rhyme and so likely to be preserved. The later Sloane MS. also preserves them. These rhymes and others are the only reliable evidence for the language of the author, and to this we now turn.

The Author's Dialect

Since rhyme evidence is in consideration, no distinction is made between the two base manuscripts. There are a number of imperfect rhymes of *m* : *n*, *ng* : *n*, *remembre* : *engendre* 1235–6, *deme* : *grene* 2143–4, *fyne* : *prime* 463–4, *tyme* : *engyne* 775–6, *doctryne* : *pryme* 1473–4, *tyme* : *nyne* 2107–8, *tyme* : *masculyne* 2669–70, *sublyme* : *myne* 3057–8, *freton* : *com* 2811–12, *ouyrstronge* : *anone*

2105–6, *aaron* : *longe* 2563–4. Though fairly frequent, such rhymes are not so bad as to undermine other rhyme evidence; similar or worse rhymes are to be found in Lydgate and Hoccleve and other fifteenth-century poets,[1] and Kökeritz referred to such rhyming as 'time-honored practice'.[2]

Some rhymes indicate a SW. pronunciation: *desire* : *hyre* 727–8 may imply SW. *hīeran, hīran*, and *mylte* : *spylte* 3055–6, requires the causative form *miltan, mieltan* (< **mæltjan*; the Anglian equivalent with i-umlaut, *meltan*, would be indistinguishable in the pr. from the strong verb). With these go: *spille* : *smylle* 2003–4, *skylle* : *smylle* 2031–2, *smyllis* : *dong hillis* 2035–6, *smylle* : *ylle* 2101–2.[3] A similar reason, SW. *ie/y*, may explain these rhymes. The spellings *smulle, smille* are common in the SW. and WMid.,[4] but also occur in the literary standard language, e.g. *Boke of Noblesse* (Roxburghe Club), *smyllis* p. 70; *Knyghthode and Bataile, Smylle* (rhymes with *kille, spille*) 1017. Both *mylte* and *smill-* could be explained as ME. *e* > *i* before *l* [Jordan, 34]. This, however, does not occur elsewhere in rhyme: *welle* : *telle* 43–4, *welle* : *dwelle* 507–8, *telle* : *concelle* 571–2, *telle* : *welle* 623–4, etc.

Of other rhymes some indicate a NMid. or N. origin, others SE. The rhyme *hadde* : *made* 2305–6 corresponds to those quoted by Jordan [156] from Mannyng and *Scottish Legends*, and cf. *Pearl* 134 ff. *hade* : *glade* : *brade* : *made*. According to Jordan the normally unstressed short vowel lengthened under stress. The same explanation might apply to *shappe* : *mishap* 1341–2, *shappe* : *myshappe* 2777–2778, but *shappe* n. retained its historically short vowel until the fifteenth century, the long vowel being by analogy with the verb *shāpen*. Dobson considers the short *a* in *shape* in the rhyming dictionaries of Levins and Poole to be a Northernism [6].

---

[1] Wilhelm Dibelius, 'John Capgrave und die englische Schriftsprache', *Anglia*, xxiii (1901), 153–94; see especially pp. 166–8.

[2] *Shakespeare's Pronunciation*, p. 312.

[3] Cf. also, not in rhyme: *smylle* n. 1959, 2006, 2011, 2025; *smylle* v. 2019, *smyllith* 2005, *Smyllid* 1958, 1965, *smyllyng* 1943, 1947, 2093, *swete smyllyng* 1967, *mylt* 1618.

[4] M.E.D. files, e.g. *Firumbras* smylleþ 2546; *SLeg*. Laud MS. smulde 3. 66, 214. 492; *Glo. Chron*. smille App. XX 23; *Kildare Gedichte* smilliþ 157.14; *P. Plowman C* smylle 8. 50; *King Alisaunder* (Lincoln's Inn MS.) smulliþ 5517; beside *Palladius* smylle 10. 122. 12. 514 (in rhyme); *Trin. Hom*. smullen p. 35, also the N. *The Visions of Tundale* (1843) smylland 2045, smylle (rhymes with telle) 1543. The tendency of *e* to become *i* [Jordan, 34] will account for the *i-* spellings and does account for the N. (Tundale) examples; however the *u-* spellings must go back to a WS. *ie/y*.

However, we may in all three cases have imperfect rhymes of the long vowel with the short.[1]

Gysse : *is* 739–40, 1865–6 may imply derivation from ON., cf. OI. *gizka*. Three instances of such a rhyme are quoted in *M.E.D.*, all from the East Midlands: these are *Handlyng Synne* 10162 *ges* : *is*, *Ludus Coventriae* 360.144 *gysse* : *blysse, Wisdom* 361 *gees* : *ys* : *þis*. *Therto* : *go* pp. 993–4. *þere-to* : *so* 1227–8, *woo* : *doo* 2593–4, *do* : *so* 2921–2, *allone* : *done* pp. 2759–60 show rhyme of ME. ǭ with ǭ; also, *fixacion* : *allon* 1607–8. Kökeritz[2] shows that ME. ǭ became ǭ in Suffolk before 1400, and Jordan [45 n.] cites spellings *noun, echoun* from Northampton documents. According to Dobson [148 and n.; cf. 152 and n.] the raising of the open to the close vowel is common in Northern and Eastern dialects, ME. examples occurring in Gower, Havelok, and the *King Alisaunder* group. The presence of similar rhymes in Chaucer shows the change in London English, e.g. *to* : *moe* : *go* : *woe*, *home* : *come* [Ten Brink, 31], and *sothe* : *wrothe, sothe* : *bothe*.[3]

Vapoure : *sure* 1805–6, *vse* : *hows* 2285–6. The rhyme might be of [uː] and [iu] from ME. *ü* [Dobson, 187], but more probably we have ME. *ū* for *ü* in words from French [Dobson, 178. 2], cf. Lydgate *St. Albon and Amphabel*, iii. 1487, *treasure* : *laboure*. Jordan [230] localizes the falling together of OF. *ü* with ME. *ū* in the North Midlands and southern areas of N.

Flowe : *howe* 1467–8, *flow(e* : *nowe* 955–6, 2299–2300, 2489–90, *now* : *grow* 387–8, *fowre* : *howre* 971–2, *socowre* : *fowre* 1453–4, 2499–2500, *fowre* : *liquor* 1765–6,: *liquour* 2183–4,: *sowre* 2119–20, show ME. *ou*, OE. *ōw, ēow* rhyming with ME. *ū*. Dobson [173] considers the vowel to be *ū*, Kökeritz[4] thinks the rhyme is on a diphthong, a diphthongization of ME. *ū* different from the standard eNE. development. Jordan [280], who also takes the rhyme as diphthongal, cites rhymes from *Palladius* and *Siege of Troy* (Harley MS.), EMid., and Lovelich, a Londoner. The orthoepists cited in Dobson include Northerners, but also Londoners; and Wright[5] records the pronunciation in several Northern counties, but also

---

[1] Cf. p. xxviii, n. 4; for rhyme of *ǎ* : *ā* not in N. or NMid. Cf. *late, translate, therate, Knyghthode and Bataile*, pp. 50–5.

[2] *Phonology of the Suffolk Dialect* (Uppsala Universitets Årsskrift, 1932), pp. 293, 295.

[3] F. Wild, *Die sprachlichen Eigentümlichkeiten der wichtigeren Chaucer-Handschriften* (Vienna and Leipzig, 1915), sec. 14, p. 72.

[4] *Shakespeare's Pronunciation*, p. 245.

[5] *English Dialect Grammar* (Oxford, 1905), pp. 168, 171.

in Kent, of the reflex of OE. *ōw* as a diphthong with unrounded first element ([au]), suggesting a late ME. *ū*.

The six N. or NMid. pr. pl. forms have already been listed. There are also a number of rhymes indicating loss of *r* by assimilation to a following consonant. These are: *owtrage* : *charge* 287–8, 991–2, 2747–8, *raage* : *surcharge* 1063–4, *aperage* : *litarge* 1133–4, *cese* : *reherce* 1437–8, *ponderous* : *cours* 2459–60, *hermes* : *verse* 2659–2660, *serche* : *speche* 1429–30, *Arnolde* : *worlde* 1251–2. This loss occurred early before *s* [Jordan, 166; cf. Luick, 772]; Dobson [401c] shows the loss before *s* and *sh* [ʃ] and occasionally other consonants. No special dialect area is indicated by the ME. examples.

One item only of vocabulary is unusual, *siselye* 1244, not in *O.E.D.* There are no other examples of this in *M.E.D.* files, and only two for the corresponding adjective, *O.E.D. sisel* [ON. *sýsl*]; both of these are from the *Northern Homilies.*[1] It may have existed further south in the Danelaw territory.

Taken together the *hadde* : *made* rhyme, the *gisse* : *is* rhymes, *vapoure* : *sure*, *vse* : *hows*, and the six *-e(s*, *-is* pr. pl. rhymes, could be thought to give the language a slight NEMid. flavour; *desire* : *hyre* : *mylte* : *spylte*, and the four *smyll(is* rhymes point to the SW. The rhymes cancel each other out, and there are in any case too few to place the author's speech far out of London. Though from a Bristol family, Thomas Norton spoke, or at least wrote, the King's English of his day, as might be expected of a member of the Royal household who was probably looking for patronage from the great.

THE AUTHOR

The Ordinal of Alchemy was written by Thomas Norton (? 1433–1513 or 1514), an esquire, of a family well known in Bristol in the fifteenth century. He has been commonly mis-identified and confused with his uncle, Thomas, notably by the author of the *D.N.B.* article on him, while in an article in *Isis* for 1932 M. Nierenstein and P. F. Chapman attempted to show that none of the four Thomases of this family in the fifteenth century could have written the work.[2] This attempt failed, but the authors have found and

---

[1] J. Small, ed., *English Metrical Homilies* (Edinburgh, 1862).
[2] 'Enquiry into the Authorship of the *Ordinall of Alchimy*', *Isis*, no. 53 (xviii. 2), 290–321.

arranged in convenient form a great deal of information about the family, and have constructed a family tree from the author's grandfather, Thomas, to his great grandson, Samuel Norton, who wrote *The Key of Alchimie* in 1577, the centennial year of the *Ordinal*. A detailed refutation of Nierenstein and Chapman's argument disqualifying any Thomas of this family from the authorship is contained in my article in *Ambix* for 1957.[1] Here we need only an outline of the evidence in proof of identification.

Samuel Norton's *Key of Alchimie*[2] contains a clear claim that his great-grandfather wrote the *Ordinal*. In the 'Preamble' addressed to Queen Elizabeth he says that in the time of Edward IV seven men possessed the art of alchemy, four religious and three laymen. The religious were: Dalton, monk of Tewkesbury (cf. ll. 913–1010), his (Samuel's) great-grandfather's master, Canon George Ripley, the well-known author of *The Compend of Alchemy*, 1471,[3] and the Archbishop of York; the three laymen 'whiche were favored of the kinge, one of them was a stranger borne in loraine, the other nighe to the middest of England, the third of them was my great grandfather, him selfe beinge of his privie Chamber, diverse tymes an ambassador for him, and one also that with him felt such fortunes frownes (as the traiterous earle then drove the kinge unto, when he was forced to flye into burgonie)'.[4] It is clear that Samuel is recalling the account of the three alchemists at Leadenhall in Chapter V of the *Ordinal* (ll. 1387 ff.), of whom the youngest and greatest was his great-grandfather. He does not say which of his four great-grandfathers it was, but one of them, as Nierenstein and Chapman have shown, was Thomas Norton, Customer of Bristol, who described himself officially as 'of the king's household',[5] a description which agrees

---

[1] 'Thomas Norton and the *Ordinall of Alchimy*', *Ambix*, vi (Dec. 1957), 59–85.

[2] Bodleian MS. Ashmole 1421, ff. 165^v–217^r. This is an early seventeenth-century manuscript, written by Thomas Robson.

[3] *The Compound of Alchymy, or the ancient hidden Art of Archemie . . . first written by . . . G. Ripley . . . set foorth by R. Rabbards . . .*, London, 1591; also printed in Elias Ashmole's *Theatrum Chemicum Britannicum* (1952), pp. 107–93. Ashmole believed that he was Norton's master, as did Francis Thynne and those who copied the group of manuscripts represented in this edition by R. But Samuel Norton makes the two distinct and there is no evidence in favour of the supposition.

[4] Quoted in Nierenstein and Chapman, op. cit. p. 315.

[5] E. W. W. Veale (ed.) *The Great Red Book of Bristol*. Text (Pt. IV), *Bristol Record Society Publications*, xviii (1953), 69.

with Samuel's phrase 'of his privie Chamber'. The gentlemen of
the privy chamber were instituted by Henry VII as forty-eight
servants of the king, but according to Samuel Pegge's *Curialia*[1]
they were the same as the 'Squyers of Houshold' mentioned in the
'Liber Niger Domus Regis Angliae' of the time of Edward IV.[2]
They were still called 'Esquires of Houshold' under Richard III,
but in the Eltham Statutes of 1526 the new name was used.[3] They
were in constant attendance on the king, but were 'likewise
employed in confidential offices without doors, as occasion
required',[4] and it is to such duties that Samuel referred in his
'diverse tymes an ambassador for him'.

Samuel, in the 'Preamble' goes on to mention his great-grandfather's book:[5]

Of whom I not a little wonder why he would not impart it to the king;
& yet in his book I find that hee was willing therto: yf some great fault
in the king had not letted it; for in his book after a mourning sort he
saith:

> Truly king Edward was nigh therto
> If sinne had not kept him therefro
> But surelie sinne jointlie with grace
> Will not be together in one place.

ffor further he addeth

> Gratia tardatur peccatum dum dominatur,

That is to say

> Grace of consolatione
> Is deferred while sinne hath domination.

Yet both in the beginning & ending of his book hee after a prophetical
kind of manner giveth out that that science shall happen to the kings of
England, where his words are found to be on this wise

> Yet once this science I understand
> shall greatly honor the throne of England
> When in this Land shall raigne a king,
> Which shall love god above althing

The Lateine verses in the beginning of his book are to many & to long
to be recited, but that which I most of all desire to come to pass, is that

---

[1] *Curialia: or an Historical Account of Some Branches of the Royal Household*,
Part I (London, 1782), p. 47.

[2] pp. 13–86 of *A Collection of Ordinances and Regulations for the Government
of the Royal Household*, published by the Society of Antiquaries, London, 1790.
For the duties of the forty squires of household see pp. 45–6.

[3] Pegge, op. cit., p. 50.   [4] Ibid., p. 51.

[5] The extract which follows from *The Key of Alchimie* is taken from a transcript in the Wellcome Historical Medical Library, London; it corresponds to
MS. Ashmole 1421, f. 171ᵛ.

which hee intimates in his 6th Chapter where speaking of the stone to be
revealed to the kings of this Land, it shall be found hee saith

> By the fortune & by the grace
> Of a woman faire of face.

None of these quotations is in accordance with the text of the
Ordinal as we have it, nor is the revelation of the stone to a king
of England made in the sixth chapter, but in the fifth. Furthermore, the lines on Edward IV were surely not written in 1477
when he was still alive. A simple explanation of these incongruities
is that Samuel had access to a copy somewhat revised, with the
Proem and Chapters I–VII renumbered Chapters I–VIII. On this
theory the Latin line 'Gratia tardatur peccatum dum dominatur'
represents a revision of line 28 of the Latin Preface: 'Propter
peccata tardantur munera grata'. The revelation to a king of
England would then be correctly in the fifth chapter as we know
the text (ll. 1423 ff.), and probably the reference to Edward IV
could well have been added here after his death, perhaps in '*Henry
the seaventh's* owne *Booke*'. The verse passage 'Yet once this
science I understand . . .' seems to be a free rendering of lines
29–30 of the Latin Preface, with an adroit shift in tense from past
conditional to future assured. The copy owned by Henry VII,
and manuscript A, which seems like a presentation copy, lend
colour to the suggestion that Norton may have revised a little for
each new patron whom he hoped to interest, and that perhaps a
prospective patroness accounted for the passage about 'a woman
faire of face', a happy chance for the writer's great-grandson when
he came to address Queen Elizabeth.

That Samuel knew of such a revised version is clear from quotations in a later section of *The Key of Alchimie*:

> 1. Tho: Nortons authorite for one; where in his 4th Chapter hee
> saith, yee may not with mettalls & quicksilver beginne, To make Elixirs
> which ye intend to winne; Small clarkship there is therin, for they are
> not for this art.

This is from Chapter III, not IV, and the first part corresponds
to ll. 1199–1200; the second part, however, 'Small clarkship . . .'
does not appear in any known manuscript. Shortly afterwards
Samuel quotes ll. 1201–4 as 'Thomas Norton his words'.[1]

> 2. . . . . Of which Thomas Norton . . . maketh mention in his sixth

---

[1] Wellcome transcript, 228–9.

chapter . . . Other men say no liquor from above / Descended better than such as cungers love.[1]

This is from our present Chapter V, ll. 2257–8.

3. . . . Thomas Norton, whose owne words are these

> I made also the Elixir of Life
> Which mee bereft a marchant's wife:
> She wrought with it a full great wonder;
> I made the quintessence which set under
> The nose of him which soundeth nie to death
> Would make hime revive thereof the only breath.

Yf of him it were asked what daies he lived; there were some lately that could well report, for he lived since the birth of my father & was provectae aetatis.[2]

This is clearly an expansion of ll. 905–7. Samuel refers to the same person as his great-grandfather in the 'Preamble', and more formally in the body of the work as Thomas Norton, and becomes a little less formal in the last quotation where family reminiscence comes in. His great-grandfather's book can be no other than the *Ordinal* with revisions by the author. The absence of the more striking changes from any of the known manuscripts seems to imply that a revised copy was preserved in the family and never let out to be copied.

It was no unknown work that Samuel laid claim to for his great-grandfather. By 1577 an alchemical poem, *The Ordinal of Alchemy*, written by Thomas Norton of Bristol in 1477 was familiar in certain learned circles in manuscript copies.[3] The author had been celebrated in Walter Haddon's *Poemata* (1567);[4] one manuscript (R) has a copy of Haddon's lines before the text, and contains descriptions of pictures 'In nortons owne bok fownd in bristowe', a phrase appearing in two other manuscripts of the same group, of which one (Longleat 178) was copied in 1574, the other (Ashmole 1490) probably about 1577. Ascham in *The Scholemaster* mentions 'Th. Norton of Bristow' in such company as Chaucer, Surrey, and Wyatt,[5] and earlier Bale had attributed to 'Thomas Norton, patria Bristollensis, alcumistarum sui temporis non ultimus' a work, *Epitomen Alchimiae*, the first words of which he quotes as 'Ad honorem Dei, in tribus personis', clearly referring

---

[1] Ibid. 239.   [2] Ibid. 297.   [3] See above, p. xxiv.
[4] London, 1567, p. 82.   [5] London, 1570, p. 60.

to the *Ordinal*.[1] When, therefore, Samuel said that his great-grandfather was a leading alchemist of the time of Edward IV, and gave quotations from his book, none of his contemporaries would doubt that he meant his great-grandfather Thomas Norton, and his book the *Ordinal*. Such a claim he must have been certain was true. His family was no more unknown than the book; his father was a knight, Sir George Norton, his mother was a daughter of the Marquis of Dorset; the great-grandfather in question had been a man of at least local prominence. He is attempting to gain the queen's favour in the 'Preamble', and seems to be somewhat on the defensive, and so is unlikely to have claimed what could be challenged. Although the *Key of Alchimie* was not printed, and presumably never seen by the queen, its author must have intended that it should be. He evidently expected no challenge, and there is no evidence that anyone of his contemporaries or immediate successors disputed him.

The author signed his work with an acrostic employing the initial syllables of the Proem and the first six chapters. This was first pointed out in print by Michael Maier in 1617,[2] but noted earlier by Francis Thynne in his own autograph copy of the *Ordinal*, probably at the time of copying, 1573–4, but certainly before his death in 1608.[3] Elias Ashmole in 1652 added the first line of the last chapter to form a couplet:

> From the *first word* of this *Proeme*, and the *Initiall letters* of the *six* following *Chapters* . . . we may collect the *Authors* Name and place of Residence: For those *letters*, (together with the *first line* of the seventh *Chapter*) speak thus,
>
> > Thomas Norton of Briseto,
> > A parfet Master ye maie him trowe.[4]

In one early manuscript (E) the first four syllables only, forming the name 'To Mas Nor TON', were copied over the corresponding

[1] John Bale, *Scriptorum Illustrium majoris Brytannie . . . Catalogus* (Basle, 1557–9), ii. 67.

[2] *Symbola Aureae Mensae duodecim Nationum* (Frankfurt, 1617), p. 467. His words are: 'THOMAS NORTONVS, *Bristoniensis, in arte perfectus magister*, (vt habent initiales syllabae illius libri capitum, quem de hac arte condidit) *agnoscitur.*'

[3] MS. Longleat 178, f. 10ᵛ. His note is in the left-hand margin at the beginning of the text: 'his name was thomas Norton of Bristowe as apperethe by the addinge together of the first syllable of euery chapter & one of ye preface for the first preface begynnethe with To: the I chap wth mas. the 2 wth Nor the 3 wth Ton: the 4. wth of the 5: wth Bris. the 6 wth Towe. & so thomas norton of Bristowe.' [4] Op. cit., p. 437.

syllables in the text, but in a much later hand of the late seventeenth century.

There was a William Norton of Bristol who in 1370 was accounted 'one of the most worthy men of the said town',[1] but the real founder of the fortunes of the Norton family was Thomas Norton, perhaps the son of William; in 1390 he inherited from Elias Spelly, burgess and former mayor, considerable property in Bristol, including a ship.[2] In 1402 he bought from one John Corne 'two messuages . . . near the cemetery of the church of St. Peter',[3] where he built one of the finest houses in the city.[4] He progressed from bailiff in 1393, to sheriff in 1402, to mayor of Bristol in 1414,[5] and represented Bristol in several Parliaments between 1399 and 1421.[6] The exact date of his death is not known, but his two sons, Walter and Thomas, were in 1435 sharing the house bequeathed to them by their father.[7] The younger brother, Thomas, has been identified with the alchemist, but, as Nierenstein and Chapman showed, this is impossible, for his will was proved and registered in 1449.[8] He must have died childless, for his half of the Great House in Bristol, and his lands in Kingston-Seymour, Somerset, went to his brother Walter.[9] He left legacies to his brother's children, Agnes, Elizabeth, and Thomas, who later was to write the *Ordinal*.[10]

The date of birth of this third Thomas, our author, is uncertain. If he was the Thomas Norton esquire who was a witness to a transfer of property on the Sunday after St. Lawrence (10 August) in 1454 at 'Sutton Maundevyle' in Wiltshire,[11] then for his signature to be valid he must have been of age, and so born in 1433 or earlier.

[1] *The Little Red Book of Bristol*, ed. Francis L. Bickley (Bristol and London, 1900), ii. 52.
[2] Revd. T. P. Wadley, *Notes or Abstracts of the Wills . . . in the . . . Great Orphan Book and Book of Wills* (Bristol, 1886), pp. 27, 28.
[3] See J. J. Simpson, 'St. Peter's Hospital, Bristol', *Trans. Bristol and Glouc. Arch. Soc.* xlviii (1926), 193–4.
[4] Ibid., pp. 203–4.
[5] Robert Ricart, *The Maire of Bristowe is Kalendar*, ed. L. Toulmin Smith (London, 1872), pp. 37–8.
[6] *Return. Members of Parliament. Part I. Parliaments of England, 1213–1702* (London, 1878), pp. 258–97.
[7] See Simpson, op. cit., p. 198.
[8] Op. cit., p. 313. See also Wadley, op. cit., p. 140.
[9] Revd. John Collinson, *The History and Antiquities of the County of Somerset* (Bath, 1791), ii. 123.
[10] F. A. Crisp, *Abstracts of Somersetshire Wills*, 1890, Series v, p. 73.
[11] *Cal. Close Rolls, Henry VI*, vol. 6, p. 434.

The identification is not certain, but probable. I have suggested
elsewhere that if he were the youngest of the three alchemists at
Leadenhall (ll. 1389 ff.), and so was born under a cross at the end
of three shires (ll. 1397–8), then he may well have been born at
Colerne, Wiltshire, the nearest village to the county boundaries of
Somerset, Wiltshire, and Gloucestershire.[1] Apart from the mention
of him in his uncle's will, 1449, and two important passages dealing
with him in *The Great Red Book of Bristol*, which we will deal
with later, we have a few records of his career. He was sheriff of
Somerset in 1476 and 1477,[2] and a member for the Commission
of the Peace for the same county in 1475 and 1476.[3] He and Thomas
Croftes were collectors of customs and subsidies in Bristol on
3 December 1477,[4] and he was still holding that office in 1479.
On 13 July 1477 he was made a commissioner to examine and
take over for the king the lands of Thomas Burdet, guilty of high
treason, in Gloucestershire.[5] He is mentioned in the will of his
father-in-law, John Shipward, 14 December 1473, where his wife
Joan is made legatee, by a possible second reversion, of the property in case the testator's son John should fail to carry out the
testator's wishes.[6] On 8 February 1476, Stephen Martyn, 'sherman' of Bristol, made a gift of all his goods and chattels to him and
to John Gourney, merchant of Bristol.[7] In other wills he is mentioned as owning property next to property in the wills, and it
appears he owned a tenement on or near 'Worshuppstrete' in
1471.[8] His will is dated 26 November 1513, and includes a bequest
'To the gyldyng of thymage of St. Jamys [cf. ll. 573–7] at the High
Auter of St. Peter's as much money as shall be necessary for
performing of the same'. His son Andrew was to find a secular
priest daily to sing for his soul and for the souls of his ancestors at
the altar of St. George.[9] At the inquisition *post mortem* at Yeovil,
24 April 1514, it was found that he died possessed of one third of
the manor of Kingston-Seymour, Somerset, and the advowson of
the church, which his son Andrew inherited.[10] He certainly does

[1] *Ambix*, vi, p. 83.
[2] Revd. William Phelps, *History and Antiquities of Somersetshire* (London, 1836), i. 72.
[3] *Cal. Pat. Rolls, Edward IV, 1467–77*, p. 629.
[4] Ibid., *1477–85*, pp. 22, 71.   [5] Ibid., p. 50.
[6] Wadley, op. cit., pp. 160–1.
[7] *Cal. Close Rolls, Edward IV*, vol. ii, item 1574.
[8] Wadley, op. cit., p. 146.
[9] Ibid., 1890, p. 73.   [10] Collinson, op. cit. ii. 123.

not appear to have been in dire poverty at the time of death, as
Pits and others following him have said.[1] He died, then, either in
late 1513 or early in 1514, either approaching his eightieth year or
past it, if our estimate of his birth date is correct; *provectae aetatis*,
as his descendant Samuel put it.

Of two incidents in Thomas Norton's life we have information
in some detail, although the exact significance is in neither case
clear. The alchemist had a younger brother, also called Thomas,
who was not in his uncle Thomas's will in 1449, and so was apparently not born then. He was certainly born by 1458, however, for
in that year their father Walter, for some unexplained reason, by
a feoffment assigned all his real property in Worcestershire and
Bristol to his two sons-in-law, directing them as feoffees to recon-
vey the estate, except half of the Great House, to his younger son,
'that he schold not be vexid ne troublyd by Thomas his Eldyr
Brother'.[2] There was a strange delay in executing the deeds, and
finally it was in 1466 that Walter brought the documents to the
Council House, and requested their enrolment according to the
custom of the city in order to assure their validity. Not content
with this formality, he requested the mayor, sheriff, and other
dignitaries to accompany him to St. Peter's Churchyard, so that
he might in their presence give possession of the eastern half of
the house to his younger son Thomas, in the name of all the estate.[3]
He had already given up all his jewels and household possessions
to this younger son, and made him 'Sieur thereoff in hys lyfe';
while in his will, dated only six days before, he had left to the
elder Thomas only a silver cup, some hangings and cushions in the
hall of his dwelling, and the standing bed in the great chamber
with its tester and curtains—the elder Thomas also to have the
western half of the Great House.[4] Walter clearly distrusted his
elder son, and wished to make certain that he would lay no hand
upon his property after his death. Yet, only ten months later,
Thomas Norton the younger was appearing before the mayor and
sheriff to complain that his father, 'by the synystre labour and

---

[1] 'In hanc vanissimam artem miser impegit . . . suam etiam sine dubio sub-
stantiam, & eorum qui ei crediderunt, bursas exhausit & exinaniuit.' *Ioannis
Pitsei Angli . . . Relationum Historicarum de Rebus Anglicis Tomus Primus*
(Parisiis, 1619), i. 666.

[2] E. W. W. Veale (ed.), *The Great Red Book of Bristol*. Text (Pt. III), *Bristol
Rec. Soc. Pubns.* xvi. 139.

[3] Ibid., pp. 139–42.   [4] Ibid., p. 112.

informacion of yll-disposid persoones hathe publisshed and noysed in dyversez Countrays that he hath enfeoffid the seyd Thomas Norton the Younger his son but of trust onely to his owne usze', and that he intended to make void the existing deeds and disinherit the complainant, 'against all right and conscience'. The younger Thomas therefore prayed the civic officials to make known what they knew respecting the matter, and they solemnly affirmed that they were witnesses to the transfer of the property.[1] There is nothing to indicate that Walter Norton took any further steps; the date of his death is unknown, but the 1466 will was enrolled in the *Great Red Book*, and does not appear to have been contested. The significance of all this is not clear; the father may have become disillusioned about both his sons, or have recovered some confidence in the elder.

The second of these incidents in Norton's life, when he accused the mayor of Bristol of high treason, is described in a long passage in *The Great Red Book*. This is a 'Remembraunce Nevir to be put in oblyvion but to be hadde in perpetuell memory of all the trewe Burgeises and lovers of the Towne of Bristowe of the Innatural demeanyng and the Inordinate behavyng of Thomas Norton of Bristowe Gentleman against the noble famouse and trewe merchaunte William Spencer beinge the thirde tyme Maire of the Towne of Bristowe', and it was compiled by John Twynyho, the recorder, who advised the mayor in the matter.[2] On Friday, 12 March 1479, Thomas Norton came to the mayor, and read him an accusation of high treason, protesting that this was not because of any dispute depending between him and the mayor but only in 'subduyng of the Renued malice and traytrous dispositioun Surgyng of thyne olde Rotyn hatefull and Traytrous hert'. The usual formal offer of trial by combat was given, and Norton gave his glove and sealed appeal to the sheriff, who was present. The next day the mayor, apparently to the great distress of the council, announced that he would not remain in office until he was cleared of the charge, and gave himself up to the sheriff to be taken to the gaol until the king heard of the case.

On the Sunday the sheriff delivered the appeal and glove to Thomas Asshe, yeoman of the King's Chamber, and Comptroller

---

[1] *Bristol Rec. Soc. Pubns.* xvi. 139–42.

[2] The whole is published in *Bristol Rec. Soc. Pubns.* xviii, 57–93, and the quotations following are from this source.

of the Port, to be given to the king, with a letter from the sheriff
stating that Norton had retained divers riotous and idle persons by
oath and otherwise, and that the previous week the mayor had
ordered five of them to be arrested for assaulting the bailiff of
Temple fee and leaving him for dead; three were arrested, two
escaped. On Monday the sheriff, bailiffs, and the rest of the council
sent a full account of Norton's conduct to the king and the Privy
Council. The letter speaks highly of Spencer's good deeds and
then launches into a denunciation of Norton. He haunts taverns,
keeps in his service 'many idell and misgouvernid persones',
neglects divine service and on Sunday afternoons plays 'at the
Tenyse and othir suche fryvolous disportes'. He has troubled his
father and mother and 'sith theire decees he hath interuptid and
broken their last willes and testaments'. He has imprisoned his
younger brother and acquired his property by forcing his father-
in-law, John Shipward, to give him the deeds to it, abusing his
authority as king's agent by threatening, or at least by falsely
letting it be known he had authority, to behead him if he refused.
He had finally driven his younger brother to fly to Spain, and
during the voyage there his brother was drowned. He had agreed
to pay a rent to his younger brother's widow, but had withdrawn
from the agreement.

When Norton arrived in London to appear before the king, the
deputies of the town had preceded him, and 'the kinge estraunged
his loke from him And he perceivid that and departid from the
Courte to Braynesforde And all the Courte hath him in suche
lothnes that no Creature accompanyed nor made him anny chere.'
When finally on Saturday, 20 March, the case was heard, Norton
had no evidence to put forward; as the 'Remembrance' puts it:
'Almighty god that is the serchere of all hertes and Knowith the
previtee of all sacresies made him so fele and understande his
oune untrue demeanyng in this matier that he coude unnethe
loke speke ne Kepe his countenaunce before the Kinge and his
Counceile but demenyd himself as a persone Ronne into fronsy.'
As a result, the case against Spencer was dismissed. According to
Adam's *Chronicle of Bristol*, the mayor was 'highly commended of
the King for his wisdom; and the said Norton was severely checked
of his malicious intent'.[1]

In a letter dated 21 March, the king informed the sheriff that

[1] *Adam's Chronicle of Bristol*, ed. F. F. Fox (Bristol, 1910), p. 73.

the charges against Spencer were dismissed, and directed him to send to him William Wilkins, 'upon whome the saide Thomas groundith the matier of his saide accusacioun'. The sheriff wrote back to inform the king that the man he required was John Wilkins, a butcher. He gave him a thoroughly bad character, related the various disturbances of the peace in which he had been involved, and sent him to the king. According to the sheriff's letter, Wilkins was a persistent and incorrigible law-breaker (and yet after several outbreaks he had been made watchman!). Some six months before the incident between Norton and the mayor, some fellow prisoners had laid information that Wilkins had often alleged that the mayor, William Spencer, was disloyal, having £400 of the late Duke of Clarence, and £300 of the Earl of Warwick's, which should have been forfeited to the king. On examination Wilkins affirmed he had only said that if he were free he would cause the mayor to come before the prince's council, but would not say why.

After accusing the mayor of treason Norton had tried to contact Wilkins, but being rebuffed by the keeper had passed messages to him through his wife. Apparently he was relying on Wilkins's evidence to sustain his suit. When the king examined Wilkins, however, he spoke well of the mayor and made no accusations against him. However, Thomas Norton was not beaten yet, and, as the 'Remembrance' puts it, 'he contrived fals froward and senestre billes of compleynt' against the mayor and presented them to the king. The 'Remembrance' includes one of these.

In this, Norton complains that after receiving the king's letter dismissing the charge of treason, Spencer has arrested him and some followers on the grounds that they were his retainers, in spite of the fact that the same charge had been laid against the same persons previously, and they had been tried by a former mayor, John Shipward, in the presence of the recorder, Spencer and others, and been acquitted. Norton claims that on this previous occasion they were 'examyned sodenly severally and secretly . . . at the which it was plainly proved and founde bi that examinacioun that all suche promise as they had made with me was no Reteignor but Rightfull playn and laufull dealinge for whiche they were then and there clerely dismissed'. He goes on to explain that as customs officer he had arranged a special search to be made by two men for cloth smuggled out of Bristol by land 'to other of youre portes uncustomed'. This had never been done before, and his two men had seized nine cloths belonging to the mayor, William Spencer. These, of course, were forfeited, and when Norton refused a bribe from Spencer of a hogshead of wine to conceal the fact, the mayor had retaliated by thus indicting his followers of wearing his livery.

Of the affray between his followers and the bailiff of Temple fee on the Sunday before his accusation against the mayor of high treason, Norton gives his account. He says that the merchants did their best to evade customs duty by shipping their goods at night, with the connivance of the sailors. The sailors were violent with his searchers, and the mayor was misusing his authority to terrorize anybody from joining with himself as customs officer to prevent this smuggling; in this he had the support of the other merchants. The arrest of his followers on the morning after the fight with the bailiff was an instance; only one was involved, the bailiff had begun the fight, and each of the combatants had a broken head and no other injury. The king, however, still dismissed the accusations, and ordered the recorder, John Twynyho, to conduct a final investigation into the matter so that all grudges might cease—an investigation for which Norton, at the abrupt close of the document, had not appeared.

What truth there was in these charges and counter-charges we cannot know. It seems that Norton was very much a man of his age in his conduct towards his opponents. He shows little love of merchants in his poem (cf. ll. 27-8, 905-6), but on the other hand we need not take too seriously the character reference which the aldermen sent to the king with the express purpose of blackening his name. It would be interesting to have a corresponding account of the way of life of that more renowned customs officer, Geoffrey Chaucer, written by a group of wine importers. The most damaging passage is that describing his behaviour toward his younger brother, and incidentally toward his father-in-law. But again we have no means of knowing the exact truth. From John Shipward's will, mentioned earlier, it might seem that his father-in-law was not on altogether bad terms with him; and his younger brother, however innocently, was a Jacob to his Esau, and it may be that their father had regretted too late his partiality for his younger son. In trying to recover his inheritance, Thomas may even have been doing what had been his father's last intention. All this, however, must remain conjecture. Also conjecture is the following attempt to relate what we know of his relations with his father and brother to some passages in the *Ordinal*.

By taking up the study of alchemy as a young man, an occupation quite certain to waste rather than augment the family fortunes, Thomas would surely have disappointed his father. These alchemical studies would have been going on during the fifties of the century, and Walter Norton would then have transferred his affections and property to his late-born child, even to the extent of giving him his elder brother's name, as if the latter were dead. He was still of the same mind in 1466, when he made his will, but by the next year he had altered and was trying to disavow his own actions. A possible motive suggests itself, namely that the elder son finally gave evidence of an ability to get on in the world. Thomas states that his master delayed giving him the final secret of the red stone because he was too young, scarcely twenty-eight (ll. 2583 ff.); if he were born in 1433, this would have been in 1461. After a period of trial he received the secret (ll. 2621–2), and then presumably set about making his elixir. It was in 1466 that 'Bryse' began his work on 'change of þe coyne' at the mint,[1] and by this time Thomas would have had ample time to complete his operations to his own satisfaction, and be ready to play his role of the youngest and greatest of the three alchemists at Leadenhall (ll. 1389 ff.). Since the devaluation of the coinage was due to a shortage of gold, a successful alchemist might well gain the king's favour, as Samuel Norton says all three of them did. Such favour, especially if it took the tangible form of an appointment as squire of household, might well have led his father to a more respectful attitude and to a reconsideration of his act of disinheritance. A further incentive toward this could have been that Thomas gave up the expensive active pursuit of alchemy, as indicated in ll. 895–8. This abandonment of his vocation would have been occasioned by the

---

[1] See l. 1383. This 'Bryse' was Hugh Brice, a goldsmith, the 'Citezeyn and Alderman of London' who paid for the printing of Caxton's *Mirrour of the World* (1480) to be presented to Lord Hastings. He was appointed clerk of the mint in the Tower of London, 2 February, 1466, where he acted as deputy to the master, Lord Hastings. The coinage was to be altered and all gold and silver coins were to be called in, Brice's duty being then to give fixed sums in exchange for the coins according to their size and weight. On Brice's activites see *Cal. Pat. Rolls, Edward IV*, p. 475; *Edward IV—Henry VI*, pp. 149, 546, 551, 556, 586; on the change of currency see Charles Oman, *The Coinage of England* (Oxford, 1931), pp. 175, 199, 219–21.

INTRODUCTION

small leisure afforded him by his appointment, and would probably have followed hard upon it.

This suggestion fits in with other information in the text. The incident of Thomas Herbert and the alchemist Dalton (ll. 913 ff.) must have occurred before the restoration of Henry VI in 1470, since John Delves, one of those involved, was beheaded after the Battle of Tewkesbury in 1471.[1] Thomas Herbert was the brother of William Herbert, first Earl of Pembroke, who was executed at Northampton after being captured at the Battle of Edgecote in 1469; in his will, made on the day of the battle, he appointed his brother one of his executors.[2] Thomas was made esquire of the body for Edward IV on 10 July 1461, receiving fifty marks a year,[3] and in 1465 he was serving as constable of Gloucester Castle while still an esquire of the body.[4] Troy house was in Monmouthshire and a seat of the Herbert family.[5] So the account in the *Ordinal* is completely consistent, and indeed appears to be that of an eyewitness for the first part of it. Thomas Herbert held Dalton for a time in Gloucester Castle, and then for nearly five years at Troy before releasing him; the death of Herbert came soon after. He died, in fact, in 1474 or possibly a little earlier,[6] and so his initial forcible introduction of Dalton to the king was in 1469 or earlier, just when, on our conjecture, Thomas Norton was squire of household and in a position to know of it. The incident confirms the king's interest in alchemists, since Herbert took the trouble to bring one to him by force and violence. We may conclude our conjectures by assuming that, once launched on a public career, Thomas Norton neglected alchemy until he wrote the *Ordinal*, to the date of which and the realm of fact we now return.

[1] For an account of his and others' execution after taking sanctuary in Tewkesbury Abbey after the battle, and in spite of a royal promise of pardon see Stow, *Annales of England* (1592), pp. 695–6. Stow has his name wrong, calling him James, whereas his source, the *Chronicle of Tewkesbury*, correctly has him as John. See also Sir Delves L. Broughton, Bart., *Records of an Old Cheshire Family* (London, 1908), pp. 36–43.

[2] William Dugdale, *Baronage of England* (London, 1675), ii. 257.

[3] *Cal. Pat. Rolls, 1461–7*, p. 8.

[4] Ibid., p. 441.

[5] *Comprehensive Gazetteer of England and Wales*, ed. J. H. F. Brabner, F.R.G.S. (London, 1894), iv. 286.

[6] The manor of Duntisborne Rouse in Gloucestershire, granted to him and to his male heirs in 1462, was granted to Sir Richard Beauchamp in 1474, after his death without male heirs. See Samuel Rudder, *A New History of Gloucestershire* (Cirencester, 1779), p. 424.

In the last two lines of the poem Norton states that the work was begun in 1477, implying perhaps that it was not completed in that year. Internal evidence agrees with this date. Gilbert Kymer is spoken of in the past tense as if he were dead (l. 1559); he died in 1463. There are references to the new currency, 1465 and 1466, and later (ll. 1383 ff.) to the Battle of Tewkesbury, 1471, and to Herbert's death, 1474 or earlier, the latest datable event mentioned. Since manuscript A is to be dated not far from 1490, there is no reason to doubt that the author gives the true date of his beginning to write.

Besides the *Ordinal*, Bale credits Norton with another work entitled 'De transmutatione metallorum' and also 'alia quaeda(m)',[1] and to these Pits adds a third 'De lapide Philosophico' and 'id genus alia multa'.[2] As to the first of these, Pierre Borel in his *Bibliotheca Chimica* attributes to Norton a work 'de transmut. metallorum, liber vnus', but since he says that Norton 'claruit anno 1447' and adds: 'Vide eius opus in Tripode aureo Michaelis Maieri' he probably knew of only one work of Norton, the *Ordinal*, and 1447 is a mistake for 1477.[3] It is probable that the title is only another name for the *Ordinal*. As to the second, 'De lapide Philosophico', there is a manuscript mentioned in the first Report of the Historical Manuscripts Commission, among the books and papers of the Earl of Winchilsea and Nottingham, described as 'Another book of Poetry, headed "Mr. Norton's work de lapide ph'orum."'.[4] This, however, is the *Ordinal*, as Nierenstein and Price first pointed out.[5] If this name was used sometimes to describe the *Ordinal*, then Pits has added to the Norton canon a name only, not a separate work.

THE ALCHEMY OF THE *ORDINAL*

Much of *The Ordinal of Alchemy*, even the technical part of it, makes straightforward reading. But no reader of the *Canon's Yeoman's Tale* will be surprised to find the heart of the matter,

---

[1] Op. cit. ii. 67.
[2] Op. cit. i. 666.
[3] Paris, 1654, p. 168.
[4] Hist. MSS. Comm. *1st Report*, 1870, Appendix, p. 32, col. 2.
[5] M. Nierenstein and Frances M. Price, 'The Identity of the Manuscript entitled "Mr. Nortons worke, *de lapide ph'orum*" with the Ordinall of Alchimy', *Isis*, no. 60 (xxi. 1) (1934), 52–6.

the process of making an elixir or philosopher's stone, extremely obscure. A little of this obscurity can be cleared up by historical study of the concepts and processes of alchemy, but only a little. The alchemists of medieval Europe took over from the Arabic world a large body of learning which convinced them of the possibility of making a philosopher's stone and of transmuting base metals into gold or silver. From their inherited scientific ideas a supporting theory and method of transmutation could be proposed which at least sounded plausible. But the practical application of the erroneous theory was impossible, and in describing practical steps the writers were of necessity, and even intentionally, vague. We cannot, then, elucidate in detail the writings of the alchemists, but we can, however, examine how their theories and misconceptions arose. The task of explaining these theories has been greatly eased by excellent studies now available in English, particularly the books by F. Sherwood Taylor and E. J. Holmyard, which will be found abundantly cited in the footnotes, and by the very recent *Origins of Alchemy in Graeco-Roman Egypt* by Jack Lindsay (1971). Only with such helps could the present Introduction have been attempted. In this brief sketch the question of a Chinese origin or a possible double origin of alchemy may be passed over, and we will begin with Egypt in the early centuries before and after Christ where we find the first alchemical writings of the Western world.

Our knowledge of Hellenistic alchemy comes from collections of writings in three manuscripts, one at Venice and two at Paris, and from three papyri at Leiden and a papyrus at Stockholm.[1] The Venice manuscript contains parts of a work *Physika kai Mystika* attributed to Democritus; this pseudo-Democritus is referred to in the Leiden papyrus, he is frequently referred to by other commentators as an authority, and his work is usually placed at A.D. 100 or earlier, the earliest known Greek alchemical text. From the sixth-century commentator Synesius we learn that the work was originally in four books on the making of gold, of silver, of gems, and of purple; the extant text preserves only two recipes for tingeing with purple, some recipes for making gold (chrysopeia) and silver (argyropeia), a polemic against another school, and an interesting account of the writer's relations with his teacher,

[1] For references see F. Sherwood Taylor, 'A Survey of Greek Alchemy', *Journal of Hellenic Studies*, l (1930), 109–39.

Ostanes. The recipes of the pseudo-Democritus and his school
have been taken together with those in the papyri[1] to show that
the alchemical writers adopted practical craftsmen's recipes for
making imitation jewellery and precious metals, and adapted them
to their own more philosophical purposes. The writers were
familiar with methods of making alloys of gold or silver and other
substances to produce something resembling gold or silver in
weight, and of superficially treating these with arsenic or antimony
to procure a white or silver-like colour, and with sulphur to produce yellowing. In the case of alloys the gold or silver was thought
of as a 'seed' or 'ferment' which would tend to grow, or transform
the 'lump' into the more precious metal.

The question of colouring or tingeing metals is more complex
and of greater importance in the history of alchemy. The pseudo-
Democritus and his followers seem to have taken the quality of
colour as an important characteristic in the metal, and hence
changing this quality effected a genuine change in the substance.
The colour sequence which became classic was black, white,
yellow, purple, and a general theory of metallic perfection seems
to underly the operations to effect this. The basic unity of all
matter was the underlying theory, but to the early alchemists prime
matter was not the indeterminate Aristotelian *hyle*, but apparently
lead, or an alloy of base metals which when melted together would
look black owing to surface oxidization. To this were applied
substances thought to be able to impart new qualities to it because
they had sympathy with it.[2] This concern with a specified sequence
of colours in the work is a permanent theme in alchemy, but by
the fifteenth century the number has been reduced to three, black,
white, and red (perhaps the original purple). The yellowing has
dropped out. Jung suggests the reason for the change from four
to three was psychological rather than chemical, a preference for

[1] The recipes in the papyri have been taken to be true craftsmen's recipes,
but according to E. J. Holmyard they are often incomplete and impractical, and
are probably collections made by alchemists (*Alchemy*, Penguin Books (1957),
p. 25).
[2] See André J. Festugière, *La Révélation d'Hermès Trismégiste*, vol. i,
L'Astrologie et les Sciences occultes (Paris, 1944), pp. 234–5. Lindsay, op. cit.,
p. 113, associates the colour-sequence of black–white–red with a 'herb of resurrection', so that the specific colour changes were perhaps sought in alchemy as
indicating a change from death to life in metals. For further analogies of the
colour-sequence with the theme of rebirth or resurrection see H. J. Sheppard,
Ambix, vii (1959), 42–6.

a trinity rather than a quaternity.[1] In any case, this trinity appears in Norton (1529–34).

Another group of early Hellenistic alchemists was the school of Mary the Jewess[2] to whom was attributed the invention of an efficient still, the water bath and even the *kerotakis*, an instrument in which metals to be worked on were held on a grating above a quantity of mercury, or in other cases, sulphur and arsenic sulphide. When this was heated the resulting fumes attacked and dissolved the metals on the grating, and the liquid flowed down into the heated mixture in the bottom. Sherwood Taylor[3] suggests how this apparatus could be used to produce a continuous blackening, whitening, and yellowing of the heated mixture. On the basis of the colour sequence and a study of the Egyptian craftsman's recipes in the papyri and pseudo-Democritus, A. J. Hopkins[4] developed a theory of the origin of alchemy as the application of Greek philosophy to the artisan's technology. The basic formless first matter was sought by fusing the base metals so that a black (oxidized) alloy resulted. By treating this with antimony or arsenic a white surface (e.g. of copper arsenide) was produced, while the coppery colour within would be taken as evidence that the mass was already being perfected towards gold (cf. the *Ordinal*, 2651 ff.). Yellowing would follow by treating the mass with sulphur fumes in a *kerotakis*. The hydrogen sulphide fumes would be thought of as a spirit or tingeing *pneuma* carrying the yellowness of sulphur to the mass, penetrating it and conveying new qualities. Neo-Platonic and Stoic conceptions of a very subtle pneuma operating on prime matter and developing it thus seemed to have a visible proof and a practical application. Later historians like Holmyard and Sherwood Taylor are more cautious and less boldly speculative in handling the early documents. But it is clear that the early alchemists were applying philosophical concepts to imitative craftsmen's technique, and their interest was in transforming metals and improving them. It is to Bolos of Mendes who lived about 200 B.C. that the credit most probably belongs for this union

---

[1] C. G. Jung, *Psychology and Alchemy*, tr. R. F. C. Hull (Princeton, 2nd edn. rev. 1968), p. 230.

[2] Sherwood Taylor, op. cit., p. 116; see also id., *The Alchemists*, (1949), pp. 38, 43 ff.; she was also known as Miriam, or Mary, sister of Moses, or of Aaron, cf. *Ordinal* 2563, 2657.

[3] *J.H.S.*, l. 133–7.

[4] *Alchemy, Child of Greek Philosophy* (New York, 1934); see esp. pp. 46–58.

of theory and practice, and from his work the *Physika kai Mystika* most probably derives.[1] However this may be, it is clear that the earliest Hellenistic alchemists, in the early centuries of our era and perhaps before, were concerned with the possibility of transmutation and improvement of metals by imparting to them new qualities of colour in a definite sequence. The materials had to have mutual sympathy, and the worker had to know the secret of combining different natures; as the *Physika kai Mystika* has it: 'The nature in such a case is charmed by the nature; in such a case triumphs over it; in such a case, dominates it.'[2]

A presentation of early Hellenistic alchemy as essentially a practical, rational, or philosophical pursuit would be very one-sided however. Festugière[3] has characterized the whole mental set of the era as tending to give up the search for knowledge by reason and to look to revelation even for scientific knowledge, and this tendency is apparent in the *Physika kai Mystika*. The writer tells us that he studied long under a master Ostanes who, however, died before he had completed his education in the art, and had taken precautions before death to ensure that the secret knowledge would come only to his own son. The baffled pupil raised his master's spirit, but the shade was silent, saying his demon forbade him to speak; all he would impart was that 'the books are in the temple'. Later, at the temple, a pillar opened and Ostanes' son explained that his father's books were there. In these the formula (quoted above, see footnote 2) that explained all to the pupil was found. Already then at this early date we can see elements of a quasi-religious nature destined to survive long: the long search for a secret knowledge and the final acquiring of it often in a very cryptic form from a master who had been himself initiated into the secret and who imposed a solemn oath of secrecy on the learner. The relationship of Norton and his master, described in Chapter II (819 ff., cf. 2583 ff.) shows much the same features.[4] The beginner in alchemy always encountered great difficulty, and Norton's account in Chapter II is somewhat amusingly confirmed

---

[1] Festugière, op. cit., pp. 230–4; cf. also Lindsay, op. cit., pp. 90–130.
[2] The rendering is that quoted by Sheppard, op. cit., p. 44; cf. Festugière, op. cit., pp. 231–2.
[3] Op. cit., Chapter I, esp. pp. 13–14.
[4] For an account of a succession of masters and pupils in fifteen- and sixteenth-century England see Sherwood Taylor, *The Alchemists*, pp. 130–5.

in the *Liber Secretorum Artis* attributed to Calid, son of Iaichus; the author tells of his pupil, Musa, who laboured long and at last begged for direction, but got only the instruction to read the philosophers' books. After reading more than one hundred he was still in the dark, 'qui tunc remansit ideo stupefactus, & quasi extra mentem positus, etiam per annum continue in ea perscrutando'. Whereupon his master wrote his book to enlighten him.[1]

Such secrecy and religious attitudes are associated then with the work from our earliest records, but in the later works of Hellenistic alchemy a further element of Gnosticism appears. The gnostic symbol of the serpent eating its tail, the *Ouroboros*, had appeared in an early text, *The Gold-making of Cleopatra*, perhaps representing the circulatory nature of a process such as distillations.[2] In another work attributed to the same author, *Dialogue of Cleopatra and the Philosophers*, mystical language is found which may refer to death and resurrection of the soul or of metals, or both,[3] and in the works of Zosimos of Panopolis (*c.* A.D. 300) the gnostic overlay had become a dominant feature. In his *Visions*, which have been translated by Sherwood Taylor,[4] a priest explains to the dreamer that he had been killed and dismembered, his bones and flesh burned until he learned to become a spirit. Later the priest appears as a man of copper, who was the sacrificer and sacrifice; all the rites take place in the presence of an altar in the form of a bowl containing people being boiled. In succeeding visions the dreamer meets a succession of figures who are cast into the waters. The whole evidently represents a form of a death and regeneration myth. As an introduction to a work on furnaces the

---

[1] In Jean Jacques Manget, *Bibliotheca Chemica Curiosa . . .*, (2 vols. Geneva, 1702), ii. 184.

[2] Sherwood Taylor, *The Alchemists*, p. 58; cf. *J.H.S.*, l. 112.

[3] See H. J. Sheppard, *Ambix*, vi (1957), 96. He is apparently thinking of passages like the following: 'The waters, when they come, awake the bodies and the spirits that are imprisoned and weak. For they again undergo oppression and are enclosed in Hades, and yet in a little while they grow and rise up and put on various glorious colours like the flowers in spring.' (Translated Lindsay, op. cit., p. 254.) An important alchemical metaphor first appearing in 'Cleopatra' is that of the marriage, implicit in the formula of the pseudo-Democritus that nature is charmed by nature, and nature dominates nature. 'From this rock take arsenic and use it for the divine process of whitening. And look, in the middle of the mountain, below the male there lies the mate with whom he is united and in whom he delights; for nature rejoices in nature and without her there is no union. . . . See the fulfilment of the art is the joining-together of the bride and the bridegroom, and in their becoming one.' (Ibid., p. 256.)

[4] *Ambix*, i (1937), 88–92; cf. also *The Alchemists*, pp. 60–5.

same Zosimos makes a specific reference to Jesus Christ as a saviour who, as son of God, made himself one with Adam. Adam had been originally a man of light, but was persuaded to put on a material Adam made of the four elements, and Jesus bore him back up to where the Men of Light dwelt before.[1] The analogies of Christ and the philosophers' stone found in later Latin alchemists (e.g. Petrus Bonus of Ferrara and Arnald of Villanova) had their origin in earlier writings.

The double nature of alchemy, as a practical art, and as an esoteric practice to be described only in veiled language with consequent mystification, remained very evident throughout the history of European alchemy, and although not much trace of it appears in Norton, yet clearly he knew of it, and the religious and arcane nature of the work with the consequent necessity for guarded speech was important to him (1181–2, 2631–2, 2649–50, 2682). This resulted in a considerable use of synonyms for the materials used. Once again this practice goes back to the earliest known Greek sources; one of the Leiden papyri contains a synonomy of thirty-seven substances and plants with their mystical names.[2] It seems likely that most, if not all, of the mysterious liquors and waters enumerated in the *Ordinal* (2209–2350) are really the same substance.

The basic alchemical theory developed in Hellenistic alchemy comprised, then, the concept of the unity of matter, the transformation of metals in a colour sequence, the concept of using gold or other precious metal as a seed or ferment to work on an alloy of base metals, and the apparatus of distilling, heating, and working on materials by a tingeing spirit or *pneuma* in an enclosed vessel, the *kerotakis*; the work had a sacred or arcane quality since the operation had analogies to the cosmos and was in fact a microcosm (like man himself) of the great cosmos, not merely in physical correspondence to the world-pneuma that operated throughout the cosmos, but in mystical analogy. The discovery of the work was often attributed to divine revelation by the Egyptian god Thoth, corresponding to the Greek Hermes. In the sixteenth and seven-

---

[1] The whole passage is available in Jung, op. cit., pp. 360–8, and in Festugière, op. cit., pp. 263–73.

[2] Sherwood Taylor, *J.H.S.*, l. 111. The practice of devising secret names for drugs is found in early Sumerian and Babylonian texts (cf. E. O. von Lippmann, *Entstehung und Ausbreitung der Alchemie*, iii (1954), 53).

teenth centuries, at the end of its long career, alchemy was known as the Hermetic art.

Greek scientific writings of all kinds, including alchemical works, were translated into Arabic in the second half of the eighth century, and the Islamic alchemists developed the science. In the writings attributed to Jabir Ibn Hayyan (whose name may appear in the medieval form Geber)[1] certain prominent alchemical theories appear, including the theory that metals are composed of sulphur and mercury. Aristotle had assigned the source of metals to the union of two vapours, one moist and one dry, congealing in the bowels of the earth; the moist vapour was the cause of their fusibility and ductility, while the dry vapour was the cause of their 'earth' and being affected by fire.[2] In the Jabirian theory these two vapours became the vapours of mercury and sulphur, and if the mixture was perfectly tempered, gold was formed. The sulphur and mercury were in some way different from the common substances passing under these names, which were known to combine to produce the red mercuric sulphide, or Cinnabar. This sulphur–mercury theory was widely, if not universally, held throughout the Middle Ages and later. It was clearly a keystone of alchemical theory; if the faulty blend in any base metal could be corrected, gold would result.

While this sulphur–mercury theory of metals is not stressed in the *Ordinal*, it clearly lends itself to a symbolic interpretation as a marriage. This appears in the 29th speech of the *Turba Philosophorum*, a translation of an Arabic work which may be as early as A.D. 900. In this speech the instruction is to join 'Citrine' with his wife, and Art is produced between them; after conjunction they are to be placed in a bath, which is not to be too much heated. Ruska in his edition equates the Citrine (*Zitronengelben*) with sulphur and the wife with mercury. Now, whatever the Litharge

---

[1] The historian of alchemy, E. O. von Lippmann, was doubtful of his existence (op. cit. i (1919), 363), and Paul Kraus (*Jabir ibn Hayyan*, 2 vols., Cairo 1942–3) argued that the works attributed to him were pseudonymous; however, E. J. Holmyard considered him a real chemist, and H. W. Stapleton argued that his genuine works were re-edited after his death during the ninth century. For references see von Lippmann, ii. 71 ff.; iii. 54–5. The major Latin works of 'Geber' have not been traced to Arabic sources. The short account of Arabic additions to the theory of alchemy given here is based on Sherwood Taylor, *The Alchemists*, Chapter VII, E. J. Holmyard, *Alchemy*, Chapter V, and the latter's 1928 edition of *The Works of Geber. Englished by Richard Russell, 1678.*
[2] *Meteor.*, 378 a, b.

and Magnesia of Chapter III of the *Ordinal* may be, as the two 'materials of the stone' they are clearly male and female elements, the brown and ruddy Litharge or Marchasite being the fiery, masculine element, and the glittering Magnesia being the female fluid element; they are apparently surrogates for sulphur and mercury.[1]

Returning to the Jabirian writings, another concept, important for later alchemy but first found in them, is that of balance of the qualities hot, cold, moist, and dry. Holmyard gives an example of the complicated way in which the amounts of these qualities in lead could be calculated.[2] But if these were known, a perfect balance could be obtained by adding correct amounts of certain qualities to achieve a proper proportion, and gold could be obtained from lead. This could be done by means of elixirs, or medicines. As a physician prescribed a medicament rich in one quality to make up the imbalance of humours causing diseases in his patient, so the alchemist could rectify the misproportion of qualities in base metals and make them gold.[3] Such a medicament could be an elixir. This concept goes back to Hellenistic alchemy, but the notion of the supreme elixir was developed by Jabir.[4] The Jabirian writings describe repeated distillations of various animal and vegetable substances to try to separate out pure qualities of heat, cold, moist, dry, to add to a mixture to gain the correct proportion of qualities for gold. In the *Ordinal*, a great part of the 'Gross Work' of Chapter IV seems to be concerned with obtaining 'pure' natures, and of the 'Subtle Work' in Chapter V with the combining of these. Norton gives a great deal of instruction on the subject of colour, taste, and smell, so that an adept could tell from these which element was dominant in the mixture at any time, and correct the imbalance with the appropriate opposite quality.

A further evidence of such a traditional method continuing to find its place in alchemical writings is the widely repeated statement of errors of other alchemists or the writer himself in the early

[1] See J. F. Ruska (ed.), *Turba Philosophorum: ein Beitrag zur Geschichte der Alchemie* (Berlin, 1931), pp. 215-16. The instruction is to join the masculine—called the Son of the Red Slave—with his fragrant wife, and after the conjunction to place Citrine with his wife into the bath. Ruska says the 'son' may be 'Quicksilver' or sulphur, or sulphide of arsenic; in a footnote on p. 216 he seems to opt for the latter, making the Citrine the sulphur and the wife Quicksilver.

[2] *Alchemy*, pp. 74-5.   [3] Sherwood Taylor, *The Alchemists*, pp. 80 ff.

[4] Ibid., p. 82; Holmyard, op. cit., p. 76. The supreme elixir, as elixir of life, most probably has its origin in Chinese alchemy.

period of his acquaintance with the art. The errors frequently consisted of experiments involving distillation of many organic substances, resulting in great waste of time and money. Norton attributes such to his interlocutor Tonsile at the beginning of Chapter III (1051–66), Ripley to himself when young in the last part—*Retractatio*—of his *Compend of Alchemy*, and Chaucer's Canon's Yeoman to his master (*Canterbury Tales*, G 790 ff.). This practice is presumably the result of the investigations by the Jabirian writers of the distillates of various substances.

Besides Jabir the world of Islam produced a great chemist in al-Razi (? 850–925), usually known to the Latin world as Rasis or Rhases, whose methods are described by Holmyard.[1] These involved a purification of the original materials, then disintegration by solution (usually in alkaline liquids) and then the solutions combined in proper proportions and blended by 'coagulation' to produce an elixir. Whether this process lay behind Norton's 'Gross Work' and 'Subtle Work', which appear to mean obtaining pure ingredients and then dividing them into their qualities and recombining them, is not clear, but the parallel is suggestive.

It is interesting that the best-known philosopher of the Arabic world, Avicenna (980–1037), while following al-Razi on the constitution of metals (the sulphur–mercury theory, with the base metals due to the inferior quality or the impurity of the ingredients) none the less rejects the possibility of transmutation:

As to the claims of the alchemists, it must be clearly understood that it is not in their power to bring about any true change of species. They can, however, produce excellent imitations, dyeing the red [metal] white so that it closely resembles silver, or dyeing it yellow so that it closely resembles gold. . . . Yet in these [dyed metals] the essential nature remains unchanged; they are merely so dominated by induced qualities that errors may be made concerning them, just as it happens that men are deceived by malt, *qalqand*, sal-ammoniac, etc. . . . Those properties which are perceived by the senses are probably not the differences which separate the metals into species, but rather accidents or consequences, the specific differences being unknown.[2]

As a result, several thirteenth-century European authorities, Albertus Magnus, Vincent of Beauvais, and Ramon Lull denied the possibility of real transformation. However, the existence of a

[1] Op. cit., pp. 84–8.
[2] E. J. Holmyard and D. C. Mandeville (edd.), *Avicennae de Congelatione et Conglutinatione Lapidum* (Paris, 1927), pp. 41–2.

work attributed to Avicenna, *De Anima in Arte Alchimiae*, supporting transformation, enabled alchemists to dismiss the *De Congelatione* as early work or a deliberate blind to conceal the great mystery from the public.

When alchemy entered Europe in the twelfth century, its theories and methods were pretty well established. The sulphur–mercury theory of metals, the elixir, the colour sequence, the ferment, the separation and conjunction of elements or qualities, the distillatory practices for achieving this, the analogies of marriage, death, and birth, the association with religious mysteries—all these conceptions were already present when the first Latin translation of an Arabic alchemical work, Morienus Romanus *Liber de Compositione Alchemiae*, was made by Robert of Chester in 1144. This was followed by Gerard of Cremona's translation of *De Aluminibus et Salibus* attributed to al-Razi, and *Aristoteles de Perfecto Magisterio*. In the next century, along with a growing literature of translation, a discussion of alchemy appears in the encyclopedic works of Vincent of Beauvais; Aquinas, Roger Bacon, and Ramon Lull treat of the subject, and as a result, not long after their deaths works under their names make their appearance.

The vast Latin literature is bewildering.[1] Even the nature of the end product is not clear. Often it is a substance produced by a combination of sulphur and mercury, e.g. in the treatise of Petrus Bonus of Ferrara, *Pretiosa Margarita Novella* (*c.* 1330),[2] where, however, the 'sulphur' merely activates an internal sulphur within the mercury, acting as a 'ferment' to render the mercury into the 'stone', itself capable of acting as a ferment on base metals, making them into gold. Arnald of Villanova also holds the theory of an internal sulphur within the quicksilver, while John Dastin in his supposed letter to Pope John XXII states that the necessary pure sulphur is in properly prepared gold and silver, which substances with quicksilver are the only basic materials required.[3] On the other hand, the emphasis in the pseudo-Lull's *Testamentum* is on the discovery of the quintessence,[4] and Johannes de

---

[1] A great deal of it is conveniently printed in two great anthologies: Lazarus Zetzner, *Theatrum Chemicum*, 6 vols. (Strasbourg, 1613–61), and Jean Jacques Manget, *Bibliotheca Chemica Curiosa*.

[2] Translated A. E. Waite, *The New Pearl of Great Price* (London, 1894).

[3] C. H. Josten, 'The Text of John Dastin's "Letter to Pope John XXII" ', *Ambix*, iv (1949), 38–9; cf. Lynn Thorndike, *A History of Magic and Experimental Science*, iii. 87.   [4] Manget, i. 707–77.

Rupescissa wrote his *Liber Lucis* (*c.* 1350) to deal with the extraction of this fifth element from the other four.[1] Again, most writers —Petrus Bonus among them, and later Norton and Ripley—insist that there is no use in beginning with substances other than metals, whereas in a commentary attributed to Roger Bacon on the *Secreta Secretorum*, the author says that vegetable and animal substances are very good, and human material best of all, especially blood 'in quo ad occulum distinguntur quattuor humores'.[2]

In general, however, some process involving the breaking down of the materials into their elements, and recombining them in a certain secret proportion is usual, though the number of stages varies. The Baconian commentary just mentioned explains that the work of alchemy is to separate out the four humours, reduce them to 'puras simplicitates suas', mix them in a certain proportion, and then add 'quicksilver' mortified and sublimed several times.[2] Petrus Bonus says of the four elements: 'They must all be . . . separated . . . purified . . . recombined in even proportions . . . then we shall have all the four indissolubly united, and the work will be perfect.'[3] Arnald of Villanova in his *Rosarium Philosophorum* speaks of different qualities as dominant at different stages of the mixture, and the need for knowledge of this when adding mercury.[4] Exactly what these proportions were is obscure, although the second part, the *Practica*, of the pseudo-Lull's *Testamentum* contains detailed accounts.[5] In Norton's contemporary, George Ripley, both Bacon and 'Ramounde' [Lull] are said to agree:

> As for ye proporcion yu muste be ware;
> lete ye bodye be sotelly fylde
> with mercury as mych, yen subtelde,
> i. of ye sonne, 2. of ye mone
> tyll all to gether lyke pappe be done.

> Then make mercury 4 vnto ye sonne
> And 2 vnto ye mone as it schulde be;
> thus thyne werke muste be [be]gonne
> in fygure of ye trynyte:
> 3. of ye bodye & of the spiritus 3,
> And for ye vnyte of ye substans spirituall,
> i. more then ye substans of ye parte corporal.

[1] Ibid. ii. 84–7.
[2] R. Steele (ed.), *Opera hactenus inedita Rogeris Baconi*, fasc. v, 'Secreta Secretorum' (Oxford, 1920), p. 117.
[3] Waite, op. cit., pp. 247–8.
[4] Manget, i. 672.   [5] See Chapters 9, 10, 11, 20, ibid. i. 765–6, 769.

Be ramoundes reportorye yis is trewe
proporcion who so lyste to loke . . .
but 3. of ye spiritus bakon toke
wnto 1. of ye bodye; for yis I wooke
many a nyghte or I it wyste;
bothe be trewe, take wyche yu lyste.[1]

Arthur Dee in James Hasolle, *Fasciculus Chemicus*, London,
1650, attempts to explain this:

Let the Bodies (*saith he*) be corrected or limated with an equall proportion of Mercury: *whence understand that the proportion of Earth and Water
must be equall, then he proceeds further and teaches*, that one Body of the
Sun be joyned with two of the Moon, *in which words are understood two
parts of Water to one of Earth. He proceeds also farther*, and joyns four
parts of Mercury to the Sun and two to the Moon; *whence observe that
four and two make six parts of Mercury, Water, or Fire, which parts are to
be mixt with one part of the Sun, and another of the Moon, which since they
constitute two parts of Earth, there shall be a like proportion to the aforesaid
six parts, viz. of Water, as one part of Earth to three parts of Water. As
appears from his following: viz.* after this manner begin thy worke in
figure of a Trinity.[2]

A fairly simple example of an alchemical process is provided
in the digest of Arnald of Villanova's *Rosarium* appended to the
Aldine edition of the *Pretiosa Margarita Novella*. This sets out the
work in four stages. Gold or silver is first dissolved in 'mercury',
by the help of prolonged pounding and heating. This solution is the
union of male and female, and the solution is heated for thirty
days, very gently, until the mixture becomes black, when it has
been reduced to its first nature, sulphur and mercury as they
occur in the earth.

The second process is separation of the elements by distillation,
and cleansing of the separated elements. By distilling with different
degrees of heat, different distillates are apparently obtained, three
representing the volatile elements, and the residue being earth.
Even more vague are the instructions for cleansing the separated
elements.

The third process is reduction, recombining the elements. The
water (now called 'mercury') is added very slowly, little by little,
to the earth—a process compared to irrigation—heating gently the
whole time. Successive sublimations are required, followed by

[1] *The Compend of Alchemy*, quoted from Bodleian MS. Ashmole 1486,
f. 55[r]; cf. Elias Ashmole, *Theatrum Chemicum Britannicum* (1652), pp. 130–1.
[2] pp. 46–7; James Hasolle is an anagram for Elias Ashmole.

repeated mixing of the residue with 'mercury'. The sublimate
should be a white flaky earth, which is the white sulphur or white
tincture.

In the fourth operation this is 'fixed' with silver to produce the
elixir, but here the instructions become too vague to follow.[1]

No clear notion can be gained of the exact nature of the processes. The whole, moreover, is based on a magical view of the
cosmos. Ashmole in a long note on the *Ordinal*, 1087–8, defends the
use of natural magic which he defines as:

the Connexion of naturall Agents and Patients . . . wrought by a wise Man
to the bringing forth of such effects as are wonderfull to those that know
not their causes.

The magician, he explains, makes use of his knowledge of the
harmony in the universe between the different levels or degrees
of existence:

But how to conjoyne the *Inferiours* with the vertue of the *Superiours* . . .
or how to call out of the hidden places into open light, the dispersed and
seminated *Vertues* . . . is, the work of the *Magi*, or *Hermetick Philosophers*
onely; and depends upon the aforesaid *Harmony*.[2]

This essential theory is summed up in the famous *Tabula
Smaragdina* or *Emerald Table of Hermes*, twice quoted and referred
to once by Norton; it runs in part:

What is below is like what is above, and what is above is like what is
below, for accomplishing the marvels of the One Thing. And as all things
were from one thing, by the mediation of one thing, so all things were
born of this one thing, by adaptation.

Its father is the Sun, its mother the Moon. The Wind carried it in
its womb, its nurse is the Earth.

It is the father of all the Perfection of the whole world.

Its power is integral, if it be turned into Earth.

Separate the Earth from the Fire, the subtle from the gross, smoothly
and with judgment.

It ascends from the earth into the Heaven and again descends into the
Earth and unites in itself the powers of things superior and things
inferior. Thus you will receive the brightness of the whole world and all
obscurity will fly far from you.

It is the strong fortitude of all fortitude, for it will overcome every
subtle thing and penetrate every solid.

Thus was the world created.

Hence there will be marvellous adaptations of which this is the means.[3]

[1] Waite, op. cit., pp. 316–39.   [2] *Theatrum Chemicum*, pp. 445–6.
[3] Lindsay, op. cit., pp. 185–6.

The magical world view of the alchemists, the vagueness of their accounts of their art, and their frequent use of religious and mythological analogies seem best explained by C. G. Jung in *Psychology and Alchemy*, and his later *Mysterium Coniunctionis*. Considering the frequent actual visions apparently experienced during the work, and the stress laid on the psychological condition of the operator,[1] Jung maintains that from the inception of alchemy, the claims made for the operations are due to the psychological processes which the adepts underwent in the course of the work, and which they unconsciously projected on to or into the material changes.[2] Many of the most overt indications come from sixteenth-century and later alchemy, but he finds, for example, in the *Liber Platonis Quartorum*, a work going back at least to the tenth century, the instruction that the worker must participate in the work, for if the investigator has not in him the likeness to the work, he will not rise to the required height.[3] Among medieval writers who stress the importance of the worker's state of soul, he quotes from Geber a passage, possibly imitated by Norton, and also from Norton himself.[4]

According to this explanation alchemy is a kind of *gnosis* and the stages of the work are symbolic of the gnostic scheme of the redemption of the imprisoned *nous* from the embrace of matter:

> In the Christian projection the *descensus spiritus sancti* stops at the *living body* of the Chosen One, who is at once very man and very God, whereas in alchemy the descent goes right down into the darkness of inanimate matter whose nether regions, according to the Neopythagoreans, are ruled by evil. Evil and matter together form the Dyad. . . . This is feminine in nature, an *anima mundi*, the feminine Physis who longs for the embrace of the One, the Monad, the good and perfect. . . . She is 'the divine soul imprisoned in the elements', whom it is the task of alchemy to redeem.[5]

Thus in the *Vision of Arisleus*, a possible chemical process of reducing a substance to its first matter by dissolving in acid and heating the solution to dryness is allegorized as the death of the philosopher Thabritius, or his absorption into the body of his wife Beya during

---

[1] *Psychology and Alchemy*, pp. 250 ff.   [2] Ibid., p. 270.
[3] Ibid., pp. 266–7.
[4] Ibid., p. 271; this passage from Geber, *Liber Perfecti Magisterii* is similar to the *Ordinal* 531–9. Jung also quotes (p. 270 n. 79) from the Latin version of the *Ordinal* 2692: 'Whethir his mynde accorde with the werke', without noticing, however, that it is the mind of the patron, not the adept, to which Norton refers.
[5] *Psychology and Alchemy*, pp. 304–5.

intercourse. The allegory corresponds also to the *nous* being entrapped into the embrace of *physis*, physical nature, which in turn is a myth symbolizing the great dread of primitive man, namely the possibility of the newly emergent conscious mind sinking back into the unconscious, with the resulting disintegration of personality and mental suffering. Whoever dared to allow this to happen, or to court its happening, might experience a fruitful encounter with the unconscious and a consequent development of personality. Mythologically the hero could undertake such a dangerous journey to the underworld and return bringing something of permanent value. Alchemically by the skilful application of the life-giving *pneuma* the matter in the alchemical vessel could be revived into a glorious stone.[1]

Along with Jung we should mention Mircea Eliade's account of the genesis of alchemy in the magic associated in the early ages of metal-work with the smith, and the initiation rites of his craft.[2] More recently, Jack Lindsay has provided us with a great deal of mythological material analogous to alchemy and illustrating the mental milieu in which the art developed initially in Hellenistic Egypt. However, the allegorical, mythical, or psychic aspects of alchemy, while extremely common, and perhaps predominant, in medieval and late medieval writers, make little overt showing in Norton's *Ordinal*. He does indeed stress the necessity for virtue and purity of motive, and of being a man adapted to the art; when he describes the 'Red work' at the end of Chapter V he professes to be fearful of touching on so sacred a mystery; he quotes or refers to passages in earlier writers about the alchemical marriage and birth. But on the whole the bent of his mind seems extremely down-to-earth and practical, as may be seen in the following account of his work.

An alchemical tract, says Thorndike, 'was likely to be in its inception a typical and stock performance rather than an original and personal contribution'.[3] *The Ordinal of Alchemy* bears out this judgement. In the Proem we have a typical account of the great number of ignorant would-be alchemists, pity for whom compels the author to write in order to warn them off—a warning repeated

[1] Ibid., pp. 327 ff.
[2] Mircea Eliade, *The Forge and the Crucible*, trans. Stephen Corrin (New York, 1962).
[3] Thorndike, op. cit., iii. 40.

in the last few lines of the poem. The difficulty inherent in understanding alchemical writings is touched on; some of these are only obscure, others have been maliciously falsified. Norton proposes to lay out the precise order of the processes, just as the ordinal sets out the order of the Church year and saints' days for liturgical purposes. Honesty and enough money are prerequisites for success. He lists the chapters and concludes with a warning that the book be read many times and other books with it. Apart from the title, all is standard material. Similarly, the first Chapter, a defence of the truth, excellence, and holiness of alchemy, based on revelation which the adept swears never to reveal to the unworthy, may be compared with similar defences by Petrus Bonus of Ferrara and Geber in the *Summa Perfectionis*.[1] There follows another standard feature, the good and evil practitioner; one privately and patiently working and paying his own way, the other out and about, advertising his powers and swindling his clientele. Norton, interestingly, denies that metals can be 'multiplied'; they are not like living things, but can be only transformed, not grown, either underground or in the alchemical vessel. The good alchemist like Ramon Lull must have wealth, patience, birth, perseverance, humility, trust in God, and devotion to learning.

Chapter II, though interesting, is again full of standard alchemical 'topoi': the examples of unsuccessful hair-brained quacks, the long process of learning the art, the difficulty of finding a genuine adept for a master, the taciturnity of the truly knowledgeable, the transfer of the secret from master to pupil, and the subsequent rapid understanding of the whole art. No less standard are the excuses for failure—untrustworthy servants and patrons who steal the completed elixir.[2] How true are the stories of the Norman monk, and of the parish priest who wished to have a bridge built across the Thames we cannot know, but the incident of Delves, Herbert, and Dalton before Edward IV, as already indicated, could well be perfectly accurate. Again in Chapter III the account of mistaken experiments with various organic substances is paralleled in other alchemical writings.

[1] Waite, op. cit., pp. 53–77; for Geber see Holmyard's, *Works of Geber* pp. 32–55.
[2] Cf. the experience of Thomas Charnock, a sixteenth-century Englishman, whose servant 'would sleepe so long till the Fire went out, / Then would the Knave that whorson Lout, / Cast in Tallow to make the fire burne quicker . . . thus was I cumbred with a drunken sott' (Ashmole, op. cit., p. 294). Ripley

It is in this third Chapter that we are introduced to Norton's alchemical theory. The two ingredients which will suffice for the 'white work', i.e. the preparation of an elixir turning metals into silver, are a 'marchasite' and 'magnesia', clearly the male and female elements in an alchemical marriage, with overtones of incest. But it is impossible to find what they are meant to be. From the description in line 1132 this substance might be the modern litharge, PbO. By heating with salt—or more likely with urine— lead chloride would be produced, which would be *somedele white* (1135). However, Rulandus gives seven meanings for 'LITH-ARGYRUM', of which one—'That which is made when silver is separated from Lead'—is the modern litharge; the others include mixtures of silver and lead, gold and lead, gold and silver, and lead and copper.[1]

The alchemists insisted that 'the stone', or at least the materials of it, were commonplace, found everywhere, and of no value in the eyes of the unlearned. Pythagoras in Speech 13 of the *Turba Philosophorum* speaks of it as 'found everywhere, being a stone, and also not a stone; common and precious; hidden and concealed, yet known by everyone'.[2] In *The New Pearl* this is listed as a diffi-culty in alchemy:

They call it the vilest and commonest of all things, which is found among the refuse of the street and on the dunghill; yet they add that it cannot be obtained without considerable expense. They seem to say in the same breath that it is the vilest and that it is the most precious of all substances.[3]

As to the female element, magnesia, the term goes back to Hellenistic alchemy,[4] and is familiar from its mention in Chaucer's *Canon's Yeoman's Tale* [G 1448–71]. It is defined as follows in Rulandus:

Magnesia generally stands for Marcasite. Artificial magnesia is melted tin when mercury has been injected into it, and the two have been mingled together until they form a brittle substance, and a white mass. It is also

describes alchemists who excuse themselves to their creditors by pleading that they have been robbed of their Elixirs (ibid., p. 156).

[1] *A Lexicon of Alchemy . . . by Martinus Rulandus* (Frankfurt, 1612; trans-lated 1892), p. 208.
[2] A. E. Waite (trans.), *The Turba Philosophorum or Assembly of Sages* (London, 1896), pp. 42–3.
[3] See pp. 111–12; cf. pseudo-Lull *Testament, Theoria* c. 38. Manget, i. 731.
[4] Lindsay, op. cit., p. 375.

silver mixed with mercury, an extremely fusible metallic compound which is liquefied as easily as wax, is of a wonderful whiteness, and is called the magnesia of the philosophers. . . . It is also the matter of the philosopher's stone. . . . The whole therein is mercury.[1]

Rulandus also calls it 'The Woman', and it is clearly the feminine principle in the work.

Rulandus's account seems to fit with Norton's statements about magnesia. As with other alchemical terms, however, the meaning varies with the user. Rupescissa makes it sulphur of the philosophers, called Roman Vitriol,[2] Rulandus defines Roman Vitriol as Green Atrament, i.e. presumably sulphate of iron. Norton and Rulandus seem to have in mind the same ideas as in Lull's *Testament*,[3] where he calls magnesia a white earth in which 'our gold' (i.e. the masculine fiery principle) should be planted, and for whose whitening time and patience are required:

> Et nostrum finale secretum est, nostri argenti vivi congelatio, sine qua namque fieri non potest certitudo scientiae nostrae, quae in principio magisterii nostri est nostri argenti vivi congelatio in magnesia nostra. . . . Nostra magnesia est argentum vivum.[4]

Beyond the impossibility of determining what these substances might have been—if any real substances are intended—there is the puzzle of Norton's denying that the first step in alchemy was a mixture of metal and quicksilver, or acid (1199–1200), as it was usually agreed that only from metal could metal be produced.

Chapter IV deals with what Norton calls 'the gross work'. The terms 'gross work' and 'subtle work' are, as far as I know, peculiar to Norton. It is clear that under 'gross work' is included the preparation of the materials of the stone and their purification, that is to say the production of the magnesia and 'chosen marcasite' of the previous chapter. It is possible, however, to equate more exactly the gross work with the initial stages of the alchemical process as described by others, and so obtain a clearer idea of what Norton meant by it, though of course it partakes of the vagueness common to almost all alchemical terms.

According to Norton the gross work is a dirty business (1273–4, 1297–8), takes a long time and requires great patience (1255–8, 1323–4), includes the processes of 'eating' and 'drinking' (1238–44), simmering (1264–72), and purifying (1277–8); the object was

---

[1] *Lexicon*, p. 216.
[2] *Liber Lucis*, c. 2, Manget, ii. 84.
[3] *Theoria*, c. 29, Manget, i. 726–7.
[4] Ibid., p. 727 (misnumbered 627).

to find 'pure natures and simple', (1220) or in other words to divide the materials into 'elementa propinqua' (1226–7).

Arthur Dee in his alchemical notes, published by 'James Hasolle' (i.e. Elias Ashmole) in 1650 in his *Fasciculus Chemicus*, has a chapter (Chapter II) on 'Preparation', in the 'Corollary' to which he paraphrases lines 1303–4, referring by name to Norton, and adds:

And according to Attaman, The second work is not made but from a clean and purified body. *And this Preparation, or first work he calleth a Sordid labour, and adjudges it not worthy a learned man, therefore not unfitly said to be the work of Women.*[1]

This appears to be a reminiscence of line 152, and it appears that Arthur Dee thought of his Preparation as equivalent, at least roughly, to the gross work. It will therefore be interesting to see what he includes in Preparation.

He includes extracts from Lull on the separation of the elements [p. 32], Avicenna on calcining and imbibing [pp. 32–3], and extracts from Arnald of Villanova's *Rosarium Philosophorum* on 'separation', 'solution', and 'putrefaction'. Now Arnald's *Rosarium* is contained in Manget, vol. i, and in it he divides his work into four stages, Solution, Purification, Reduction, and Fixation. It seems that the gross work corresponds to the first two of these, and takes the process as far as the separation into the four elements (or qualities) and their purification, so that the subtle work can begin with the joining of the qualities together to form the elixir, or, as Arnald puts it, the joining of the water and earth, which is his third stage.[2]

The reference to 'Porta' (1235 ff.) is to the *Porta Elementorum*, an alchemical work, not really by Avicenna.[3] The Latin passage quoted by Norton seems to apply to the early part of the work, in which in order to reduce the original materials thoroughly to their first matter, a process of solution, distillation, pounding of the remaining solid, and redissolving in the distillate was carried out. The passage in *Porta Elementorum* is very obscure, representing the process under the figure of a cooked hen; the words are: 'Non comedas festinanter, nec comedas quod non bibas, nec bibas quod non manduces.'[4]

[1] p. 38.
[2] *Rosarium Philosophorum*, II, c. 1, 8, 9, 14, Manget, i. 667–70.
[3] Printed in *Artis Chemicae Principes, Avicenna Atque Geber, Hoc Volumine Continentur*, ... Basileae, Per Petrum Pernam M.D.LXXII, occupying pp. 1–23.
[4] Ibid., p. 3.

The pseudo-Bacon in the *Tractatus Trium Verborum*, having given an account of the separation of the elements very similar to that in Part II of the *Rosarium Philosophorum*, refers to the frequency of the distillations, and adds that if the process is repeated the vessels will break: 'Vnde sequitur omne, quod est vitra, a malo est. Comede vt bibas, & bibe vt comedas &c.'[1]

The simmering of the work appears to be the same as what Arnald calls 'Inhumation', by which after the solution of the original solids (gold or silver) in the 'mercury', it is left to putrefy and digest for thirty days: 'Decoquas ergo complete, ut ebulliant omnia levi igne, & in suam materiam primam redeant, & sint argentum vivum.'[2] The slow fire reduces the danger of combustion, as would be the case with butter and oil (1267–70), and when it is complete the mass will be black, 'in odore foetida, & in tactu subtilis et discontinuata'.[2] The style is allusive, as if Norton expected his readers to be familiar with alchemical writings, and his only task was to remind them of the relevant passages.

In Chapter V, after an initial anecdote Norton approaches the 'subtle work'. The materials must have been divided into four elements—the process he calls the gross work—and the method for this, if the reader has not already discovered it, is in 'Ortolane'. The stone will have to have every quality, be flexible yet fixed (1463–8) and be of fixed colour. But in the processes of combining the elements, the colour sequence of red–white–black is important; consequently the combinations of elements which produce these colours must be known. Moreover, in the combination of elements it is important for the worker to know which is the 'reigning' or dominant element, so that the counter-element or quality may be added to temper the mixture to a perfect balance. Colour, taste, and smell indicate which qualities are dominant, and so Norton spends a great deal of this chapter (including 1473–1544, 1777–1872, 1943–2036, 2107–66) in instructing his readers in certain well-known medieval lore. Much of this on colours, tastes, and odours is very close in language and arrangement to Books iv and xix of Bartolomaeus Anglicus's *De Proprietatibus Rerum*, a work

---

[1] The *Tractatus Trium Verborum* is printed in *Sanioris Medicinae Magistri ... Thesaurus Chemicus*, Frankfurt, 1620; see pp. 293, 299. The *Tractatus* is also known as *Epistolae Tres ad Johannem Parisiensem*.

[2] Manget, i. 668.

so popular that copies could be hired by students at Paris.[1] Why
Norton included this comparatively elementary instruction if he
was convinced that only the learned could undertake alchemy is
one of the minor puzzles of his work.

However that may be, Norton turns to composition or conjunction (1547–1688). Each of the four elements contributes its special
effects: earth supplies generation, fixation, and multiplication; fire
extendibility, penetrability, and multiplication; air causes generation of colours and helps in liquefaction; water is revivifying and
cleansing. By tempering the degree of each quality accurately the
perfect substance can be generated, and the correct proportions are
in the works of Bacon and 'Lully'.[2] The references to conjunction
in accordance with principles of grammar, rhetoric, music, etc.
(1637 ff.) may be taken as purely metaphorical, or perhaps as a hint
that the 'real' alchemy is some mental or spiritual discipline. The
process is designed to change the originally black material towards
white; and according to Bartholomaeus (xix. 5), the different
degrees of strength of the qualities in a substance are the causes
of their colours. The elixir in the making must pass through all
grades of colour before ending in white, for it is to be a microcosm
and so have experienced all the material possibilities of the cosmos.
The alchemist must therefore know the various degrees of admix-
tures of qualities to produce this sequence. Such a spectrum of
colours is referred to symbolically in alchemical writers as a rain-
bow or peacock's tail. There were four degrees of each quality.[3]

[1] Thorndike, op. cit., ii. 405. As a short example of Norton's indebtedness to
Bartolomaeus, compare the *Ordinal* 1501–7 with the following in Trevisa's
translation, taken from B.M. MS. Add. 27944: '. . . white colour is y-gendred
of scarsete of humour and druye matiere by maystrie of hete . . . as it fareþ in
lymes and in bones y-brende and in oþere suche.' [xix, c. 3, f. 304 v/a.] 'And if
colde haþ þe maistrie in moist matiere þanne is white colour y-gendred as it
fareþ in snowe, in hore frostes, and in horenesse of her.' [xix, c. 4, f. 304 v/b.]

[2] The real Ramon Lull did not believe in transmutation, as E. Allison Peers
shows (*Ramon Lull, a Biography* (London, 1929, p. 407 n.). See Ramon Lull,
Ars Generalis Ultima etc., Venice, 1480 (B.M. Catalogue no. I. A. 20185), pt. XI,
sect. v, c. 15 for Peers's note, and the earlier pt. IX, c. 8, para. 8. Norton refers
twice to Lull's *Art General* (1558, 1674), but is apparently referring to the
pseudo-Lull *Testament*, see p. lx n. 4.

[3] No precise methods of measuring these 'degrees' was known in the Middle
Ages. Lanfranc describes four degrees as first, body heat; second, as hot as can
be handled without feeling pain; third, painful but endurable; fourth, sufficient
to burn the body. The first three are natural ('kyndely'), the last, 'unkyndely'.
(*Lanfrank's Science of Cirurgie*, ed. Robert V. Fleischhacker, E.E.T.S., O.S. 102
1894, pp. 11–12.)

When conjunction is properly made a process of 'digestion' begins. Human digestion was understood as a process of the decomposition of food by heat and its changing into substances used by the body. The alchemical process is taken as similar, so that the materials are now to be heated in a closed vessel and matured, the external heat exciting the intrinsic or internal heat within the materials to digest the 'stone'. It is during this process, the intermediate stage between black and white, that the various colours appear, and by means of colour, taste, and smell the alchemist can tell the dominant element or quality and temper it by adding its contrary. Norton cites a number of liquids useful for tempering the mixture (2185–2276, 2313–50), some recognizable, like sea-water, others not. Again, it is impossible to say what these substances may really be, or whether they are all one.

There follows a passage on 'means' and 'extremes' (2367–2408) and 'circulations' (2409–66), terms frequent in alchemy of the Lullian tradition. The simplest account of the 'means' and 'extremes' is that in Hasolle.[1] Nature, the author explains, goes in small steps; the extremes are 'naturall Argent vive, and perfect elixir'. The means are of three kinds: material, operative, and demonstrative signs such as colours. Circulation was essentially a process of passing a material from solid to liquid to vapour and back, or, as the alchemists understood it, from one element to another. From the time of the Jabirian writings onwards the idea that frequent repetition of a process could effect something different from one such process, especially distillation and redistillation, had been part of alchemical practice. As the author of the Lullian *Codicillum* puts it: 'Eleganter dixerunt Philosophi quod opus magnum non est nisi solutio et congelatio: sed ista fiunt per viam circulorum.'[2]

The doctrine of the white stone is now complete. It is a true Microcosm containing all qualities knit together, and with it metals can be transmuted—Norton goes further than other alchemists and calls it transubstantiation (2520). One half of it must be set aside to work on the 'red' stone, which can transmute base metal into gold. Of this process Norton says he learned from his master, but only after considerable further persuasion, and he himself apparently feels the matter so sacred and awful that he

[1] Op. cit., pp. 201–5.   [2] Manget, i. 908.

hurries over it with only hints and obscure quotations from older
writers. The red is hidden in the white, like Bonus of Ferrara's red
sulphur in the mercury, is produced from it, joins with it in
(incestuous) marriage, and the perfect union is consummated, the
red element controlling and changing the white into a permanent
red.

The sixth Chapter deals with five 'concordances', namely, the
suitability to the work of the financial backer, of the workmen or
servants, of the instruments, of the place, and of the astrological
situation. The first two are wholly practical. The other three are
less so, and some elements of magical ideas appear: the shapes
and materials of the vessels must have natural 'sympathy' with
the processes for which they are used. But Norton then goes on
to complain that nobody in England can make sufficiently hard
and impervious pottery. He mentions an illustration he provides
of several furnaces—presumably represented by that on folio 1ʳ of
manuscript A—but two, and perhaps three, of his own design he
has excluded from the illustration. Different localities are suited to
different chemical operations according to the nature of the place;
windy places and those which are haunts of lechery are always to
be avoided. The work must be timed to obtain favorable astrological influences, and another illustration—presumably represented by that on f. 67ᵛ of A—shows a suitable horoscope. He
concludes with a warning against the forbidden arts of geomancy
and necromancy.

The last Chapter concerns the control of the fire to produce
various degrees of heat. Some of these are roughly specified, as the
heat used to boil goose or pork, others only vaguely described. He
recommends a bellows worked by the foot and protection for the
face for certain high degrees of heat, and sums up by saying that
regulating the draught of a furnace, especially at the supreme
moment of projection, can be learned only by experience. The
poem is now complete. Norton has shown the course of the work
in order; nothing has been omitted; with this *Ordinal* and the
books to which he has referred a wise man can succeed in the art.
With a final apology for his English style, a final caveat that the
ignorant desist from their useless attempts, and a final plea to the
reader to pray for his soul, he makes an end by dating his work,
1477.

THE ORDINAL OF ALCHEMY

All abbreviations have been expanded without comment.
Superscript letters have been brought down: $þ^t$ is rendered as *þat*; $þ^e$ *as þe*; *shew^t* as *shewith*. *ff* initially is
written as *F*. The abbreviations *-con* and superscript *c*
are rendered as *-cion* and *-ec-* as in *humectacion*. A dot or
line at the end of a word is written *-e*. When parts of a
compound word are separated by a space—often less than
a normal word space—a hyphen is inserted; e.g. a-side,
a-boute, to-gedir.

Preface

Liber iste clericis monstrat scientiam,
Liber sed laicis auget insciciam;
Liber honores iuuans per copiam,
Et liber pauperum fugans inopiam.
Liber fiducie est et veritatis,   5
Regibus consilium, doctrina prelatis;
Et liber vtilis viris beatis
Viuere qui cupiunt absque peccatis.
Liber secretus, liber doni dei,
Electis semita viris boni spei,   10
Valens constantibus firme fidei.
Ve non credentibus verbis oris mei!
Querunt alchymyiam falsi quoque recti;
Falsi sine numero, sed hij sunt eiecti.
Et cupiditatibus heu! tot sunt infecti,   15
Quod inter Mille Milia vix sunt tres electi.
Istam ad scienciam multi sunt vocati,
Nobiles et pauperes, inscij, litterati;
Qui nolunt labores neque tempus pati
Ideo non perficient quia sunt ingrati.   20

1vb Liber artis filios docet iste satis
Quibus hec percipere deus dedit gratis;
Versiclis propheticis quatuor hijs credatis;
Omnia dat gratis diuine fons pietatis.
Hec nobilis sciencia est tamen illis data   25
Qui diligunt iusticiam mente cum beata;

f. 1ᵛ *Columns separated by double bar divided at line* 10 *and coloured blue, gold, gold, pink* 1 *Initial Capital* L *in gold on leaf-shaped background, blue and brown with green and red in centre. This leaf wholly in margin, 3 lines deep and rising clear of first line. From it a spray of green leaves across the top margin and down the left below text; among the green leaves some blue* (? *fruit*) *and gold spots* 5 liber] Lliber MS. 9 Liber] Lliber MS. 11 firme fidei *written together, divided by hair-line* 15 *Last* i *of* infecti *in line with left border-line of centre bar* 16 Mille Milia] M. M. MS.; le, lia *inserted above by another hand* 22 percipere] *second* per, *written* .p., *almost effaced by small hole, through which can be seen red and blue line-end markings from text on the back of the illumination now stuck to* f. 1ʳ, *but originally probably at the beginning or end of Chapter VII* 24 *Whole line within a scroll outlined in pink; letters in gold but much worn and now mainly white*

Dolosis & raptoribus sed est denegata,
Propter peccata tardantur munera grata.
Sepe reges anglie decorasset hec res,
Firma si in domino fuisset eorum spes.   30
Ille sed qui capiet per hanc rem honores,
Antiquos mores mutabit in meliores.
Iste, cumque venerit, regnum reformabit
Virtutibus & moribus, & exemplum dabit
Sempiternum regibus; plebs tunc iubilabit,   35
Et mut[u]o se diligens laudes deo dabit.
O rex hec facturus! deum regem ora,
Et eius auxilium pro re hac implora.
Tunc regi iusto fulgenti mente decora,
Grata superuenient qua non sperabitur hora.   40

28 *See note on 24*   32 *See note on 24*   meliores] melios MS., *no mark*
representing re *any longer visible*   36 mutuo] muto MS.   40 *See*
note on 24

To the honour of god oon in persones þree
this boke is made þat lay-men shuld it se,
And clerkis al-so aftir my decese,
wherbi al lay-men which puttith them in prese
To seche bi alchymy grete riches to wynne   5
May fynde goode concelle ar þei such werk bigyn,
And grete deceptis thei may herbie eschew,
& bi þis doctryne know fals men fro þe trewe.
Nethirles clerkis grete secretis here may leere,
But al lay-men shal fynde here cause to feere,   10
And to be ware of fals Illusions
which multipliers worch with theyre conclusyons.
But for that I desire not wordly fame
But your gode preyers vnknowe shalbe my name,
þat no man shuld þer-aftir serche ne looke,   15
But wisely consydire þe flowris of thise booke.
Of euery state which is within mankynde
If ye make serche moche peple ye may fynde
which to alchymy theire corage doth addresse
Only for appetite of lucour and richesse;   20

As popis with cardynales of dignitee,
Archbissopis & bissoppis of hye degree,
with abbottis & priours of religion,
with freris, heremites & prestis many on,
And kingis, with princis, lordis grete of blode,   25
For euery estate desirith after goode;
And merchantis al-so which dwelle in fyre
Of brennyng couetise haue therto desire;
And comon workmen wil not be owt lafte,
For as wel as lordis þei loue þis noble craft,   30

5 seche] serche BEW, sek R   wynne] fynde EW   8 þe] *om.* EW
10 al] also B   here] *om.* E   12 theyre] fals BR   15 no man]
none B   17 state] estate B   19 corage] myndes R   21 of
dignitee] of hey dignitee EW, of great dignitie R   22 hye] every W
25 lordis] *om.* W   & *inserted above with caret* A   29 wil not be owt
lafte] therof wyll haue part R   30 craft] art R

As goldsmythis whom we shuld leest repreve,
For sightis in theire craft movith hem to bileve.
But wondir is that wevers dele with suche werkis,
Fremasons & tanners with pore parish clerkis;
Staynours & glasiers wil not therof cese,   35
And yet sely tynkers wille put theyme in prese
with grete presumpcion, but yet som colour was
For alle suche men as gife tyncture to glas.
But many artificers haue be ouer swifte
with hasty credence to fume a-wai theire thrifte,   40
And alle be it that losse made them to smerte,
yet euer in hope continuede theire herte,
Trustyng somtyme to spede right welle.
Of many such truli I can telle
which in such hope contynued al there lyfe,   45
wherbi thei were pore & made to vnthryfe.
It had be good for theym to haue left of
In seson, for noght thei fownde but a scoffe;
For truly he that is not a grete clerke
Is nyse & lewde to medle with that werke.   50
Ye may trust wel it is no smale engyne
To know al secretis perteynyng to the myne,
For it is most profunde philosophie,
The subtile science of holi Alchymye;
Of which science here I entende to write,   55
How be it I may not curyously endite,
For he that shuld al commyn peple teche,
He most for theym vse playne & comon speche.
Thogh that I write in playn & homely wise,
No good man shulde suche writyng despyce.   60
Al mastirs which write of þis soleyne werke,
Thei made theire bokis to many men ful derk,
In poyses, parabols, & in methaphoris alle-so,
which to scolers causith peyne and wo;
For in theire practice when thei wold it assay,   65
Thei leys their costis as men see al day.

f. 3ʳ

f. 3ᵛ

36 yet] also R   40 hasty] over hastie R   49 grete] good R
52 perteynyng] belongyng R   58 &] *om.* W   59–60 *om.* E
59 Thogh that I] Trowth if I S₃   playn & homely] an homely W
62 theire] *om.* B   65 it] *om.* EW   66 al day] all waye W

Hermes, Rasis, Gebere, and Auycenn,
Merlyn, Ortolane, democrite, & morien,
Bacon, & Raymonde, with many auctours mo
write vndir covert, & Aristotille alle-so; 70
For whate herof thei wrote with theire penne,
Theire clowdy causis dullid many men.
Fro lay-men fro clerkis & so fro euery man,
Thei hidde this arte that no man fynde it can
Bi theire bokis, thofe thei shew reson fayre, 75
wherby moche peple be broght in-to despeyre.
Yet anaxagoras wrote playnyst of theym al,
In his boke of conuercions naturalle.
Of al the olde faders that euer I fownde
He moste disclosid of this sciens the grownde. 80

f. 4ʳ wherof Aristotille hadde grete envye,
And him rebukith vnrightfullye
In many placis, as I can welle reporte,
Entending that me to him shuld not resorte.
For he was large of his connynge & loue, 85
God haue his sowle in blys with hym a-boue.
And such as sowide envyous seed,
God forgife theym theire mysdede,
As the monke which a boke dide write
Of a Ml. receptis in malice for despite; 90
which be copied in many a place,
wherbi hath be made pale many a face,
And many gownys hath be made bare of hue,
And men made fals which bifore-tyme were true.
Wherfore my pitee doith me constrayne 95
To shew the trouth in few wordis & playne,
So that ye may fro fals doctryne flee,
If ye geve credence to this boke & to me.
Avoide youre bokis writen of receytis,
For al such receptis be ful of deceytis; 100

f. 4ᵛ Truste not such receptis, & lern wel þis clause:
No thing is wroght but bi his propre cause;

---

72 causis] clawsis S₃R   84 me] men BES₃RW, n *inserted above with
caret* A   85 large] *om.* E, fre W   89 the monke] he W   93 bare]
pale B   94 men] ny *inserted above with caret after* mē A, many BT
98 to me] me BERW   101 receptis] deceiptes R

wherfore practice fallith ferre behynde
where knowlich of the cause is not in mynd,
wherfore remembre euyrmore wisely,   105
To werch nothing but ye know how & whi.
Also he that wold in this arte procede,
To eschew falshode he hath grete nede;
For trowth is good which þis arte most gyde,
wherfore to falshode ye may neuyr slyde;   110
But stedfastly your myndes most be sett
Fals colorid metalle nevir to conterfett;
As thei that seche blanchers or citrinacions
which will not abyde alle examynacions,
where-with fals plate þei make as thei can,   115
Or monay to begile som good trew man.
But god hath made þat of his blessid arte
Al þat be fals shal haue therof no parte.
He must haue grace þat wold for þis arte sewe,
Therfore of right hym nedith to be trewe.   120

f. 5ʳ   Also he may not be trowbled in his mynde
with owtward chargis which this arte wold fynde;
And he that wold haue his entent
He must haue riches sufficient.
In many wayis he may not loke,   125
But only pursue the ordire of this boke,
Namyd of Alchymye the ordinalle,
The crede michi, the standarde perpetuall;
For like as the Ordinalle to prestis settith owte
The seruyce of the dayes as þei go abowte,   130
So of al the bokis vnorderide in Alchymye
Theffectis be here set owte ordirlye.
Therfore this boke to an Alchymystre wise
Is a boke of incomperable price,
whose trowth shal nevir be defilede,   135
Thofe it appere in homly wise compiled.

103-4 *interchanged* R   103 wherfore] wher R   ferre] verye farr R
104 where] ther R   106 but ye] but yt ye (yt *ins. above with caret*) S₃
109 trowth is good which] god is trouthe who R   123 he that] he BT,
if he R   124 sufficient] Inowghe suffycyent W   131 bokis] good
workes W   vnorderide in] vnderight in B, vnorderyde of E, wrytten in R
133 Alchymystre] alchymystery S₃   135 be] *om.* B

And as I hadde this arte bi grace fro hevyn,
I geue you the same here in chapiters sevyn,
As larglie as I bi my foialte may,
Bi licence of þe dredful Iuge of domysdai.   140

f. 5ᵛ

The first chapitere shal al men teche
whate maner peple may this science reche,
And whi the trew science of Alchymye
Is of olde faders callid blessid & holye.
In the seconde chapiter may be sayne   145
The nyce Ioys therof with the grete peyne.
The thrid chapiter for the loue of oone
Shalle truly disclose þe maters of oure stone,
which the Arabies doyn Elixer calle,
wherof is it there vndirstond ye shalle.   150
The iiij chapiter techeth þe grose werke,
A fowle laboure not kyndly for a clerke,
In which is fownde ful grete trauayle,
with many perilis and many a fayle.
The v chapiter is of the subtile werke   155
which god ordeynyde only for a clerke,
But ful few clerkis can it comprehende,
Therfore to few men is this science sende.
The vj chapiter is of concorde and love
Bitwene low naturis & hevynly spere above,   160

f. 6ʳ

wherof tru knowlige auauncith gretly clerkis
And causith fortherance in our wondre werkis.
The vij chapiter truly teche yow shalle
The doutfulle regymentis of your firys alle.
Now souerayn lord god me gyde and spede   165
For to my maters as now I wil procede,
Prayng al men which this boke shal fynde,
with deuowte prayers to haue my soule in mynd;

---

139 larglie] large S₃   bi my foialte] by fryaltee BT, by my fealtie RW
140 of] on W   142 maner] maner of BE   146 therof with the] wt W
149 Arabies] Arabiens BW   Elixer] the Elixer S₃ W   150 there] *om.* W
151 iiij] th *inserted above with caret* A   153-4 *om.* W   155-6 *follow*
162 W   155 v] th *inserted above* A, 6 W   chapiter] *om.* R   159 vj]
te *inserted above* A, 5 W   160 naturis] matters B   162 wondre]
wonderous R   163 vij] th *inserted above* A   truly] *om.* BTW   165 *small*
ornamental capital N   lord] *om.* S₃   166 to my maters as now] nowe to
my matter R

And that no man for better ne for wors
Change my writyng, for drede of goddis curs;   170
For where quyck sentence shal seme not to be,
þere may wise men fynd selcouth priuyte;
And changing of som oone sillable
May make this boke vnprofitable.
Therfore trust not to oon reding or tweyne,   175
But xx. tymes it wolde be ouer-sayne;
For it conteynyth ful ponderose sentence,
Al be it that it fawte forme of eloquence.
But the best thing that ye do shalle
Is to rede many bokis, & then this with-alle.   180

f. 7ʳ   Capitulum 1

Mastrie ful mervelous & Archymastrie
Is the tyncture of holye Alchymye,
A wonderful science, secrete philosophie,
A singuler grace & gyfte of almyghtie,
which neuir was fownde bi labour of man,   185
But it bi teching or reuelacion bigan.
It was neuir for money sold ne boght
Bi any man which for it hath sowght,
But govyn to an able man bi grace
wroght with grete cost with long leiser & space.   190
It helpith a man when he hath nede,
It voidith vaynglorie hope & also drede,
It voidith ambyciousnes extorcion & excesse,
It fensith aduersite þat she do not oppresse.
He that therof hath his fulle entente   195
Forsaking extremytees with mesure [is] content.
Som peple wold not haue it callid holy,
And in this wyse thei do replye:
Their sei [how] paynyms may this sciens haue,
Such as oure lord god wol neuir save   200

170 drede] feare R   172 fynd] fynd owt W   174 this boke] this hole
booke R   178 Al be it that it] althoughe it R, albe yt W   184 &]
the R   190 cost] craft W   194 fensith] quenshythe W   196 is]
inserted above with caret A   199 how] *inserted above with caret* A, *om.* S₃

f. 7ᵛ For theire wilfulle fals infidelite,
Then cause of goodnes possessours may not be;
Al-so it makith noon othir thinge
But gold or syluere for monay, cuppe, or ring,
which of wise men is prouyde & wel fownde 205
Leest vertuys thing that is vpon the grownd;
wherfore, concludyng, alle men of that secte
Say how this science nys holy in effecte.
To this we say, & witnes as we can,
How that this science was nevir taght to man 210
But he were prouyd perfitly with space
whethir he were able to receyve this grace
For his trouth, vertu, & for his stable witt,
which if he fawte, he shal nevir haue itt.
Al-so no man cowde yet this science reche 215
But if god sende him a master hym to teche,
For it is so worshipfulle & so selcowth,
That it most nede be taght fro mouth to mouth;
Also he shalle, be he nevir so lothe,
Receyve it with moste sacred dredfulle othe, 220
f. 8ʳ That as we refuse grete dignite and fame,
So he must nedely to refuse the same;
And also that he shal not be so wilde
To tech this secrete to his owne child,
For nyhenes of blode ne consanguynyte 225
Be not acceptide to this dygnyte;
So blode as blode may haue no parte,
But only vertue wynnyth this holi arte.
Therfore streytly he shal serche and se
Al maners & vertuys, with the abilite 230
Of the person which shal this science leere,
And in like wise make him streytli swere;
So that no man shal leve this arte behynde
But he an able & a prouede man can fynde.
When age shal greve hym to ride or go, 235
One he may teche but then nevir no mo.

210 to] by W   211 were] well W   216 hym] m *over erasure*
218 nede] *om.* B   220 sacred] *om.* BRW   222 to] do S₃, *om.* B
224 secrete] syence W   229 streytly] secretly B   232 swere] to
swere S₃   236 teche] *om.* B   no] *om.* ERW

For this science most evir secrete be.
The cause wherof is this, as ye may se,
If oon evil man hadd herof alle his wille,
Alle christian pees he myght hastly spille,   240

f. 8ᵛ   And with his pride he myght set a-downe
Rightful kingis & princis of renowne;
wherof the sentence, perile, & Iupardie
vppon the techer restith dredfullie.
So then for dowte of such pride and wrech   245
He must be ware þat wil this science teche.
No man therfore may reche þis grete present
But he that hath vertuys excellent.
So thofe men ween possessours to not ayde
To halowe this science as is late forsaide,   250
Nothir seme not blessed effectuallie,
yet in hyr ordir this science is holie;
And forasmoch that no man may hir fynde
But only bi grace, she is holi of hir kynde.
Also it is a worke and cure dyvyne   255
Fowle copyr to make gold or syluere fyne.
No man may fynde such changis bi his thoȝt
Of diuers kyndis which goddis hondis wroȝt;
For goddis coniunccions man may not vndo,
But if his grace consent fully therto   260

f. 9ʳ   Bi helpe of this science which oure lorde above
Hath govyn to such men as he doith love;
wherfore olde faders conuenientlye
Callide this sciens holye Alchymye.
wherfore no man shulde be to swifte   265
To caste a-way oure lordis blesside gyfte,
Consideringe howe that almyghty god
From grete doctours hath this scyence forbood,
And grawnte it to few men of his mercy,
Such as be feythfulle, trewe, and lowlye.   270
And as there be but planetis sevyne
Amonge the multitude of sterris in hevyne,

239 man] *om.* B   alle] *om.* B   240 pees] princes B, peeres R   245 dowte]
dread R   wrech] *om.* B   249 thofe] those B, *om.* W   possessours]
possessions R   to] doo B   253 that] as BRW   no] *om.* B
255-60 *om* B (T *adds in margin*)   261 helpe] meane R   265 to]
so EW

So a-monge mylions of mylions of mankinde
Scarsely vij men may this science fynde.
Wher-of lay-men ye may leere and see   /   275
How many doctours of grete auctorite
with many serchis haue this science soghte,
yet al theire labours haue tornyde in-to noghte;
If thei [did] cost, yet fownde they noon avayle,
For of theire purpose euery tyme thei fayle.   280

f. 9ᵛ   And in despeire thei cesyn and departe,
& then thei say how their is no such arte,
But feynyd fabuls thei name it where thei go,
A fals fownd thinge thei sai it is also.
Such men presume to moche vpon their mynd;   285
Thei ween their witt suffice þis arte to fynde.
But of theire sclandre & wordes of owtrage
we take their-of truly litille charge;
For such be not convided to oure feest
which wenyth theym-silf wise & can do leest.   290
Al be it such men list not lengire to pursew,
yet is the science of Alchymye fulle trewe;
And al be it som prowde clerke say nay,
yet euery wise clerke wel considre may
How he which herof no trouth myght see   295
May not herof lawful witnes be.
For it were a wondir thing & queynt
A man that nevir had sight to peynt;
How shulde a borne blynde man be sure
To write, or to make goode port[r]eture?   300

f. 10ʳ   To bild powlis stiple myght be grete dowte
For such prowd clerkis to bring a-bowte;
Such myght wel happe to breke their crowne,
Ar thei cowde wisely take it downe.
Wherfore al such [be] ful ferre behynde   305
To feche owte þe secretiste poynt of kynde.

275 leere] learne BERW   277 serchis] serchers BR   soghte u *inserted above between* o *and* g A   279 did] dide *inserted above with caret after* thei A
288 truly litille] lyttell or small W   289 convided] counted B, convytede
S₃R   291 men] *om.* BT, men ne W   297 wondir] wonderfull R,
wondrus W   305 be . . . behynde] *so* S₃W; ful ferre be hynde, *with a second*
be *inserted after* ferre A; shall ferre be hynde B; full fer be behynde ER
306 feche] serche W

Therfore al men tak their fortune & chance;
Remitt such clerkis to theire ignorance.
Now ye that wille for this science pursue,
lerne ye to know fals men fro the trewe.   310
Alle trew sechers the science of Alchymye
Most be ful lerned in their firste philosophie,
Els al her labour shal hem lett and greve
As he that fecchith watir in a seve.
The trew men serche & seche alle a-loone   315
In hope to fynde oure dilectable stone;
And for thei wold þat no man shuld haue lost,
Thei prove and serche al at theire owne cost;
So theire awne pursis thei wille not spare,
Thei makith theire cofers þere-bi fulle bare.   320

f. 10ᵛ   With grete pacience thei do procede,
Trustyng only in god to be theire spede.
The fals man walkith fro towne to towne,
For the moste parte with a thredbare gowne,
Euyr serching with diligent a-wayte   325
To wyn his pray with som fals disceyte.
Of swering and lesyng such wil not cese,
To say how thei can siluer plate encrese;
And euyr thei rayle with periurye,
Sayng how thei can multiplye   330
Gold and siluer, and in suche wise
with promyse thei please the covetyse,
And causith his mynde to be on hym sett;
Then falshode and couetyse be fully mett,
But afterwarde, within a litille while,   335
The multiplier doth hym begyle.
With his faire promyse and with his fals othis
The covetise is broght to thredbare clothis,
But if he can hasteli be welle ware
Of the multipliere & of his cheffare,   340

308 Remitt such clerkis] remyttynge soch men R   309 *Small ornamental
capital* N   311 sechers] serchers BRW   the] of this EW, of ye R
312 ful] firste B, fully R, *om.* W   315 serche & seche] serchythe & serchythe W   320 Thei] which R   þere-bi] to be BE   325 diligent
a-wayte] diligence & awayte E   326 fals] *om.* W   327 lesyng] lienge R
329 periurye] Inivrye EW   334 couetyse] covetus B, covetousnesse R
fully] well EW

f. 11ʳ Of whose deceptis moche can y reporte,
But I darre not, lest I gife comforte
To such as be disposide to tregedie,
For so moche hurte myght growe therbye.
wherfore avise yow and be wise   345
Of theym which profre such seruyce,
If thei had connynge, haue ye no dowte
Thei wolde be lothe to shewe it owte.
When such men promyse to multiplye,
Thei compas to do som felonye,   350
Som trew mannys goode to bere a-waye.
Of such felons whate shulde I say?
All such false men where evir thei go,
Thei shulde be punyshide, thei be not so.
Vppon nature thei falsly lye,   355
For metallis do not multiplye.
Of this sentence alle men be sure:
Euermore arte most sewe nature.
Nothing multiplieth, as auctours says,
But bi one of these two waies: 360
f. 11ᵛ One bi rotyng callide putrefaccion,
That othir as bestis bi propagacion.
Propagacion in metallis may not be,
But in oure stone moch like þing ye may se.
Putrefaccion most destroy and deface   365
But it be doon in his convenient place;
Metallis of kinde grow low vndre grownde,
For above erth ruste in theym is fownde,
So above erth apperith corrupcion
Of metallis, & in longe tyme destruccion;   370
wherof no cause is fownde in this case
But that above erth thei be not in her place.
Contrarie placis to nature cavsith stryfe,
As Fishis owte of watir lesith lyfe,
And man with birdys & bestis lyue in Ayere,   375
But stone & mynerallis vndre erth repaire.

343 tregedie] treacherye R   345 avise] I adwysse W   and] to W
348 it] theyr cunnynge R   350 felonye] vilanye EW   357 sentence]
science R   358 sewe] folowe R   366 be] must be B   370 destruc-
cion] dissolutyon R

Phisicians & poticaris fawte appetite & will
To seche watir flowris on an hye drye hill,
For god hath ordeyned of his wisdom & grace
Al thinges to growe in theire naturalle place. 380

f. 12ʳ Ageyne this doctryne som men replie,
And say that metalis do multiplie,
For of siluyre, ledd, tynne, & also brasse
Som veyne is more, & som veyne is lasse;
Of which diuersite nature shuld cese, 385
If metallis dit not multiplie & encrece;
wherfore, thei say this reson shewith now
How that vndir erth thei multiplie & grow;
whi not then aboue erth in vessels close & fayre
Such as shal preserue hem from fyre water & aire? 390
Here-to we sai this reson is but rude,
For this is no parfite simylitude.
For cause efficient of metals fynd ye shalle
Only the vertu mineralle,
which in euery erth is not fownde, 395
But in certeyne placis of eligible grownde,
In-to which placis the heuenly speere
Sendith his bemys directly euery yeere,
And as the maters there disposide be
Such metallis therof formed shalle ye se. 400

f. 12ᵛ Fewe growndis be apte to such generacion,
How shulde then a-boue grounde be multiplicacion?
Also alle men perceyuyn that be wise,
How watire congelid with colde is yse;
And bifortyme it hardide was, 405
Som lay in more placis & som lay in lasse;
As watir in fossis of the carte whele
were vaynes smale when thei bigan to kele,
But watir in dichis made veynes more
For plentie of mater þat was therin frore; 410
Heruppon to say it were no good aduyse
That therfore of yse shuld multipli more yse.

377 fawte] lack R   393 efficient] suffycyent E   396 placis] *om.*
BR of] *om.* R   399 maters] metales E   409 in] of EW   veynes]
veynes of ise R   410 mater] water RW   therin frore] in theym before
R, thare before W

So thofe þere be of metalle veynes more & las,
It previth not that thei encrece more þen it was.
Also ye may trust withowt any dowte, 415
If any multipliyng shuld be broȝt a-bowte,
Al þe ingredientis most draw to symplicite,
And breke composicion, a[s] yerly ye may se
For multipliyng of herbis how nature hath prouidid
That al thing onyd in the seed be diuidede; 420

f. 13ʳ Els stalkis & levis which vertually þere-in be
May not com forth actually þat Eye myght hem se;
But metalle holdith his hole composicion
when corrosyfe watirs hath made dissolucion,
Therfore seth yse is nere to symplicite 425
Then is metalle, & may not encreside be,
Truly ye may truste, as I seide bifore,
How of I vnce of syluer may siluer be no more.
Also nothing multiplied shal ye fynde,
But it be of vegetatife or of sensityfe kynd; 430
where metallis be only elementatife,
Havyng no seed nethir feldyng of lyve.
Wherfore concluding al multipliers most cese,
For metalle ons metalle shal not more encrese.
Netherles one metalle transmutide we fynde 435
vnto a metalle of an nother kynde,
For propinquyte of mater that in theyme was,
As it is know bitwixte yre and brasse.
But to make tru syluer or gold is no engyne,
Excepte only the philisophers medicyne; 440

f. 13ᵛ wherfore such lesyngis as multipliers vse
Clerkes reprove and vttirly refuse.
Such arte of multipliyng is to be reprovid,
But holy Alchymye of right is to be louyd,
which tretith of a precious medicyne 445
Such as trewly makith gold & siluyr fyne.
Wherof exemple for testymonye
Is in a cite of Catylonye,

414 encrece] entreat B   418 as] s *inserted above with caret* A   420 onyd]
vnyd S₃, vnited R, Joynyd W   421 vertually] naturally BT   425 seth]
seyng W   nere] more BS₃   435 transmutide we fynde] of another kynd
W   436 in to another mettall transmvtyd we fynd W   444 louyd]
beloued BER

C 9205   C

which Raymunde lully knyght, men suppose,
Made in vij ymagis the trowth to disclose.   450
Thre were good siluer in shape like ladies bright,
Euerych of iiij were golde & like a knyght;
In borders of theire clothinge litteris did appere
Signifiyng in sentence as it shewith here:
Of olde hors-shoys, seid one, I was Ire;   455
Now am I siluere as good as ye desire.
I was, seid a nothire, yre fet fro the Myne,
But now I am golde pure, perfite, and fyne.
Whilom I was copir of an olde rede panne,
Now am I good siluere, seid the thrid woman.   460

f. 14ʳ   The iiij said: I was copir grow in filthi place,
Now am I perfite gold made bi goddis grace.
The v seid: I was siluere, perfite throwgh fyne,
Now am I golde excellent, better þan the prime.
I was a pipe of lede welnere CC. yere,   465
And now to alle men good siluere I appere.
The vij seid: I, lede, am gold, made for a Mastrie,
But truly my felows be nere therto than I.
This science berith hir name bi a kinge
Callid Alchymus with-owte lesynge;   470
A glorious prince of moost noble mynde,
His noble vertuys holpe him þis arte to fynd;
He serchid nature, he was a noble clerke,
He left extorcion, he sought & fownd þis werk.
King hermes also he did the same,   475
which was a clerke of excellent fame
In his quadripartite made of Astrologie,
Of phisike, & of this arte of Alchymye,
And also of magike naturalle,
As of iiij science in nature passing alle;   480

f. 14ᵛ   And there he saide that blessid is he
which knowith thingis truli as thei be;
And blesside is he that makith dewe profe,
For that is rote of connyng and roffe.

450 disclose] s inserted above with caret A   461 iiij] th inserted above A
grow in] yt grewe in R, & greve in a W   463 v] th inserted above A
464 prime] myne BT   467 vij] th inserted above A   469 S₂ begins
470 lesynge] any lesynge ES₂   474 extorcion] exhortacon S₂   he sought]
om. BT   475 hermes] Caildrex B, Calid T, Ptolomeus R   480 iiij] our S₂

For bi opinion is many a man 485
Deceived, which herof litille can.
An olde proverbe: in a bushel of wenynge
Is not fownde one hanfulle of connynge.
with dewe profe & with discrete assay,
wise men may lern new thingis euery day; 490
Bi connyng [men] k[n]owe theym-silf & euery thing,
Man is [but a] beste & wors with-owten connyng.
But litil fauour hath euery man
To science wherof he litille can,
And litille connyng makith men prowd & wild, 495
Sufficient connyng makith men ful mylde.
Noble men now in maner haue despite
Of theym that haue to connynge appetite,
But noble kingis in Auncien dayes
Ordeyned, as olde auctours sayes, 500
f. 15ʳ That the vij science to lerne and can
Shuld noon but only a noble man;
And at the leest he shulde be so fre
That he myght studye with liberte;
wherfore olde sagis dide theym calle 505
The vij sciencis liberalle;
For he that wolde lerne hem perfitly and welle,
In clere libertee he must dwelle.
Fro wordly werkis he muste withdrawe
That wolde lern but mannys lawe; 510
Moch more the worlde he must forsake
which many sciencis wold ouyrtake.
And for [that] cause men may welle se
whi connyng men despisid be,
yet noble memorie shal neuyr cese 515
Of him which connyng doith encrece.
He that lovith connyng, Iustice, & grace
Is set a-syde in many a place;

487 wenynge] wynnynge ES₂R   488 hanfulle] d inserted above after n A
491 men] inserted above with caret A   knowe] n inserted above A   492 but a]
inserted above with caret A   493 euery] any ES₂R   495 prowd] full
prowde ES₂   509 wordly] l inserted above after r with caret A   muste]
must hime S₂   513 that] inserted above with caret A   517 Iustice]
Iustely E

But who to cowrte bringith in with gyle
Profett or present, he is a man that while;   520
f. 15ᵛ   wherfor this science & many gracis mo
Be lost, and be departed alle yow fro.
And ferthermore remembre whate I say,
Synn callith fast for his endyng day.
Couetyce & connyng haue discorde bi kynde;   525
who lucour coveti[t]h this science shal not fynde;
But he that lovith science for hire owne kynd,
He may purchace both for his blessid mynde.
Of this Chapiter more I nede not teche,
For here apperith what men may it reche;   530
That ys to remembre only the trew,
And he that is constant in mynde to pursew,
And is not ambycious, to borow hath no nede,
And can be pacient not hasty for to spede,
And that in god he sett fully his trust,   535
And that in connyng be fixid al his lust,
And with al this he lyve a rightful lyfe,
Fa[l]shode subduyng, support no synful stryfe.
Such men be apte this science to atteyne.
The Chapiter folowing is of Ioy and peyne.   540

f. 16ʳ   Capitulum ii

Normandie norshide a monke now late
which deceyuede men of euery state.
But bifore that, he in his fantasye
Wenyde he hadde cawght this arte fully.
Such reioysing therof he hadde,   545
That he be-gan to dote & to madde.
Of whose ioyes, al be it thei were smale,
For an exemple y write this tale.
This monk had walkide a-bowte in france,
Rangyng apostata in his plesance,   550

519 *The early part of* S *begins*   520 present] pleasur R   525 Couetyce]
Covetuos BES   534 hasty] hastely B   536 be fixid] he fyxe ESS₂
538 Falshode] l *inserted above with caret* A   543 that] that done R
three (?) letters erased after that, *apparently* -on A   546 madde] be
mad ESS₂

And after he came in-to this londe,
willing that men shulde vndirstonde
How that of Alchymye he had the grownde
Bi a boke of receptis which he had fownde;
In sewertie therof he set alle his mynde 555
To leve som noble acte behynde,
wherbi his name shuld be immortall,
And his grete fame in lawde perpetuall.
And ofte he muside wherto begynne
To spende the riches which he shuld wynne. 560
f. 16ᵛ And evir he thoght: lo, this y can,
where myght y fynde som trusty man
which wolde accorde now with my will,
And helpe my purpose to fulfylle;
Then wold y make vppon the playne 565
Of Salisbury, glorious to be sayne,
Fyften Abbeys in a litille while,
On abbey in thende of euery myle.
Heruppon this monke to me resorted,
Of trust, he seid, which men of me reportide 570
His forseid myndis he dide to me telle,
And prayed me to kepe his grete concelle.
I saide bi-fore an ymage of seynt Iame
That I wolde nevir disclose his name,
yet I may write with-outen alle vyce 575
Of his desires that were so nyce.
when he hadde discouered his grete connyng,
He said that he fawtide nothinge
But a goode meen for his solace,
To labour to the kyngis good grace, 580
f. 17ʳ To gete licence of his estate,
And of his lordis mediate,
To purchace lond for the Abbeys forsaide,
For which al costis shuld be welle paide;
But yett he had grete dowte and fere 585
How to purchace, of whome, and where.

567 Fyften] ffyftye BT   578 he] om. BT   fawtide] wantyd SS₂   579 a
goode meen] of good men SS₂   581 gete] purchace S₃   582 mediate]
ymedyate S

When I had herd of this grete werke,
I serchid to wite whate maner clerke
was he, & whate he knewe of scole,
And therin he was but a fole;   590
yet y soeffrede, and helde me stille,
more to lerne of his lewde wille.
Then seide I it were a lewde thing
Such maters to shew to a kynge;
But if the profe were resonable,   595
He wold thynk it a folish fable.
The monk seid how that he hadde in fyre
A thing which shulde fulfille his desyre,
wherof the trouth within xl dayes
I shuld wel know bi trew assayes.   600

f. 17ᵛ   Then I seid I wold no more that tyde,
But xl dayes y seid y wolde abyde.
When xl dayes were goon and paste,
The monkis crafte was clene ovircaste.
Then alle his abbeys & alle his thoght   605
was turned to a thinge of noght,
And as he came he went fulle lewde,
Departing in a mynde fulle shrewde.
For sone aftir, within a litille while,
Many trew men he dide be-gile,   610
And afterward went in-to frawnce.
Lo, this was a pitefulle chawnce
That xv abbeys of Relygion
Shulde in this wise falle to confusion!
Grete wondre was what thing he ment,   615
And whi he sett alle his entent
Abbeys to bilde, then was it wondre;
why nolde he lyve obedience vndre,
But be apostata and Rayle abowte
This blesside science to fynde owte?   620

f. 18ʳ   But as I wrote a-boue in this boke,
Late no deceyver aftir this sciens loke.

588 clerke] a clarcke BT, of clarke ESS₂R   594 shew] open SS₂
600 trew] good SS₂   601 I wold no more] I wolde abide B   602 om.
B   603 goon] cvme SS₂R   613 xv] fyftie BT   614 confusion]
conclusion B   615 wondre] om. B   618 nolde] wolde BSS₂
obedience] obedyent B   619 Rayle] range R

Another exemple is goode to telle
Of one that trustide to do as welle
As Raymonde lully or bacon the frere,   625
wherfore he namyd him-silfe saunz pere.
He was persone of a litylle towne
Not ferre fro the Cite of londone;
which was take for half a leche,
But litil connynge had he to preche.   630
He wenyd him sure this arte to fynde,
His name he wolde haue euer in mynde
Bi mene of a Brigge, ymagined in dotage,
To be made ovir Tamyse for light passage,
wherof shulde growe a comone ese   635
Al the contray there a-bowte to plese.
Yet thof he myght that werke fulfille,
It myght no wise suffice his wille.
Wherfore he wolde sett vp in hight
That Brigge for a wondirfulle syght,   640
f. 18ᵛ   with pynaclis gilte shynyng as golde,
A glorious thinge for men to beholde.
Then he remembrede of the newe
How grettir fame shuld him pursewe
If he myght make that brigge so bright   645
That it myght shyne also bi nyght,
And so contynew, and not breke,
Then al the londe of him wolde speke.
But in his mynde ranne many a dowte
How he myght bringe that werke abowte;   650
He trowid that lampis with light of fyre
Shulde wel performe his nyce desire,
wherfore lampis for that entent
He wolde ordeyne sufficient;
But then he fille in ful grete drede   655
How that after the tyme that he were dede
That light to fynde men wolde refuse,
And change the rente to some othir vse;

---

623 *Small ornamental capital* A   625 *om.* E   634 Tamyse] the tames
ESS₂   637 Yet thof] He thought S   638 suffice] fulfill BT   643 of
the newe] agayn of newe R   645 bright] light R   649 dowte]
thought SS₂   654 He wolde] He thought he wold SS₂

Then thoght he wel is him that wiste
In whom he myght sett alle his truste.   660
f. 19^r   At the last he thoght to make that light
For that bryge to shyne by nyght
with carbuncle stones to make men wondire,
with dowble refleccion a-boue and vndire.
Then newe thoghtis trowbled his mynde,   665
Carbuncle stonys how he myght fynde;
And where to fynde wise men and trewe
which wold for his entent pursue
In seching alle the worlde a-bowte
Plentye of Carbuncles to fynde owte.   670
For this he toke so mekille thoghte,
That his fatt fleshe wastide nye to noght.
And where he trustid with-oute despeire
Of this sciens to haue been heyre,
whe[n] the yere was fully come and go,   675
His crafte was loste and thrifte alle-so.
For when that he toke vp his glasse,
There was no matere for golde ne brasse.
Then he was angrye & welnere woode,
For he hadde wastyde a-way his goode.   680
f. 19^v   In this wise endid alle his disporte;
whate shuld I more of hym reporte;
But that lay-men & clerkis in scolis
May know the dotage of these twoo folys?
Remembre these exemples where ye goo,   685
For in such myndes be truly many moo;
Thei lewdly beleve euery conclusion,
Be it nevir so fals Illusion;
If it in boke writen thei may fynde,
Thei weene it trew þei be so lewde of mynde.   690
Such lewde and hastye confydence
Causith pouertee & lewde expence;

---

659 thoght he wel is him] thought him wel ys he SS₂   669 seching]
searching BSS₂S₃R   672 wastide nye to] fylle to S₃   673 where]
om. BT   675 when] n *inserted above with caret* A   676 thrifte] trust
SS₂   678 matere] watter B   for golde ne brasse] butt gold or brase E
679 woode] dede B   681 wise] om. BT   683 that] thay B
688 fals Illusion] false or faynyd illusyon SS₂

Of trust of this arte arisith Ioyes nyse,
For lewed hope is folys paradyse.
The trew taught children made this confession: 695
Lorde with-oute the alle is degression,
For as thow arte of oure science bigynnynge,
So with-owte the may be no good endyng.
Confiteor altissime nullus ista rapit,
Licet prius didicit, absque te nihil sapit;
Nam tanta stat gracia te deum semper apud,
Perficere sicut capere nam finis es et caput.

f. 20ʳ As of the Ioyes of this arte ye haue seyne,
So shal ye now hire somdele of the peyne, 700
Alle be it contrarye to the appetite
Of theym that hath to this science delyte.
The firste payne is to remembre in mynde
How many sechene & how fewe may fynde;
And yet no man may this science wynne, 705
But it be tawgthe hym bifore þat he bygynne.
He is welle lernyde and of fulle clere witte
whiche bi techynge can sewrly lerne itt;
Of many diuersites he most be sure
whiche secretis wolde know of worching of nature. 710
yet techynge may not so sewrlye availe
But that somtyme shalle happe a man to faile,
As alle that be now dede and goone
Faylide bifore they fownde owre stone,
Oon tyme or othir, firste tyme other last, 715
Alle men faylide tille dewe practyce were past.
No man soner failithe in hete and colde
Then doithe the mastire whiche hasty is & bolde;
f. 20ᵛ For no man soner may oure werkis spill
Then he þat is presumyng his purpose to fulfill. 720
But he that shalle trewly do the deede,
He most vse prouidence, & euer worche with dreede,

694 folys] folysche ESS₂   696 degression] dyrysyoun S, transgression R
698 *The following Latin lines in gold lettering within a scroll; see Introduction*
699 *Small ornamental initial capital* A. *After* haue, y *struck through with vertical
stroke* A   700 ye now hire] you knowe here S   704 may] ytt E, *om.* ST
709 many diuersites] dyuers scyences SS₂   715 other last] or laste ESS₂R
720 purpose] workes SS₂   721 do the] worke in S, worke the S₂

For of alle paynys the most grevous payne
Is for oon fayle to begynne alle agayne.
Euery man shalle grete peyne haue   725
when he shalle firste þis arte covyte & crave.
He shalle ofte tymes chaunge his desire
with new tydyngis whiche he shalle hyre;
His concelle shalle often then hym begyle,
For that sesons he dredithe no subtile wyle;   730
And often tymes his mynde to & fro
In new opinions he shalle change in woo,
And so longtyme contynewe in fantasie,
A grete a-venture for hym to com therbye.
So of this arte be ye neuir soo fayne,   735
Yet ye most taaste of many a bittyr payne.
Of paynes yet I most shewe more,
Ageyn your appetitis thofe it be soore.
It is grete peyne as alle wyse men gysse,
f. 21ʳ   To wite where a trew mastir is;   740
And if ye fynde hym yet it wille be peyne,
Of his trew love to be certeyne;
For as moche that no man may teche but oone
Of the makyng of oure delycious stoone.
And alle be itt ye fynde hym þat wil you teche,   745
yet moche trowble & peynes ye may reche,
For if youre mynde be vertuysly sett,
Then the deville wille labour yow to lett.
In iij wisys to lett he wille a-wayte,
with haste, with dispeyre, & with disceyte,   750
For drede of vertue whiche ye may do
when ye shulde atteyne this grace vnto.
The firste perile forsaide is of haste
whiche cawsithe most destruccione & waste.
Alle auctours wrytynge of this arte   755
Say haste is of the deville his parte.
The litill boke wrete of þe philosophers fest,
Seythe: omnis festinacio ex parte diaboli est.

724 oon fayle to] one to fayle and SS₂   729 concelle] Conceyte SS₂
732 he] *om.* SS₂   735 ye] he B   736 ye] he B   737 *Small
ornamental initial capital* O   741 ye] he B   749 iij wisys] thre maner
of wayes SS₂

f. 21ᵛ Wherfore þat man shalle sonest spede
which with grete leysere wisely wille procede. 760
Vppon assay ye shalle trewly knowe
That who most hastith he trewly shalbe slow,
For he with hast shall bryng his werke arere
Somtyme a monyth, & somtyme an hole yere;
And in þis arte it shal euyre be so, 765
That hasty mane shal neuir fayle of woo.
Also of haste ye may trewly be sure,
That she leuythe no thinge clene & pure.
The devill hathe none so subtile wyle
As with hastynes yow to begyle; 770
Therfore ofte tymes he wille assawte
youre mynde with hast to make defawte.
He shall fynde grace in towne & londe
whiche can hastynes alle tymys withstonde;
I say alle tymes, for in oone puncte of tyme 775
Haste may destroye alle youre engyne;
Therfore alle haste eschewe & feere
As if that she a deuille were.

f. 22ʳ My witt trewly may not suffice
Haste sufficiently to despice. 780
Many men haue be caste in grete care
Bi-cause þei wolde not of haste be ware,
But euyre calle vpon to see an ende,
Whiche is temptacion of the feende.
No more of haste at this present, 785
But blessid be the paciente.
When with haste þe fende hathe noone auaile,
Then with despeire your mynde he wil assaile,
And often present þis sentence to your mynde—
How many sechithe & how few may fynde 790
Of wisere men then euyr were ye;
what sewrtie then to yow may be?
He wille move yow to dowte alle-so
whethir your techere had it or no;

766 fayle of] lacke SS₂, *om.* of E   780 Haste] ye hurt of hast R   786 the]
euery ESS₂   787 *Small ornamental initial capital* W   789 present]
call B   790 may] dothe ES₂R, *om.* S   793 yow] *om.* BT

And alle-so how it migthe so falle   795
That parte he tawgthe you, but not alle.
Suche vncerteynte he wille caste owte
To sett your mynde in grevous dowte,
f. 22ᵛ   And so youre paynes he wille repeyre
With wanhope & with suche despeyre.   800
A-gayne this assawte is no defense
But only the vertu of confidence,
To whome resone shalle yow lede,
That ye shalle haue no cause to drede;
If ye wysly calle to youre mynde   805
The vertuous maners, suche as ye fynde
In youre mastire and youre techere,
So shalle ye haue no nede to feere.
If ye considre alle circumstancis a-bowte,
Wheþer he taghte you for loue or for dowte,   810
And whethir þe mocione of him biganne—
For it is harde to truste suche a man;
For he þat proferthe hathe more neede
Of yow than ye of hym to spede;
This wise certeynte ye may welle wynne   815
Bifore þat ye your werkis do bigynne.
When suche certeynte ye trewly haue,
Fro dispeire ye may be sewre & save.
f. 23ʳ   But who can fynde suche a mastire owte
As my mastir was, he nedethe not to dowte;   820
whiche was riȝt noble & fulli worthi lawde,
He louyde Iustice, & he abhorride frawde;
He was fulle secrete when other men were lowde,
Lothe to be know þat herof augthe he cowde;
when men disputide of colours of the rose,   825
He wolde not speke, but kepte him-silfe close.
To whome I laboride longe & many a day,
But he was soleyne to preve with straite assay,
To serche & know of my disposicioun,
with manyfolde provis to know my condicion;   830

800 suche] *om.* E, great SS₂   808 haue] fynd SS₂   810 he] ye B
813 proferthe] provith ESS₂   815 certeynte] certeyn ESS₂ certaynly R
821 fulli] much SS₂, full R   828 soleyne] hard SS₂ soleme R   829 know]
prove more ESS₂

And when he fownde vnfeynyde fidelyte
In my grete hope whiche yet no thing dide see,
At the last I conqueride by grace dyvyne
His love whiche did to me inclyne.
wherfore he thoght sone aftir in a tyde   835
That lengire delaied I ne shulde abyde;
My many-folde letters, my hevy hert & chere
Movid his compassyon, þei persid hym ful nere;
f. 23ᵛ   Wherfore his penne he wolde no more refrayne,
But as here folowith so wrote he agayne: 840
My verray trustye, my dere bilouyde broder,
I most yow awnswere, it may be noon other.
The tyme is come ye shalle receyue this grace,
To youre grete comforte & to youre solace.
Youre persone with youre grete confidence,   845
Youre uertue provide with your sapience,
Youre love, your trowithe, your longe perseuerance,
Your stedfast mynde shalle your desire a-vaunce.
Wherfore it is nede that with-in shorte space
We speke to-gedire, & see face to face;   850
If y shuld write I shulde my foialte breke,
Therfore mowthe to mowthe I most nedis speke.
And when ye come, myn heyre vnto þis arte
I wille yow make, & fro this londe departe;
ye shalle be bothe my brodire & myn heyre   855
Of this grete secrete wherof clerkis despeire.
Therfore thanke god whiche gevith þis renowne,
For it is bettir then is to were a crowne;
f. 24ʳ   Nexte a[f]ter his seyntis our lord doith hem calle
which hath þis arte to honour him with-alle.   860
No more to you at þis present tyde,
But hastely to see me dispose you to ryde.
This lettre receyving, I hastid ful sore
To ride to my master a hundred myle & more;

832 whiche . . . dide see] when . . . dyd he see R   834 inclyne] declyne SS₂
841 *Small ornamental initial capital* M   trustye] trewe SS₂   dere] wel S
842 yow] nowe SS₂   845-6 your honest desyre, with so great confydence /
your vertue approvyd with so moch sapience R   848 your desire]
you ESS₂   851 foialte] seale SS₂   858 then is to] then
to BESS₂S₃   859 after] aster A   his seyntis] this science BT
863 receyving] Received BESS₂R

And þen fowrtie dayes contynually   865
I lerned al the secretys of Alchymy;
Alle be it philosophie of me was vnderstond
As moch as of many othir in this londe.
Netherles folys which for þis science soght
weene þat in xl dayes it wolde be wroght.   870
Bitwene xl dayes werk, now ye may see,
And xl dayes lernyng is grete diuersitee.
The[n] derke dowtis to me aperide pure;
There fownde I disclosid þe bondis of nature;
The cause of wondirs were to me so faire,   875
And so resonable that I ne cowde despeire.
If your mastir & ye resemble alle abowte
My goode mastir & me, then take ye no dowte.

f. 24ᵛ   The thride Impedyment deceyte we calle,
Amongist other to me the worste of alle;   880
And that is of seruantis which shuld awaite
vpon your werkis, for som can moche deceite;
And som be necligent, [som] slepyn bi the fyre,
Som be ilwillid, such shal lett youre desire;
Som be folyche, and som be ovirbolde,   885
Som kepe no concelle of doctrine to them tolde;
Som be filthi of hondis and of slevis,
Suche meddille strange maters þat greteli grevis;
Som be dronklew, & some vse moch to Iape,
Be ware of these if ye wille hurt escape.   890
The trew be folyshe, the witty be fals,
That one hurt me sore, & that other als.
For when I hadde my werkis wel wroght,
Such stele it a-wey, & lefte to me noght.
Then I, Remembring þe coste, þe tyme, the peyne   895
which I shulde haue to begynne ageyne,
with hevy hert, fare well, a-diew, saide I,
I wil no more of Alchymye.

873 Then] n *inserted above with caret* A   879 *Ornamental capital* T, *not in gold*   880 other] all other ESS₂   to me] *om.* ESS₂   882 can] vse R
883 som] *inserted above with caret* A   884 ilwillid] il witted B, evyll wyllyd S₂, ill willinge T   886 of doctrine] *om.* ESS₂   to them tolde] which to them is told SS₂   887-8 *om.* S₂   887 be] to S [*inserted above line;* be *struck out*]   889 dronklew] dronken lewed B, dronkely E, drvnken SS₂
890 hurt] greeff R   891 folyshe] folis BT   898 of] medle with SS₂

f. 25ʳ   But how that chaunce bifille that sesoun
Few men wolde it bileve bi resoun;   900
yet ten persons be witnes trewe alle
How that myshappe dide me bifalle,
which mowght not be only by man
with-owte the deville, as thei telle cane.
I made also the Elixer of lyfe,   905
which me birefte a marchaunt his wife;
The quynte essence I made also,
with other secretis many mo,
which synful people toke me fro,
To my grete peyne & to my grete wo.   910
So in this worlde there is no more to seyne
But þat euery ioye is medlide with grete peyne.
Of peyne there is a litil yet behynde,
which is convenient to be had in mynde,
That fille vppon a blesside man,   915
wherof the trouth reporte I can.
Thomas dalton this good man hight,
He serued god bothe day and nyght;
f. 25ᵛ   Of the Reede medycine [he] had grete store,
I trowe nevir englishe man had more.   920
A squyer for the body of kyng Edwarde
whose name was Thomas herbarde
Toke this dalton a-gayne his desire
Owte of an Abbey in gloucestre-shire,
And broght him in presence of the kinge;   925
wherof delvis had sone tydinge,
For dalton was whilome deluys clerke.
Deluys disclosed of dalton his werke.
Deluys was squyere in confidence
with kinge Edward, ofte in his presence;   930
Delvis reported that in a litille stownde
How dalton had made to him a Ml. pownde
Of as goode golde as the Ryalle was,
within half a day and somdele las;

908 with other] with dyuers other SS₂   909 om. S   912 medlide]
myngled R   grete] om. SS₂   913 Small ornamental initial capital O
919 Reede] gret S₃   he] inserted above with caret A   925 presence] presentes
S₃   927 whilome] willm̄ SS₂

For which deluys swere on a boke.   935
Then dalton on deluys caste his loke,
And seid, deluys, sir, ye be forswore,
wherof your herte hath cause to be sore.
f. 26ʳ   Of nothing, seide he, that I now haue tolde,
witnes oure lord whome Iudas solde.   940
But ons, seid deluys, I swore to the
How thu shuldeste not be vtterid bi me,
which y may breke wel I vnderstonde,
For the kingis wele, and for al his londe.
Then seide dalton ful soberly: 945
This answere voidith no periury.
How shulde þe king in you haue confidence,
youre vntrouth confesside in his presence?
But sir, seid dalton to þe kingis grace,
I haue be trow[b]lid oft in many a place   950
For this medicyne greuosly and sore,
And now I thoght it shuld hurt me nomore;
wherfore in þe abbey where I was take
I cast it in a foreyn, a comyn lake,
Goyng to þe Ryver which dothe ebbe & flow;   955
There is destroied as moche riches nowe
As wolde haue seruyd to þe holi londe
For xxti thowsand men vppon a bonde.
f. 26ᵛ   I kepte it longe for oure lorddis sake,
To helpe a kyng which þat Iournay wold make.   960
Alas dalton, then seide the kynge,
It was fowle done to spille suche a thinge.
He wolde haue dalton to make it [a]gayne.
Dalton seid it myght not be, certeyne.
Whi, seide the king, how came ye therbye?   965
He seid bi a chanon of lichefeld truly,
whose werkis dalton kepte diligently
Many yeres til that chanon moste dye;
And for his service, he seid in that space,
The chanon gave him al þat therof was.   970

935 on] apon BESS₂R   942 how] yt R   bi me] for me ESS₂   944 wele]
welth SS₂   945 seide] answerid S   950 trowblid] trowlid A
954 foreyn a comyn] fowle common SS₂, forayn of a comon lake R
960 make] take SS₂R   963 agayne] a inserted above with caret A

The kyng gave to dalton markis fowre
with libertie to go where he wold that howre;
Then was þe king in his herte sore
That he had not know dalton bi-fore.
And euer it happith with-owte lesynge   975
That Tiraunys be ful nye to a kinge.
For herbert lay for dalton in a-wayte,
And broght him to Stepneth with desceyte;
The seruantis of herberd þe monay toke away
which the kinge gaue to dalton that day;   980
And after herbard caried dalton ferre
Fro thens to the Castelle of Gloucetter.
The[re] was dalton prisonere ful longe,
Herberde to dalton dide mekille wronge.
Fro thens he hadd hym to prisone faste   985
To troy, tille iiij yeres were nye paste,
And after he broght him owte to deye;
Dalton to deth obeyed lowly,
And seid: lord ihesu blessid thu be!
Me think y haue be to longe fro the.   990
A science thu gave me with ful grete charge,
which I haue kepte with-owte owtrage;
I fownde no man yet apte therto
To be myn heyre whan I am go,
wherfore swete lorde now am I fayne   995
To resigne this thi gifte to the agayne.
Then dalton made devowte prayers & stille;
with smylyng chere he seid: now do your wille.
When herberde sawe him so gladde to dye,
Then ran watire fro herberde his Eye;   1000
For prisone ne deth cowde not him availe
To wynne this arte, his crafte dide him faile.
Nowe late him go, seide herberde than,
For he shalle nevir hurte ne profite man.
But when dalton fro the bloke shuld ryse,   1005
He lokide forth in fulle hevy wise;

f. 27ʳ (line 979)
f. 27ᵛ (line 999)

978 Stepneth] stepney BESS₂R   983 There] re *inserted above with caret*
986 troy tille] Twitill B   987 owte] *om.* B   992 kepte] kepte &
vsyd R   owtrage] comtrage B   1001 not] *om.*BSS₂S₃   1004 he]
om. B

And so departide with ful hevy chere;
It was not [his] wille to lyve oon yere.
This was his payne as I yowe tell,
Bi men that hadd no drede of helle.   1010
Herberde dyed so[ne] after in his bedde,
And delvis at Tewkesburye lost his hedde.
This wise grete payne, as ye may see,
Folowith this arte in euery degre.
Here loste the kinge alle his entent,   1015
For herberde was prowde and violent,
So noble a man to oppresse with pryde,
And like a felon hym leede and gyde;

f. 28ʳ   where þat bi goodnes pacience and grace,
There moght haue growe ful grete solace   1020
As wel to þe kyng ye may vndirstonde,
As for the ease of commons of the lond.
But wondire not þat grace do not falle,
For synne regnyth in this londe ovire alle.
Lo, here was grace ful redy at honde   1025
To haue ceside taxis & talagis of the londe;
wherbi moch love & grace wolde haue be
Bitwene knyghthode, prestehode, & comynalte.
Here ye may see how vicious violence
May not purchace the vertue of sapience;   1030
For vice and vertu be thingis contrarye,
Therfore þe vicious may not com therbye.
If vicious men myght lerne this science,
Thei wolde therwith do wondre violence;
And with ambiciosnes grow evirmore   1035
wors of condicions then thei were bifore.
Now is the Chapiter of ioye & peynys gone.
The chapiter folowing shewith maters of oure stone.

f. 28ᵛ   Capitulum iii

Tonsile was a laborere in fyre
Thre score yere & more to wyne his desire;   1040

1008 his] *om.* A   1011 sone] ne *inserted above with caret*   1017 pryde]
great pryde SS₂   1024 regnyth in] reygneth E, rangith S₂   1025 ful]
om. R   1032 not] *om.* E   1034 wondre] wonderous SS₂   1038 stone]
noble stone S₂   1039 was] *om.* SS₂   laborere] great Laborer SS₂

Bryan was a nother, with holton in the west;
These were euer besy, cowde practice with þe best.
But yett this science thei nevir fownde,
For thei knew not the maters ne the grownd,
But rombled forth, & euermore thei sowght,   1045
Thei spend their life & their goode to noght;
Moch lost, moch cost, moch angwish þei boght
Amonge their receptis which þei had wroght.

Then made Tonsile to me his grete compleynt;
with weping teris he seid his herte was feynt,   1050
For he had spendide al his lusty dayes
In fals receptis & in such lewde assayes
Of herbis, gummys, of rotis, and of grasse,
Many kyndes bi hym assaid was,
As crowfote, salandyne, & mezereon,   1055
Verbayn, lunarye, and mortagon,
In heere, in eggis, in merdis, & vryne,
In Antymonye, arsenek, in hony, wax, & wyne,
f. 29ʳ   In calce vive, sondyfere, and vitrialle,
In marchasites, Toties, & euery mynerall,   1060
In malgams, in blaunchers, in citrinacions,
Alle fille to nogthe in his operacions.
For he considerid not how he did raage,
when to goddis proporcione he layde surcharge.
After alle these he thogthe no thing so gode   1065
To worche vpone as shuld be mannys blode,
Till þat I seide how blode wil wast & fume
In mygthy fire, & vttirly consume.
For criste is love, then seide he, teche me
wherof þe substance of our stone shuld be.   1070
Tonsile, saide I, whate shuld it you availe
Suche thing to know? your lymmes do you faile
For verray age, therfore cese youre lay
And love your bedis, it is hy tyme to pray;

1042 besy] best B   cowde] and could SS₂   ;1043 science] noble science
SS₂   1044 ne] in SS₂   1045 thei] om. S₃   1046 & their goode]
& goodes S₃   1052 assayes] wayes S₂   1056 Verbayn] In varvayne S
mortagon] also mortagon SS₂   1057 vryne] in vrin SS₂   1059 vitrialle]
also vitrioll SS₂   1062 operacions] great operacons SS₂   1064 sur-
charge] suche charge ESS₂R   1068 mygthy] myghty and great SS₂
1074 hy] om. ESS₂

For if ye knew the materials of our stone,   1075
Ar ye cowde make it your daies wold be gone.
Thereof no charge goode mastir, saide he,
It were sufficient comforte now to me
f. 29ᵛ To know þe trew materials with-owte wrong
Of þat stone whiche I haue sowgthe so longe.   1080
Tonsile, seide I, it is no litille thinge
wherof ye wolde haue trew tidynge;
For many auctours write of þat dowte,
But none of them shewith it clere owte.
For auctours whiche of þis arte do write   1085
Besogthe gode, as witnessithe democrite,
That he vnpeyned wold fro þis world take
Ther sowlis whom he tagthe bokis herof to make.
For gretly dowtid euermore alle suche
þat of þis science thei migthe write to moche;   1090
Eueryche of þem tagthe but oon poynt or tweyne,
wherby his felows were made certeyne
How þat he was to theyme a brodyre,
For eueryche of þem wel vndirstode þat odir.
Alle-so thei wrote not euery man to teche,   1095
But to shew them-silfe bi a secrete speche.
Truste not therfore to redyng of oon boke,
But in many auctours werkis ye most loke;
f. 30ʳ Liber librum aperit, seide arnalde þe grete clerke,
Anaxagoras seithe þe same for þis werke;   1100
who þat slowfulle is many bokis to see,
Suche oone in practice prompte shal neuir be.
But tonsile, for almis I wil make no store
Playnly to disclose it whiche neuir was do bifore,
Bi way of answere for your recreacion   1105
If ye can wisely make interrogacion.
Gode mastire, saide he, then teche me trewly
whethir þe maters be sol & mercurie,
Or whethir of Sol and Lune it may be,
Or whethir I shal take theme alle three,   1110

1076 daies] good dayes SS₂   1088] herof] om. SS₂   1094 wel
vndirstode] will vnderstond ESS₂, vnderstode S₃   þat odir] another ESS₂
1097-1102 om., with caret in left margin S₃   1105 your] om. SS₂
1108 In right margin nota in later hand

Or sol bi it silfe, or Mercurie allone,
Or sulfur with them for maters of our stone,
Or whethir I shal Sal armonyake take,
Or myneralle meenys our stone þere-of to make.
Here be many questions tonsile, seide I,   1115
wisely remembrede, & fulle craftily;
ye name it not yet but only in generalle,
for ye most take somdele of þes þinges alle;

f. 30ᵛ   Of þese & of odire ye most take a parte
Oon tyme or othir to ministre þis arte.   1120
Many þinges helpithe to apte our stone,
But .ij. be materialle, & yet our stone is oon;
Bitwen whiche .ij. is suche diuersitee
As bitwen þe modir & þe child may be;
Another diuersite bi-twex þem finde ye shal   1125
Suche as is fownde bitwen male & femal.
These ij kindes shal do alle youre seruyce
As for þe white werke, if ye can be wise.
Oon of þese kyndes a stone ye shal it fynde,
For it bidith fire as stones do of kynde;   1130
But it is no stone in towching ne in sygthe,
But a subtile erthe, browne, rody, & not briȝt;
And when it is seperate & brogthe to his aperage,
Then we name it our groundid litarge.
Firste it is browne, rody, & after somdele white,   1135
And þen it is callid our chosen marcasite.
Oon vnce þereof is bettir þen fyvety pownd,
It is not to be solde within al cristen grownd.

f. 31ʳ   But he that wolde haue it he shal be fayne
To do it make, or take him-self the payne.   1140
But one grete grace in that labour is seyne,
Make it onys wel & nevir no more ageyne.
Olde faders callid it thing of vyle price,
For it is noght worth bi wai of merchandise;

1114 for to our stone many thinges we must make SS₂   1117 not] *om.* S₃
1122 ij. be materialle] ij materialles E   1124 may] shuld R   1128 þe]
your S₃   1129 it] *om.* SS₂S₃   1133 his aperage] hyr age S₃
1135 browne rody] ruddy browne SS₂ after] *om.* SS₂   1141 labour] labours
A   1142 no] *om.* SR; He yt makes it ons well nedes neuer more agayne S₃
1143 vyle] light SS₂

No m[e]n that fynde it wil bere it a-way,   1145
No more then thei wolde take a vnce of clay;
Men wil not bileve þat it is of hye price,
No man knowith it therfore but he be wise.
Here haue I disclosid a grete secrete wondir
which neuir was write bi them which ben erthe vnder.
Another stone, Tonsile, ye most haue with-alle,   1151
Or els ye fawte your chyef Materialle.
which is a stone glorious, faire, and bright,
In handlyng a stone, & a stone in syght;
A stone glitiryng with perspicuyte,   1155
Beyng of wondirful diaphanyte;
The price of a vnce conveniently
Is xx. *shillings*, or welnere therbye.

f. 31ᵛ   Hire name is Magnesia, few peple hir know;
She is fownd in hye placis as wel as in lowe.   1160
Plato knew hir propertie, & callid hir bi hir name,
And chawcer rehersith how titanos is þe same,
In þe Canon his tale, saynge: whate is thuse
But Quod Ignotum per magis ignocius?
That is to say, whate may this be   1165
But vnknow bi more vnknow named is she?
Netherles, Tonsile, now I wil trewly teche
whate is Magnesia to say in oure speche:
Magos is grue, mirabile in latyne it is,
Es in money, ycos science, A is god i-wis.   1170
That is to say it is suche a thinge
wherin of monay is wondire dyvyne connyng.
Now here ye know whate is Magnesia,
Res eris in qua latent sciencia diuinaque mira.
These ij stonys, Tonsile, ye must take   1175
For youre materials, Elixere if ye make.

1145 men] man ABESS₂S₃   1146 take] *om.* ESS₂, take vp S₃   1147 Men]
you B   hye] so heigh S₃   1148 but he be] but they that be wyse SS₂,
but if he be R   1151 *Small ornamental initial capital* A   1153 faire]
om. S   1155 stone] goodly stone SS₂   glitiryng] glysterynge SS₂
1156 wondirful] wounderfull and excellent SS₂   1162 chawcer] chawncers
A, chaunter (r *above with caret*) S₂   1163 Canon] chanons yemans R
thuse] this SS₂   1164 Quod] Quid AS₃   magis] *om.* R   ignocius] ignotus S
1167 now] *om.* SS₂R   1170 god] good SS₂   1172 wondire] wounderous
SS₂   1173 *om.* B   1174 *Latin in gold letters within scroll in green and
text ink. In left margin a hand with blue sleeve points to Latin*

Alle be it the first tyme Materials be no more,
yet many thingis helpith as I sayde bi-fore.

f. 32ʳ   This secrete was nevir bi-fore this day
So trewly discouerede, take it for your pray.   1180
I pray god that this turne not me to charge,
For I drede sore my penn goith to large;
For thofe moch peple perceyve not þ[is] sentence,
yet subtile clerkis haue to moch evidence;
For many clerkis be so clere of witt,   1185
yf thei had this grownde, þei were sure of itt;
where our lord hath ordei[ny]de þat no man it fynde
But only he þat is of vertuys mynde;
wherfore olde faders coveride for grete reson
The maters of oure stone disclosid at þis seson.   1190
Other materials ye shal none take
But only these ij. our white stone to make;
Excepte sal armonyak, with sulphur of kynde,
Such as owte of metals ye can fynde.
These ij wille abide to fulfille youre desyre,   1195
The Remenant wille voide when þei com to fyre.
Sulphur wille brenn & change colours faste,
But oure litarge abidith firste and laste.

f. 32ᵛ   Ye may not with metalle or quyk syluere begynne,
To make Elixer, if ye entende to wynne;   1200
yett if ye destroye theire hole composicion,
Som of theire componentis wil helpe in conclusion.
And that is nothing els of þat oon or that odire,
But only Magnesia, & litarge hir brodire.

f. 33ʳ   Capitulum iiij

Of þe Grose werk now I will not spare,   1205
Thofe it be secrete, largily to declare.

1178 *in* S₃ *followed by 1199–1204, completing f. 34ʳ; 1179–98 follow on f. 34ᵛ;*
1180 discouerede] dislosyd S₃   1182 sore] *om.* S₃   1183 þis] is
inserted above   1184 to] *om.* S   1185 for] Bycause SS₂   1187 or-
deinyde] ny *inserted above with caret;* i *may originally have been* r   1188 is
of] ys of a godly and SS₂   of vertuys mynde] is vertuous of mynde S₃
1189 coveride] coouered it BE   1190 oure] this SS₂   1193 nota *in
right margin*   1196 voide] avoid BR   1199 or] and SS₂   1205 I
will] wyll I ES₂S₃   not] noyer S₃

To teche yow trouth is myn entent,
As ferforth as I darre for goddis commaundement.
I wil enforme and gyde yow on the waye
In such wise as ye may fynde youre praye,   1210
If ye considre how the parties of werkis
Be owte of ordre set bi the olde clerkis.
As I seid bifore, the mastirs of this arte
Euerych of theyme discloside but a parte;
wherfore thofe ye perceyuyd theym as ye wolde,   1215
yet ye can not ordre & Ioyn theyme as ye shuld.
Arnalde shewith in his writynge
How oure fynal secrete is to know the thinge
where-vpon oure werk shuld take hir grownde,
And how pure naturis & symple may be founde;   1220
In his boke bigynnynge multipharie,
He seith in oure growndede mater ij kyndis be;
But how to fynde them he kepte þat in store,
ye haue theire names þe laste chapiter bifore.

f. 33ᵛ   Frere bacon disclosid more of that poynte   1225
when he seid: departe ye euery ioynte
In elementa propinqua, take goode hede þere-to;
But vnwise doctours worchyn neuyr so,
But hedlye thei procede as men welnere madde;
To þe mater dyuysible mo maters they adde.   1230
So when þei wene to bring forth a flowre,
Thei do nothing but multiplie Erroure.
There ceside bakon, and so do other suche
For verray drede lest thei shewid to moche.
Auicenna in porta wrote, if ye remembre,   1235
How ye shulde procede perfeccion to engendre,
Truly techinge as þe pure trowthe was:
Comedas ut bibas, & bibas ut comedas;
Ete as it drinke, & drinke as it doith Ete,
And in the meene sesons take it a perfite swete.   1240
Rasis sett the dietarie & spake somdele ferre:

1207 trouth] throughe B   entent] mynd and intent SS₂   1213 the
mastirs] by maysters SS₂   1216 & Ioyn theyme] then & yoyne E, theym
and done S, them and Joyne S₂   1218 oure] euer the SS₂   1220 &
symple] in symples ESS₂   1222 kyndis] thynges S₃   1230 adde] hadd S₃
1236 perfeccion] perfect man S₃   1237 pure] om. S₃   1239 it . . .
it] I . . . I SS₂, ye . . . ye R   1240 it] I SS₂   a] om. S

Non tamen comedat res festinanter;
Lett not youre maters ete ouyrhastelie,
But siselye consume theire foode leyserlye.

f. 34^r

Herof the prophete made wondre mencion,   1245
If ye applye it to this intencion:
Visitasti terram et inebriasti eam,
Multiplicasti locupletare eam;
Terram fructiferam in salsuginem,
Et terram sine aqua in exitus aquarum.
If it haue plentye of mete and drynke,
Men must wake when thei desire to wynke;
For it is labour of wacch and peynes grete.
Also the food is ful costelewe mete;   1250
Therfore al pore men be ware, said Arnolde,
For this arte longith for grete men of þe worlde.
Trust to his wordis ye pore men alle,
For I am witnes that so ye fynde shalle.
Esto longanimus et suauis, said he,   1255
For hasti men the ende shal nevir see.
The length of clensinge of maters infectide
Deceyvith moche peple, for it is vnsuspectide,
wherfore pore men, put you not in prese
Suche wondirs to seche, but in seson cese.   1260

f. 34^v

Excesse for on half quarter of an howre
May destroye alle, therfore chiefe socowre
Is, primum pro quo & vltimum pro quo non,
To know of the sympring of owre stone.
Til it may no more sympre do not cese,   1265
And yet longe contynuance may not cause encrese;
Remembre that watire wil bubbil & boylle,
But buttir shulde sympire, & also oyle,
And so with longe leysere waste,
And not with bubbilyng made in haste,   1270
For dowte of perilis many mo then oon,

1244 siselye] softly SS₂   1246 ff. *Small ornamental initial capitals* V, T
for Visitasti *and* Terram   1249 grete] very great SS₂   1250 ful
costelewe] full costely BR, very costly SS₂   1252 longith for] longeth to B,
belongyth to SS₂R   1254 fynde] fynde it S₃   1258 Do so prolonge the
tyme that they are reicted SS₂   vnsuspectide] suspected B   1260 seche]
search BSR, setche S₂   1262 therfore] therfore the SS₂, your S₃, ther former R   1267 Remembre that] *om.* S   &] & also S   1269 so] *om.* SS₂
waste] yt will wast SS₂   1270 haste] great hast SS₂   1271–1664 S₂ *missing*

And for superegression of oure stone.
Among grose werkis the fowlist of alle
Is to clarifie oure meenys Mineralle.
Extremytees may not be wel wroght   1275
withe-oute many meenys wisely soght;
And euery meen most be made pure
If youre werke shulde be made sure;
For fowle & clene bi naturalle lawe
Haue grete discorde, & so hath Ripe & rawe;   1280

f. 35ʳ   Stedfast to stedfast wil it-silfe combynde,
And fletynge to fletyng wil drawe bi kinde;
And euyre where þe concordance is more,
Naturis wil drawe þat were elswere bi-fore.
This grose werke is fowle in hir kynde,   1285
And ful of perils ye shal it fynde.
No mannys witt can hym so moche a-vaile
But that some tyme he shal make a faile;
As wel as þe lay-man so shalle the clerk,
And alle that labour the grose werk,   1290
wherof Anaxagoras saide trewly thuse:
Nemo prima fronte reperitur discretus.
And ons I herd a wise man say
How in Catilonye at this day
Magnesia, with myneral meenys alle,   1295
Be made to sale, if ye for theyme calle,
wherby the handis of a clenly clerke
Shal not be filyde a-bowte so fowle werke,
And longtyme sonyre your werk, I vndirstonde,
Shulde be ferre onwarde bi-fore-honde.   1300

f. 35ᵛ   For if ye shulde make al thingis as I can,
ye myght be wery bi-fore your werk bigan.
The philosophers werke do not begynne
Til al thingis be pure withoute & within;
we that most sech tyncture moost specious,   1305
Muste nedly avoid al vyle thingis & vicious.

1272 superegression] supergression BERS   1283–4 *om.* S   1284 wil] will
that B   1290 the] ys of the S   1298 fowle vyle S   1299 And] and
so B   your werk] *om.* SR   1300 Shulde] your worke should SR ferre] *om.* R
1303 philosophers] philisophers AS₃   1304 thingis] *om.* BR   1306 ned-
ly] nedes R   vyle thingis & vicious] all thinges that be vycious S &] *om.* E

Of manyfolde meenys eche hath his propurtie
To do his office after his degree;
with theym hydde thingis be owte fett,
Som that wold helpe, & som that wyl lett. 1310
Oure Apotecarys to dresse hem can no skylle,
And we for to teche them haue no manere of wille;
wherof the cause trewly is none odire
But thei wolde contrefet to be-gile her brodir,
Rather than thei wold receyve the peyne 1315
Therto perteynyng ar thei shuld it atteyne.
It is theire vse, wherof my herte is soore,
Moche to desire and lityle do therfore.
Who wold haue trew werk he may no labour spare,
Nethir yet his purs thof he make it bare; 1320
And in the grose werke he is firthist behind
That dayli desirith thende therof to fynde.
If the grose werke with al his circumstance
were done in iij yeris it were a blessid chaunce;
For he that may ende it ons in certeyn 1325
Shal neuyr haue nede to begynn a-gayne,
If he his medycyne wisely can augment,
For that is the maistrie of al oure entent.
It nedith not to name þe meenys Mineral,
For Albert writith opinly of theym alle. 1330
Moche I myght write of naturis of Mynys,
which in this grose werk be but ingynys;
For in this werk nothing fynde ye shalle
But handcrafte callid arte Mechanycalle;
wherin an hundrede wysis and mo 1335
ye may committ a faylle as ye therin go.
Wherfore beleve whate olde Auctours telle,
with-oute experience ye may not do welle.
Considre alle circumstance & set your delite
To kepe vnyformyte of al thing requisite; 1340

f. 36ʳ

1308 his] his owne S   1309–1310 om. S   1312 for crossed through,
later hand   1312 manere of] om. S   1315 receyve the peyne]
refrayne the payne S   1318 om. B   do] to do ES   1321 in] om. S
1326 begynn] begyne it BSS₃R   1329 nedith] nedith it A (it lightly om. S
crossed through)   1331 Mynys] myndes E   1332 ingynys] grosse
Ingyns S   1335 wysis] waise BSR   1337 whate] as BR   olde] om.
ES   1338 experience] gret experience S₃

f. 36ᵛ　vse oon maner vessel in matere & in shappe,
　　　　Be ware of comixtion that no þing mishap.
　　　　An hundred defawtis in specialle
　　　　ye may make vnder this warnyng generale.
　　　　Nethirles this doctryne wil suffice　　　　　　　1345
　　　　To him that can in practice be wise,
　　　　If youre Mynystres be witty and trewe,
　　　　Such shal not nede your werkis to renewe.
　　　　Therfore if ye wil voyde alle dreede,
　　　　In the grose werke do bi my reede:　　　　　　　1350
　　　　Take nevir therto no howsholde man,
　　　　Thei ben soone wery as I telle can;
　　　　Therfore take no man therto
　　　　But he be wagide, how evir ye do,
　　　　Not bi the monthe as nye as ye may,　　　　　　1355
　　　　Ne bi the weeke, but bi the daye;
　　　　And that your wagis be to theire mynde
　　　　Bettir then thei elswere can fynde;
　　　　And that thei nede not for wagis sewe,
　　　　But that their payment be quyke & trewe.　　　1360
f. 37ʳ　For that shalle cause theym to loue and dreede,
　　　　And to their werkis to take goode hede,
　　　　For dowte leste thei be put a-waye
　　　　For negligence of theym in oon day.
　　　　Howsholde men wille not do so;　　　　　　　　1365
　　　　For this werk therfore late theym go.
　　　　If y hadde know this & hadde do so,
　　　　I hadde a-uoydide mekille woo.
　　　　Alle-so in this werke most be libertie
　　　　withowte Impedyment in euery degre,　　　　　1370
　　　　with dyuers confortis, peynys to relesse
　　　　Of labour contynualle which may not cese;
　　　　Els angwishe of labour & melancolye
　　　　Might be cause your werkis to destroye.

1342 that no þing] yt be no S₃　　**1342** *Space for three letters after* that; *probably one letter erased*　　**1344** make] voide S　　**1349** voyde] avoide BSR
1351 no] *om.* ES　　**1355** as nye as] nor as S　　**1356** but] ne ES
1363 dowte leste] dovbtlese S　　**1364** negligence of theym] theyr negligens R　　**1366** For] ffrom S　　**1367** &] I E　　**1368** I hadde auoydide] & soo I might avoided S　mekille] great & mykyll S　　**1374** be] *om.* S　cause] causes R　your werkis] of your werkys S₃

Caplm.

ryse when þ chaug of þ covr was had
made som men sory & som men glad
And as to moch peple that chunge
semyd a new thing and a strauge
So that seson be fill a wondir thinge
Towdcmg this science wolvte lesynge
þat iij mastris of this science alle
lay in con bed nye to ledeu halle
which hadd &frtero ꝑtte white and redd
a wondir such iij to rest in con bedd
And that withm the space of dayes ten
While hard is to fynde con i azihons of men
Of the dewkdom of lorcyn vndirstoude
was wune þ odir ny the mydaill of ynglod
vndir a crosse in thende of shrve three
The iij was worn þ vonguit of them is he
which bi his nativryte is bi clerkis foúnde
That he shuld horio alt englishe grounde
A man myght walke all the world alwyte
And fayll such iij masters to fynde owte

nota

British Museum MS. Add. 10302, f. 38.

Of the grose werke it nede to shew no more,   1375
For olde men haue taght the remenant bi-fore;
And whate is necessarie that thei lefte owte
This boke shewith it withowten dowte;
wherfore this litille boke, the Ordynalle,
Is in Alchymye the complement of alle.   1380

f. 37ᵛ   The chapiter folowing, convenient for a clerk,
Shewith the concels of the subtile werk.

f. 38ʳ   Capitulum v.

Bryse, when þe change of þe coyne was had,
Made som men sory & som men glad.
And as to moch people that chaunge   1385
Semyd a new thing and a strange,
So that seson be-fille a wondir thinge
Towching this science withowte lesynge,
That iij mastris of this science alle
Lay in oon bed nye to leden halle;   1390
which hadd Elixers perfite white and redde.
A wondir such iij to rest in oon bedde,
And that within the space of dayes tene,
while hard is to fynde oon in Milions of men.
Of the dewkdome of loreyn [oon], I vndirstonde, 1395
was borne; þat odir ny the myddill of ynglond;
vndir a crosse in thende of shirys three
The iijde was born, þe yongist of them is he;
which bi his natyuyte is bi clerkis founde
That he shuld honour alle englishe grounde.   1400
A man myght walke alle the world a-bowte
And faylle such iij masters to fynde owte.

f. 38ᵛ   Tweyn be fletyng, þe yongist shalle abyde,
And do moch good in this londe at a tyde;

1379 litille] *om.* R   1381–2 *om.* S₃   1383 Bryse] *add.* whose surname
S   change of þe coyne] *om.* S *(with space for some seven letters left blank)*
1386 a strange] verye strange S   1389–90 *Vertical line at end,* nota *in*
right margin   1390 nye to] at BT   1392 wondir] wonder thinge B
rest] reste all S   1394 hard] *om.* B   is] yt ys E   1395 oon] *inserted*
above A, *om.* R   1396 was borne] one was born R   1402 And] To E
1404 good] *om.* BT

But synn of princis shal lett or delay   1405
The grace which he shulde do on a day.
The eldist master chantyd of hym a songe,
And seid þat he shuld soeffre moche wronge
Of theym which were to him gretely beholde;
And many thingis mo this mastir tolde   1410
which seth that tyme hath trewly falle,
And som of theym hereafter shalle;
wherof oon is trewly, seid he,
After trowbles grete ioy shalle be
In euery quarter of this londe,   1415
whiche alle good men shalle vndirstond.
The yongir askid when þat shulde be.
The olde man seide when men shalle se
The holy crosse honouryde both day & nyght
In the londe of god in the lond of lyght;   1420
which may be do in welle good seson,
But longe delayed it is withowte resone;
f. 39ʳ   when that bigynnyth note wel this thinge,
This science shal draw towa[r]de the kynge;
And many mo gracis ye may be bolde,   1425
Mo then of vs shulde now be tolde.
Grace on that king shalle descende
when he olde maners shalle amende;
He shal make ful secrete serche
For this science with dowcet speche,   1430
And a-monge the solitarie
He shalle haue tidingis certeynlye.
So soght king kalide of many men
Til he mett with Morien,
which helpid kalide at his nede,   1435
His vertew causide him to spede.
Now of such maters late vs cese,
And of the subtile werke reherce.

1409 Of] by R   were] *om.* E   1411 seth] sayeth B, *om.* T
1414 trowbles] troles S   ioy] trobyll ES   1421 welle good] right good
ES   1424 towarde] r *above with caret; slight tear in MS. through* d
1430 dowcet] gentill S   1432 *om.* S   1433 many] dyuers R
1434 Til] vntyll tyme S   1435 at his nede] ofte at his great nede S
1436 vertew] vertuus S   1437 *Small ornamental initial capital* N   cese]
leue & cease S   1438 of]*om.* B   reherce] let vs somthing rehearse S

Greet nede hath he to be a clerke
That wolde perceyve the subtile werke;   1440
He must know his first philosophie,
If he trust to com by Alchymye.

f. 39ᵛ And first ye shalle welle vndirstonde,
Al that take þis werke in honde,
when youre materials bi preparacione   1445
Be made wel apte for generacione,
Then thei most be departed a-twynn
In-to iiij elementis if ye wolde wynne;
which thing to do if ye ne can,
Go and lerne it of ortolane,   1450
which made his boke of that doctryne,
How ye shulde parte þe elementis of wyne.
Morouyre ye most for youre socowre
Know theffectis of þe qualitees fowre,
Callid hete, colde, moisture, & drynys,   1455
Of which iiij al thinge compownyde is.
And seth in this arte your chief desyre
Is to haue colour which shulde a-bide fire,
ye muste know, bifore ye can that see,
How euery colour engendride shalle be,   1460
For euery colour which may be thoght
Shal here appere bifore þat white be wroght.

f. 40ʳ Yet more ye wolde haue to this summe,
Swi[f]tly to melte as wax or gumme;
Els myght it not entre and perse   1465
The centres of metalle as auctours reherce;
So ye wolde haue it both fyxe & flowe
with coloure plentye, if ye wiste howe.
Such iij contraries ioyntly to meete
In one accorde is grete secrete;   1470

1439 clerke] good clark S   1441 his first] first his R   1442 trust]
look R   Alchymye] this art Alchymye S   1443 first] now R   vndir-
stonde] perceive & vnderstonde S   1444 take] euer taik S   werke] noble
worke S   1444 þis] þ *over erasure*   1445 preparacione] great
preparacone S   1446 for generacione] for to mak generacon S
1447 departed] departyde & separatyd S   atwynn] atwein SR   1448 wolde
wynne] purpose to wynne E, purpose any thing to wyn S   1449 can]
maie nor cann S   1450 ortolane] one namyd ortulane S   1452 parte]
om. E, parte & separat S   1453 socowre] comforthe & soccur S
1459 can that] cannot E   1464 Swiftly] Switli A

Netherles he that is clere of mynde,
In this chapitere may it welle fynde.
And firste to geve you a shorte doctryne
Of the forsaid iiij qualitees pryme.
Hete and colde be qualitees actyve,   1475
Moistour and drynys be qualitees passyve;
For thei suffren the actyuys evirmore,
As stonys to be lyme, & water to be frore.
Herupon to Iuge ye may be bolde,
Nothing is fulle wroght but bi hete or colde;   1480
Nethirles the passivis haue some actyuyte,
As in handcraftes men dayly see,

f. 40ᵛ   In baking, brewing, & other craftis alle
Moysture is operatyfe, & so drynes be shalle.
Aristotille in phisikis & other many mo   1485
Saide: Ab accionibus procedit speculacio;
Thei say þat practice is rote & bygynnynge
Of speculacion and of alle connynge.
For the properties of euery thynge
Be perceyvide bi his worchynge,   1490
As bi colours in vrynys we be bolde
To geve sentence of hete and colde.
Bi these forsaide iiij qualitees prime
we sech coloure with lengh[t] of tyme.
Of white colour we be not ful sure   1495
To sech it but in a substance pure.
Grete doctryne therof lerne now ye may
when ye know how colours grow al day.
Colour is the vtmoste þing of a bodie clere;
Clere substance wel termynyd is his mater here.   1500
If hete haue mastry in mater that is dry,
white colour is evir therof certeynly,

f. 41ʳ   As it aperith in sight of brent bonys,
And in making of alle lyme stonys;

1474 forsaid iiij qualitees] iiij qualites aforsaied ES   1478 frore] fore S
1482 men dayly] you maie dailye S   1484 Moysture is] re *over erasure*
1485 phisikis] phisike is E   1486 procedit] *a letter erased after* t, *thick*
oblique down stroke added   1488 of alle] all other S   1492 of] to E
1494 lenght] t *above with caret*   1495 colour] *om.* ES   1496 but]
om. E   1499 *Small ornamental initial capital* C   1500 his] this ES
1501 If] In S   1504 alle lyme stonys] Lyme and stones S

where colde werchith in mater moyst & clere,   1505
yett of such worching whitnes wil apere,
As it shewith in Ise and frostis hore;
The cause is sett owte in philosophie bifore.
I write not here of comon philosophie,
But bi exemple to teche alchymye;   1510
That one may be perceivide bi that odire
As is the childe perceivid bi the modire.
If hete in moiste mater & gros with-alle
worch, therof black colour gendire shalle;
Exemple therof yf ye of me desyre,   1515
Beholde when ye [se] grene wode sett afyre.
When colde worchith in mater thik & drye,
Blak colour shal be, this is the reson why:
Such mater is compactid & more thykke,
with cold con[s]treynyng, enemye to al quykke.   1520
Thiknes made derknes with priuacion of light,
So colour is priuate, then blak it is to sight.

f. 41ᵛ   Therfore euirmore remembre this—
How clere matere is mater of whitnes.
The cause efficient may be manyfold,   1525
For somwhile it is hete, & somtyme it is cold.
But white & blak, as alle men may se,
Be colours contrarie in mooste extremyte;
wherfore your werk with blak most begyne,
If the ende shuld be with whitnes to wyne.   1530
The middil colour, as philosophers write,
Is rede colour bitwene blak and white;
Netherles trust me certeynlye,
Rede is last in werke of alchymye.
Also thei sey in theire doctryne   1535
How these ij colours, Rufe and citryne,
Be meen colours bitwene white & redde;
And how that grene & colour woone as ledde

1505–6 om. S (no gap)   1505 Ise & frostis hore (underlined), maner moyst
& clere (inserted above) E   1506 in left marg. E   1507 in left marg. E
As it shewith in Ise] where colde workithe in yse S   1516 se] inserted
above with caret   1520 constreyning] s above with caret   1527 as
om. B   1531 philosophers] philisophers A   1536 Rufe] rife S
1537 Be] therbe S
C 9205   E

Bitwene rede & blak be colours meen,
And freshiste colour is of mater moost clene.   1540
Phisicians in vrynes haue colours nynteen
Bitwene white & blak, as they ween,

f. 58^r   wherof colour vndirwhite, subalbidus, is oon
Like in colour to Onychyne the stone;
Of such like colour magnesia fownde is,   1545
But magnesia gliterith with clernys.
In owre subtile werke of Alchymye
Shal be alle colours that hath be seyn with Eye,
An hundreth colours mo in certeyne
Than evir was in vreyne seyne;   1550
wherin so many colours myght not be,
But if oure stone conteynede euery gree
Of al composicions fownde in werke of kynde,
And of al composicions ymaginable bi mynde.
Of as many colours as shal therin be seyne,   1555
As many graduacions your wisdom most atteyne.
And if ye knowe not such graduacions alle,
Lerne theym of Raymonde in his arte generalle.
Gilberte kymere wrote after his devise
Of xvij proporcions, but they may not suffice   1560
In this science which he covde neuir fynde,
And yet in phisike he hadde a noble mynde,

f. 58^v   where the royalte of the nature of man
Auawncith ofte medicyns of þe phisician,
And so honowrith oft tymys his craft,   1565
when þat his medicyns per aventure myȝt be laft.
But hit is not so in þe phisik of mynys,
For that arte excedith al othire engynys,
And restith only in the wisdom of man,
As bi experiens wise men witnes can.   1570
And so of Alchymy þe trewe fundacion
Is in composicion bi wise graduacion
Of hete and colde, of moyste and drye,
Knowing othir qualitees engendride therbye,

1543 subalbidus] subalbuerus S   1544 Onychyne] onithe R 1559 kymere]
kinere BT   1567 phisik of mynys] phesick myndes S   1569 restith
risithe S

As harde and softe, hevye and lyght,   1575
Rough and smoth by ponders right,
with nombre & mesure wiselye soght,
In which iij restith al that god wroght.
For god made al thing, & set it sure
In nombre pondire and in mesure;   1580
which nombres if ye do change and breke,
vpon nature ye muste do wreke;

f. 59^r   wherfore Anaxagoras seid, take good hede
That to coniunccion ye not procede
Tille ye know the pondres ful complete   1585
Of al componentes which shuld herin mete.
Bacon seid that olde men nothing did hyde
But only proporcion, wherin was no gyde;
For noon olde auctour, king, prince, ne lorde
writyng of this science with other dide accorde   1590
In the proporcions, which if ye wolde reche,
Raymond with Bacon with Albert doon it teche,
with olde Anaxagoras, of theym iiij. ye shalle
Haue perfyte knowlich, but not of oon haue alle.
And if ye wolde Ioyn iiij qualitees to entent,   1595
Then must ye conioyne euery element,
As watir and erthe after youre desire,
welle compowned with Ayre and fyre,
knowing the worthiest in his actyuyte,
The ijde, the thridde, euerych in his degree.   1600
The iiij and the viliste may not be refuside,
For it is profitable & best to be vside;

f. 59^v   And best may extende his multiplicacion,
In whome is the vertu of oure generacion,
And that is the erthly litarge [of] oure stone;   1605
with-owte him generacion shal be noon,
Nother of oure tincturs fixacion,
For nothing is fix but erth allon.
Al other elementis moveable be,
Fire, Ayer, & watir as ye daily se,   1610

1576 right] light B   1580 and in mesure] & true mesure E, & in trewe
measuir S   1584 ye not] ye do not BSR   1590 with other dide]
in ordre doth R   1595–6 interchanged S   1601 iiij] th added above
1605 of] inserted above with caret

But fire is cause of extendibilite,
And causith maters permyscible to be;
And clere brightnys in colours faire
Is causid of kynde euirmore of Ayre;
And Ayer also with his coaccion   1615
Makith thingis to be of light liquefaccion,
As wax is, & buttir, and gummys alle,
A litil hete makith theym to mylt & falle;
watir clansith with ablucion blyve,
And thingis mortified causith to revive.   1620
Of multipliyng of fire is no gretter wondre
Then is of multipliyng of erth set vndre;

f. 60r For erth berith herbis dayly new and newe
withoute nombre, therfore it is trewe
That erth is wondirful as wel as fyre,   1625
Thofe oone sparkil may soon fille a shire;
If al a shire were fillid with flexe,
Oon sparkille then wold wonderly wexe.
Fire and erth be multipliers allone,
And thei be causers of multipliyng of our stone.   1630
Of this erth shewith Alberte, oure grete brodire,
In his Minerals whiche litarge is better then odire;
For the white Elixer he doithe it there reherce,
And the boke of Metyre shewith it in a verce.
Now to coniunccion late vs resorte,   1635
And some wise concelle therof to reporte.
Conioyne your elementis Grammatically
with alle theire concordis conueniently;
whiche concordis to helpe a clerke
Be chief Instrumentis of alle this werke;   1640
For no thing may be more contrary nowe
Then to be fixe and vnperfitly flowe.

f. 60v Alle the gramarians of Inglond & of fraunce
Can not teche yow those concordance;

1612 permyscible] permisible BES   1613–14 *Interchanged S, preceded by*
Diadema Regis terra compositi rubei / Lapis non Lapis aqua sulpharis benedicti
1626 soon] *om.* S   fille] spyll S   1627–8 *om.* S   1628 sparkille]
sparcke R   wonderly] wonderfullye R   1630 causers] causes R   of
our] our R   1635 *Small ornamental initial capital* N   1636 wise]
wittie R   to] *om.* ESR   1639 concordis] Accordes B   1642 be]
om. B   flowe] slowe B

This ordynalle tellith where ye may it se, 1645
In phisike, in the boke de arbore.
Ioyne them also in Rethoricalle gyse
with naturis ornate in purifiede wyse;
Sethen oure tincture most be moste pure & fair,
Be sure of pure erth, watyr, fyre, and ayer. 1650
In logicalle wise, be it erlye other late,
Ioyne trewe kyndes, not sophisticate;
Ignorance herof hath made many clerkis
lewdly to lese theire labour & theire werkis.
Ioyne them to-gedir also Arismetically, 1655
Bi subtile nombres proporcionally,
wherof a litil mencion made there was
when Boicius seid: Tu numeris elementa ligas.
Ioyne your elementis Musicallye,
For ij causis: one is for melodye 1660
whiche theire accordis wil make to your mynde
The trewe effecte when þat ye shalle fynde;
And al-so for like as Dyapason,
with diapente & with diatesseron,
with ypate ypaton & lekanos Muse[d], 1665
with accordis which in musike be [vsed],
with theire proporcions cawsen Armonye,
Moch like proporcions be in Alchymye,
As for the grete nombres actualle;
But for the secrete nombres intellectuall, 1670
ye most seche them, as I seid bifore,
Owte of Raymonde & owt of Bacons loore.
Bacon shewith it derkli in his iij litteris alle,
An[d] Raymonde better bi his arte generalle.
Many men ween which doith them rede 1675
That thei vndirstond, when thei [do] not in dede.
With astrologie ioyn Elementis also,
To fortune theire worchingis as thei go;

f. 61ʳ

1647 gyse] wise R   1648 wyse] gvise R   1649 Sethen] Seing SR
1651 erlye] arthilye S   1655 Arismetically] Arythemetycallie SR
1658 Boecius] om. S   1663 as] of BT   1664 diapente] diapenter BT
1665 S₂ recommences   Mused] Muse ABESS₂S₃R   1666 be vsed] be
ABESS₂S₃R   1669 As for] But for SS₂   grete] om. B   1670 But]
And SS₂   nombres] nombre B   1674 And] d above with caret   1676 do
inserted above with caret   1678 fortune] for to sie S   go] do S₃, doo go R

Such symple kindis, vnformyd & vnwroȝt,
Most craftly be gidid til þe ende be sowght;   1680
Al which seson thei haue moost obedience
Aboue formed naturis to sterris influence.

f. 61ᵛ   And science perspectyfe gevith grete euydence
To al the mynysters of this science;
And so doon othir sciencis many mo,   1685
And specially the science de pleno & vacuo.
But the chief mastres a-monge sciencis all
For helpe of this arte is magyke naturall.
When the iiij elementis wisely ioyned be,
And euerych of them sett in his degre,   1690
Then of dyuers degrees & of diuers digestion
Colours wil a-ryse towarde perfeccion.
For then worchith inward hete naturalle,
which in oure substance is but intellectuall;
To sight vnknow, hand may not it feld,   1695
His worching is know of few men & seld.
And when this hete naturall movid be shall
Bi oure outward hete artificiall,
Then nature excitid to labour will not cese
Many diuersitees of degrees to encrece;   1700
which is one cause bi reson ye may see
whi in oure werkis so many colours bee.

f. 62ʳ   Therfore it causith in this arte grete dowte
Ignorance of hete within & eke withowte,
To know how these both hetis shuld accorde,   1705
And which of them in worching shuld be lorde.
Digestion in this werk hath grete lyknys
To digestion in thingis of quyknys;
And bifore othir, as I witnes can,
It [is] most like to digestion of man.   1710
Therfore, seid morien, our stone in generacion
Is moste like thing to mannys creacion;
In whom, seith Raymonde, the iiij degrees all
Of the iiij complexions to-gedir fynd ye shall;

1681–2 om. SS₂   1684 science] noble science SS₂   1685 sciencis]
sciens S   1689 Small ornamental initial capital W   1693 inward]
inwardes S   naturalle] naturallye B   1696 of] to R   1707 Small
ornamental initial capital D   1708 in] of SS₂   1710 is] inserted above
with caret   1710 like] like thinge ESS

And that actually, which ye can not fynde   1715
Among creaturis in none othir kynde;
wherfore a-monge creaturis these ij alone
Be callid Microcosmos, man & oure stone.
Now of digestion the Alyment & the fode
Perfitly to know is nedful & fulle goode.   1720
It is humour solide, constant with siccite,
Mightly medlide after some degre,

f. 62ᵛ   In opposid passivis commixtid dewly,
Engendrid bi inward & outward hete truly;
So nothing els is oure digestion   1725
But of humour substancial a create perfeccion.
I pray yow lay-men haue me excuside
Thofe such wordis be not with you vside;
I most vse them, for alle Auctours affermys
How euery science hath his propre termys.   1730
Digestion somtyme avauncide may be
Bi outward colde, as yerely ye may se
How in wyntir men eten more mete
Then in somer, when expansid is hir hete;
For cold makith hete inward then to fle,   1735
And ligge nye to-gedir, then strenger hete is he;
which, bi his strength, his poware is more
To make digestion then he myght bifore.
But oure chief digestere for oure entent
Is virtualle hete of the matere digerent.   1740
Nethirles hete of the digestible thinge
Helpith digestion & hir worching.

f. 63ʳ   Fevirly hete makith no digestion;
Baynys may helpe, & cause also destruccion;
wyne digested hath more hete naturalle   1745
Then hath new must whose hete is accidentalle.
Coagulacion is no forme substancialle,
But only passion of thing materialle.

1716 none] one S   1717 creaturis] creatores S   1718 Microcosmos]
Micocrosmos ABES₂S₃, mycorasmos S   1719 Alyment] elemente BSR
1720 fulle] *om.* BSS₂R   1726 create] great BR   1728 wordis]
termes BR   1729–30 *om.* SS₂   1732 Bi] But B   1734 ex-
pansid] extreme R, expulsid S   1735 fle] feel S, fleete S₂   1736–8 *om.*
SS₂   1737 which bi his] by which R   1739 digestere] digesture ES₂
1743 Fevirly] fauerlie S, faverly S₂   1745 digested] disgested B

More ye must know when colours appere,
who is principalle agent in that maters clere;   1750
For sumtyme it is hete, & sumtyme cold it is,
And sumwhile moystour, & sumwhile drynys.

The principal agent to know at euery seson
Requirith grete serch made bi subtile reson;
which is not perceived but of masters fewe,   1755
For thei marke not how colours a-ryse bi rew.

The principalle agent of the qualitees fowre
hath power Royalle, as lord of moste honour,
The remenant qualitees to conuerte to his kynde;
Of which conuersion Anaxagoras makiþ mynd   1760
In his boke of conuersion naturalle,
wherof Raymunde shewith cavses specialle.

f. 63ᵛ   It is no iape, nother light to lerne,
your principal Agent al sesons to discerne;
which I tech yow to know be signes fowre,   1765
Bi coloure, sapoure, odoure, and liquour.

And first bi coloure to serve youre entent,
To know bi colowre your principal agent.

Loke in your vesselle which colour shewith moste;
He þat causith him is principalle of the hoste,   1770
As for that seson, whose pride ye may swage
Bi this oure doctrine, if ye see him rage;
which ye may do when ye welle vnderstonde
The cause of alle colours which ye haue in honde;
which I wil tech you now shortly with-alle,   1775
Bicause here & there sech hem ye ne shalle.

Whitnes is causid of many maters clere
In a nother thing termynede, & so it is here;
Blaknes is when parties of a body derke
with thiknes oppressith þe clernys of the werke;   1780
Or els it is of a combuste terrestreyte,
But of suche combustion grete hardnes shalbe.

1749 *Small ornamental initial capital* M   1755 not] *om.* BT
1756 not] *om.* S   1758 lord] lordes E   1759 to] be R   his] this SS₂
1765 I] *om.* R   signes] thinges SS₂   1767 *Small ornamental initial*
capital A   1776 ye] *scribe altered* n *to* y   1777 *Small ornamental*
initial capital W   1778 a nother] one BT   1779 *Small ornamental*
initial capital B

f. 64^r   And bi commixtion of derke, clere, and clene,
Shal be gendrid alle the colours meen.
Euery clere thinge, perspicuate and faire,   1785
Standith bi the maters of watire & of Ayre
whom a pure erth doith apprehende,
Such as shalle not theire clerenys offende.
And if in suche clernes and perspicuyte
ye can no specyalle colours se,   1790
Theruppon to Iuge ye may be bolde
The cause of such thingis was excellent colde;
As cristalle, berille, and other many mo;
Diuersite be-twene hem lerne ar ye go.
Cristalle hath watire declynyng toward Ayer,   1795
wherfore it is clere, specyous, and fayre;
But w[h]ere it declynyth toward watire more,
It is derker as berille, or yse harde frore;
But when maters drawith toward siccite,
Derknes with hardnes engendrid shal be;   1800
As it apperith in the Adamant stone,
And in other thingis many one.

f. 64^v   Twynkelinge & glitring as in Magnesia is,
Light is cause therof, within matere of cleernys;
which is superducid vpon watirly vapoure   1805
Bifortyme incensid with hete, be ye sure.
Now after clernys & colours in extremyte,
Of meen colours a litil shew will we.
Rubye colour is of a thyne fume succendid,
In a clere bodye, which also is amendid   1810
when in that bodie regnyth plenty of lyght,
For more or las therof makith more or las bright;
As the Amatyste folowith the Rubie in dignyte,
In las clernys, & in more obscuryte;
And a calcidonye in slymye substance   1815
Folowith the berille with grees of variance.

1783 commixtion] commixion BT, coniunction R   1785 clere] cleane B
1787–8 om. SS₂   1790 ye] He ye A   1797 where] h *inserted above*
towarde watire] toward mor R   1799 drawith] dryveth R   1803 *Small*
ornamental initial capital T   1804 cause] matter SS₂   within] as SS₂
1805–6 om. SS₂   1806 Bifortyme] by fortune B   1808 will
we] wilbe BT   1809 *Small ornamental initial capital* R   succendid]
fuccendid A   1811–12 om. SS₂   1815 a] in B   slymye] Shynyng SS₂
1816 with grees of] in grosse R

Grene as a smaragde is of watire clere,
with erthly substance combust mixte ful neere;
And the cleryre substance that the erth be,
The cleryre grenys therof ye shalle see.   1820
Tawny is of clernys termynate,
Infuside with a thikke fumosite congregate
f. 65ʳ   Of water & also of erth succendide,
wherby the clernys of Ayre is suspendide.
Wone or ledy colour engendride is   1825
Of watirly & erthy parties withowte mysse;
And where such parties be colde & thyk,
Evire wone coloure theron wille styk;
As it apperith in olde layne ledde,
And in men that be welnere dede.   1830
This wone colour, callide lyuydite,
In envious men vsith moche to be;
Natural hete & blode doon resorte
To theire herte, hym to comforte,
And levith colde and drye the face,   1835
For hete & blode is partyd fro that place.
Likwise when fevirs be in extremyte,
The nailis of hondis of this colour wille be.
The saphire colour that orient blewe,
Like in colour to the heuynly hewe,   1840
Is moch fairere then wone colour to syght,
For therin is more of Ayre, watir, & lyght,
f. 65ᵛ   Then is in wone colour, & that bi manyfolde;
wherfore such colour is more derere solde.
Al other blewis, þe sadder that they be,   1845
Thei haue las of Ayre & more terrestreite.
Siluer to Azure sone broght wil be,

1817 watire] watry ESS₂   1817 *Small ornamental initial capital* G
1818 erthly] earthye R   1819 substance] substance combust R   erth]
erth combuste BT   1820 *om.* SS₂   grenys] grennesse R   1821 *Small
ornamental initial capital* T   1824 *om.* B.   1825 wone or] whan S,
wan S₂   1825 *Small ornamental initial capital* W   1826 watirly]
watry ESS₂ erthy] erthly BT   1828 Evire wone] every wone BRT, Euer
one ES₂, euery mans S   1831 wone] one SS₂   colour] *om.* BT   1836 &]
in ESS₂   is] as E   1839 *Small ornamental initial capital* T   1841 Is]
it is SS₂   1843 is] *om.* SS₂   1844 *om.* S   more derere solde]
Derer then golde S₂   1846 terrestreite] terrestre E

The cause therof is perspicuyte;
Which is in syluer causede of Ayre,
wherfore it turnyth to hevynly colour fayre.   1850
And quyke siluer plenty which in him is
Causith in syluer al his brightnes.
Subtile erth, pure water, with clernys of Ayre,
Causith such brightnys to quyk siluer repaire.
Citryne colour, yelow as ye se in golde,   1855
Is colour most likinge for som men to beholde;
Causide of myghti & stronge digestion,
For humour in him hath strong decoccion.
Such colour with hete engendride be shalle,
As it is in hony, vryne, lye, & galle.   1860
The shynyng of gold is causid, as I telle,
Of pure & subtile water, termynede ful welle,
f. 42ʳ   Perspicuatly condenside, for watir pure & fyne
The more it is condensid þe better it wil shyne;
For of a mirrour the cause no nother is   1865
But Moistour termynat, as al clerkis gisse,
So that it be pollible with-alle;
For Ayre figuris receyve nevyr shalle;
For Ayre may not be termynat in his kinde,
So cause of shynyng in watire ye shal fynde.   1870
With white and rede wel medlide, pure & fyne,
wil be engendred fayre colour cytryne.
So diuers commixtions of Elementis
Makith diuers colours for diuers ententis;
with diuers digestions, and diuers degrees,   1875
Al colours be made which youre Eyen seeis.
Of elementis ye must the propre colours lerne,
wherbi of colours ye may bettir discerne.
Phisicians say of good herbis and soote,
Som be colde owtward, & hote within þe rote;   1880

1847 to] of S₃   Azure] aire BT   1848 perspicuyte] brightnes & perspy-
cuitie SS₂   1849 is] *om. with caret* S₃   1853 Subtile] Subtyltie S
1855 *Small ornamental initila capital* C   1856 Is] it ys SS₂   1858 in]
of SS₂   1861 *Small ornamental initial capital* T   1863 Perspicuatly]
in perspicuitie R   1865–8 *om.* SS₂   1869 Ayre] Ayer also SS₂ be]
om. S₂   1871 With] Off S₃R   1872 wil be] it wilbe SS₂   1873 com-
mixtions] coniunction S₂   1876 Eyen]eie B

Exemple herof if ye lyst to gete,
Beholde the wirching of gentille violete.

f. 42ᵛ   Comon philosophie the cause doith disclose
whi colde is within, & redde withoute the rose;
Anaxagoras seid in his conuercion naturalle,   1885
Inward & owtward be contrarie in thingis alle;
which is trew excepte such thingis as be
Of litill composicion, and nye to simplicite,
As is scamony, & laureolle the laxatife,
whiche be not norisshing to vegetatife.   1890
Remembre how in euery mixte thinge,
Euermore oon element desirith to be kinge;
which prowde appetite of elementis & vicious,
Mouyth men to be ambycious;
wherfore oure lord that best dispose can,   1895
Hath made ordinance for synful man,
Al prowde appetitis to equalite bring,
when requiem eternam the church shal synge;
Then shal every ambycious thoght
Playnly apere how that it was noght.   1900
Lordis and beggers and alle shalbe
In the Charnelle broght to equalite.

f. 43ʳ   Youre principalle agent so rebate shalle ye,
when he vsurpith a-boue equalite.
Therfore Aristotille seide: compown ye our stone   1905
Egally, that in hym Repugnance be none,
Nothir diuysion as ye procede;
Take hede therto for it is grete nede.
And when it fallith that ye shalle see
Alle colours at ons that named may be,   1910
Then soeffre nature with hir operacion
At hir owne leysere to make generacion;

1883–90 om. SS₂   1884 withoute] is E   1887 as] om. E   1889 is
scamony] insquamonye B   1890 norisshing] second s and first part of h
over erasure   1891 mixte] commyxte E   1893 prowde appetite]
proved abetyd S   1894 ambycious] verye Ambicyous SS₂   1897 prowde]
proved S   appetitis] qualities R   1900 how] whowe S   1902 Char-
nelle] carnell SS₂   1903 agent] om. BT   1905 compown] compounde
BTS₂R   our] your BTS₂R   1906 Egally] Equallie SS₂ R   1908 grete]
om. SS₂   1909 And] for S   when] om. ESS₂   fallith that] followeth
as S   1912 leysere] pleasure BT

So that amonge so many colours alle
Nature may shew oone principalle,
Such as shal draw toward youre entent   1915
According to youre desired element.
This wise bi colours ye may proviyde
How in youre werkis ye shal yow gyde.
Many mo thingis of colours I myght write,
But this sufficith my promyse to acquyte,   1920
As ferforth as colours may serue your entent,
Bi theym to knowe your principalle agent.

f. 43ᵛ But many clerkis wonder whi ye may se
So many colours as in our stone wille be,
Bifore that perfite white and clere   1925
And vnchangeable wille appere,
Considerynge the fewnes of þe Ingredientis.
I wil that answere to plese theire ententis,
And tech them the trouth of þat grete dowte.
Bi kynd of Magn[e]sia such colours passe owte,   1930
whose nature is of such conuertibilite
To euery proporcion and to euery degre,
As cristalle to his subiecte is fownde;
For of euerych thing þat is vpon grownde
which that ye wil cristall set vndre,   1935
Such colour hath Cristal, þerfore cese to wonder;
wherfore hermes said not vntruly ne envious:
Ad perpetranda miracula rei vnius;
God hath so ordeyned, seid hermes þe kinge,
To fulfille the Miracles of oone thinge.   1940
Comon philosophers þerfore can not fynde
The vertuys of our stone exceding fer þere mynd.

f. 44ʳ Smyllyng may helpe forth your entent
To know youre regnyng element,
And be with coloure a testymonye   1945
To know youre principalle agent therbye.

1915-16 om. SS₂   1919-22 om. SS₂   1924 stone] stoonys S₂
1929 tech them] then SS₂   grete] om. R   1930 Magnesia] e inserted above
with caret   1937 ne envious] om. R   1938 rei vnius] vnius rei R
1941 philosophers] philisophers AS₃   1942 vertuys] vertue SS₂   fer þere]
for the B   1943 Small ornamental initial capital S   1945 And with a
color for a testymonye SS₂ coloure] colors E   1946 therbye] bye R

And ye which wolde bi smyllyng lerne
Of youre principalle agent truly to discerne,
As white and black be colours in extremyte,
So of odours soote and stynkinge be.   1950
But where that fyshes know not be sight
No meen colours, bi cause theire Eyen bright
Haue noon Eye ledis for theire sight closing,
So meen odours shal not bi smyllynge
Be know of yow; this is the cawse why: 1955
For nostrels be opyn as is the fysh ys Eye.
Therfore meen odours be not in certeyne
Smyllid bi nose, as meen colours be sayne.
Heuy smylle is not, as clerkis thinke,
The myddille odour, but only the las stynke.   1960
Olde faders wrote bi theire doctryne
Of theire experience, which is not myne,
f. 44ᵛ   That if ye meddille swete savour & reddolent
Egally with stynking to prove your entent,
The soote shalbe smyllid, þe stynking not so;   1965
The cause ye may lerne now ar ye go.
Al swete smyllyng thing hath more purite,
And is more spiritual then stynking may be;
wherfore it is in Ayre more penetratife,
And more extendible, & is also to lyfe   1970
More acceptable, as frende to nature,
And therfore rather receyvid be ye sure.
Odour is a smokish vapour resoluyd with hete
Owte of a substance bi a Invisible swete,
which in the Ayre hath free entringe,   1975
And changith the Ayre & youre smyllinge;
As Sapour of metis changith your tastinge,
And as sowndis changith youre hyringe,
And as colours changith youre sight,

1948 truly] for S, *om.* S₂   1952–3 *om.* B, *in margin* T   1952 Eyen
bright] eyn be bright SS₂   1953 Haue] they haue SS₂   sight] eye SS₂
1955–60 *om.* SS₂   1956 fysh ys] eh *inserted between two words*
1964 Egally] Equallie SS₂R   1967–72 *om.* SS₂   1967 Al] as BT, a R
1973 with] by R   1973 *Small ornamental initial capital* O   1974 swete]
heat SS₂   1977–8 *om.* SS₂   1977 tastinge] herynge E   1978–9 *interchanged* E

So odour changith smylling be his myght.   1980
The cause of odours to know if ye delyte,
Fowre thingis therto be requysite:
f. 45ʳ First that subtile matere be obedient
To the worching of hete, to present
Bi a fume the liknes of the same thinge   1985
From whome that fume had his bigynnyng;
Also to bere forth that pure fume & faire,
There is requyride a clene thyne ayre,
For thikke ayre wil not bere it ferre,
But it wil reteyne it moche faster;   1990
And so thikke maters obediens hath none
To þe worching of hete, as it shewith in stone.
Hete makith odour, cold shrynkith bi reson;
Donge hillis in somyr stynk more then wynter seson.
Plesante odours engendrid be shal   1995
Of clene & pure substance & fumygalle;
As it apperith in Ambre, narde, & Myrre,
Good for a woman, such thingis plesith her.
But of pure substance with a meen hete
Be temperate odours, as in violete.   2000
Of a meen hete with substance impure
Is odour mysliking, as Aloes & sulphure.
f. 45ᵛ But when natural hete begynnyth to spille,
Then therof a-risith hevye smylle;
As fyshe smyllith which is kepte to longe,   2005
Natural hete rotith, so þe smylle is stronge.
Stynche is a vapour, a resolued fumosite
Of thingis which of eville complexion be;
And when humour only is in corrupcion,
So that the substance be not in destruccion,   2010
Therof shal only hevi smylle aryse,
But not verray stynch com in that wyse.
Of verray stynch the cause of that chance
Is only corrupcion of the selfe substance;

1984 to]for to BER, to be SS₂   1984 for *inserted above after* hete AS₃
1985 the liknes] by a lyknes S   by the licknes S₂   1988 clene] clere SS₂R
thyne] thing S   1990 it] *om.* R   1994 wynter] in winter BSS₂R
1995-8 *om.* SS₂   2000 temperate] temperyd S   2002 odour] other S
2004 smylle] spell S₂   2005-6 *om.* SS₂   2007 Stynche] Stynke
ESS₂   2007 *Small ornamental initial capital* S   2009-12 *om.* SS₂

And when euyl substance shal putrifie,   2015
Horrible odour is gendred therbye;
As of dragons & men that long dede be,
Theire stynche may cause grete mortalite.
It is not holsom to smylle to som cole,
For quenching of som snofe a mare wil cast her vole.
When the qualitees of a thing according is   2021
To your nature, good odour wille not mys;

f. 46ʳ   But when the substance is contrarie to your kynd,
The odour therof odious ye shalle fynde.
Fishis loue soote smylle, also it is trewe   2025
Thei loue not olde kidels as thei do þe new.
Al thing that is of goode odoure
Hath naturalle hete for his socoure.
Thofe Camfere rosis & thingis colde
Haue soote odours, yet auctours tolde   2030
How hete virtually incloside is the skylle
with purenes of substance whi thei so smylle.
This olde opinion ye may tech your brodire
How no good odour is contrarye to a nothire;
But it is not so of stynking smyllis,   2035
For stynch of garleke voidiþ stynch of dong hillis.
Of odours this doctryne is sufficient
As in alchymye to serue youre entent,
youre werkis to vndirstond therby,
when thingis bigyn to putrefie.   2040
Also bi odours this ye may lerne
Subtilnes & grosnes of maters to descerne.

f. 46ᵛ   Alle-so of meen substance knowlich ye may gete,
with k[n]owlich of corrupcion of natural hete,
& knowlich of diuersite bi good attendance,   2045
when humour corrumpith & when þe substance.
But our substance was made so pure & clene,
And is conservid bi vertu of the meene,
That ye no stynch therof shal fynde,
Al be it that it putrifie fro his owne kynde.   2050

2016 gendred] engendred ESS₂R   2017–20 *om.* SS₂   2020 wil]
doth E   2029 colde] olde SS₂   2031 virtually] virtuously R
2036 voidiþ] avoidithe SS₂R   2044 knowlich] n *inserted above with caret*
2046 corrumpith] corrupteth BER   2049 therof] therfor S

The iijde signe & the iijde testimonye
To vnderstond your principal agent therby
Is sapour callid, of mouthe the taste,
which euyrmore is cause of waste
Of the substance of the same thinge   2055
wherof ye make profe bi tastyng.
Sapour shuld be moch better Iuge
Then colour or odour, and more refuge,
were not taste a perilous thing
while oure stone is in worching,   2060
For it is hurtyng to helth and lyfe,
It is so gretely penetratyfe.
f. 47ʳ   Aboue alle subtile thingis it hath victorie,
And persith solide thing hastely.
Wherfore it is perile and not goode   2065
Moche or ofte to taste of that foode.
It confortith metallis as we wel fynde,
But it is perilous for alle mankinde
Til perfite rede therof be made,
Such as in fyre wil nevir faade.   2070
A lewde man late that seruyd this arte
Tastyd of the white stone a parte,
Trustyng therbi to fynde relyefe
Of alle seknes, and of alle grefe,
wherbi the wreche was sodenly   2075
Smytt in a stronge paralisie;
whom my master with grete engyne
Curide with Bezoars of the myne.
Therfore thogh taste bi comon reson
Shuld be best Iuge at euery seson,   2080
yett for that taste is abhomynable,
Sapoure is here not profitable.
f. 47ᵛ   Yet of som parties seperable
A taste may wel be covenable

2051 *Small ornamental initial capital* T   2052 therby] bye R
2054 waste] som wast R   2055 same] *om.* S₃   2058 more] better R
2062 gretely] great S   2063 subtile] soled SS₂   thingis] thynge S₃
2064 solide] holy BT   thing] thinges SS₂, solidam rem R   2069 Til]
to S   2076 paralisie] palysye E, paulsye SS₂   2078 Curide]
turnyd R   2084 covenable] conveniable SS₂

Bifore coniunccions, to make a-say   2085
whether thei be wel wroght or nay.
How be it a wise man hath helpe sufficient
Bi colour and odour to haue his entent;
For many men can chose good wyne
Bi colour and odoure when it is fyne,   2090
But for new wyne, not fynyd in generalle,
The trew taste is moste suerte of alle.
For smyllyng hath of organallis but oon,
No thing discernyng but fumose thing allone,
But taste hath .vj. organallis withowte dowte,   2095
To felde qualitees of thingis within & with-owte;
which nature ordeyned geyn perel & stryfe
For moste sewertie of thingis hauyng lyfe.
An Ape chosith hir mete bi smyllynge,
Men & popyngayes trustith to tastyng.   2100
For many thingis be of goode smylle,
which to taste be fownde ful ylle;
f. 48ʳ   For thei may be abhomynable sowre,
ouyrsharpe, to bitter, or of grete horrour,
Or venenous stynging, or ouyrstronge,   2105
The taste is Iuge & voidith such a-none.
Olde men wrote in avncyen tyme
How that of sapours there be fulli nyne;
which ye may lerne within half an houre
As sharpe taste, vnctuous, and sowre   2110
which iij do subtile mater sygnifye;
And other iij do Meen mater testifye,
As byting taste, saltish, & werish alle-so;
Othir iij came thikke substance fro,
As bitter taste, vndersowre, and dowce,   2115
These ix be fownde in many a noble howse.
v. of these ix. be engendrid with hete,
vnctuous, sharpe, salt, bitter, and dowsett;

2085 coniunccions] commicions BS   2089–90 om. B, in margin T
2089–92 om. SS₂   2091 But] om. B, in margin T   2092 suerte] sure
BT, surest E   of alle] in generall E   2093 For] om. SS₂   organallis]
originals S₂   2095 organallis] oryginalles S₂   2096 felde] fele SS₂R
2097–8 om. SS₂   2102 fownde] om. SS₂   ylle] evyll S₂   2103–6 om.
SS₂   2105 stynging] stynkynge BES₃   2112 om. E   yf you will mark
of theym ye concavite SS₂   2113–15 As bytinge taiste & wyde or sower &
douce SS₂   2114 came] conne B   2117 ix.] om. SS₂

But of the .ix., the remenant alle fowre
Be made with cold, as is the sapour sowre,   2120
And so is sowrishe taste, callid sapour pontike,
And leest sowre also, callid sapour stiptike;

f. 48ᵛ   Also is werish taste, callid vnsauerye,
with colde engendride effectuallye.
Sapour of ij thingis hath hir concepcion,   2125
Of dyuers substance, & of dyuers complexion.
Of hote & moyste in the seconde degre
with a thik substance, dowcet taste wil be;
The same degrees of the same complexion,
To a meen substance knytt bi connexion,   2130
vnctuous sapowre engendre euer shalle,
But where it is hote & dry with-alle;
with a meen substance, & in the secunde degre,
The taste therof most nedys saltishe be;
when a thing in the iijde gre hote & dry is,   2135
with a substance thikke, there is bittirnys;
But in the iiij degre mater hote and drye
with a subtile substance, sharpe taste is therby;
So .v. tastis, as I seid bifore,
Be gendride with hete, & not oon more.   2140
Of colde and drye in seconde gre bi kynde
with a subtile substance, ful sowre ye shal fynd,

f. 49ʳ   As bi facis of peple ye may deme
when thei taste grabbis while thei be grene;
The same complexion in the same degre,   2145
In a thing which of meen substance shalle be,
Of that is gendride, ye may wel suppose,
A bityng taste as is of the rose;
But sowre, & sowrishe, & leest sowre al thre
Be of cold & drye in hye and lowe degre.   2150

2121 And so] & also E, Also in S, Also is S₂   2122 leest] lesse SS₂R
2123 Also is] also ther ys a SS₂, And so is S₃   2125 thingis] thinges and E
2126 of] om. ER   2127 Small ornamental initial capital O   2129–32 om.
SS₅   2131 vnctuous] vnctouus A; u and suspension mark for us
over erasure   engendre] engendred E   2135 gre] degree BESS₂R
2137 th added above iiij   2140 gendride] ingendred R   2141–8 om.
SS₂   2141 gre] degree BR   2142 shal fynd] shall it fynde S₃
2146 substance spelled as sbstance, with dot after b upstroke   2147 gend-
ride] engendred R   2149 sowre al thre] sorowe of all iij SS₂   2150 hye
and lowe] his lowe SS₂

And colde & moist in the first degre of alle
A werish taste engendre evire shalle;
As of an Egge it shewith in the gleire,
And in pale women ovir white & faire;
For such be colde, and of humydite   2155
Thei haue trewly grete superfluyte;
Therfore to men they haue las delyte,
Colde rebatith luxurious appetite.
Ysaac seid there be but tastis sevyn,
For sowre & las sowre was oon but vnevyne,   2160
But in complexion thei were of one fundacion,
And vnsauory was but of taste pryuacion.

f. 49ᵛ Compownyde tastis be fownde alle-so,
As dowsegyre & other many mo.
So bi tastis men may craftly knowe   2165
Diuers substancys, complexions, & grees hye & low.
And when ye dowte bi taste to make reporte,
Then to your other testymonyes resorte.
As in phisike trust not to vryne
Only, but also take witnes & doctryne   2170
Of youre pulsis, & wisely consideryng
vj thingis not natural the bodi concernynge;
Hauyng respecte all-so therwith-alle
Unto the sevyn thingis naturalle;
And take hede, if ye wille be sure,   2175
Of iij thingis contrarie to nature.
Complect these xviij wisely for your grownde,
A lewde phisician lest þat ye be fownde;
For so of hadd-y-wist ye may be ware,
And helpe the seek man from his care.   2180
So of this science, if ye wille avance
your werkis, take hede to euery circumstance,

f. 50ʳ wisily considering your testimoniys fowre;
Thre be now passid the fourth is liquour.

2152 engendre] engendred BESS₂   2153 gleire] clear R   2158 re-
batith] debateth BR   2159 there be] therbye S   2163 Compownyde]
compounded SS₂   2165–6 om. SS₂   2166 grees] degrees BR   2167 ye]
your S   2168 your] om. R   other] om. BT   resorte] ye most resort R
2169 phisike] visyck S   trust not to] taiste not SS₂   2171 pulsis]
pylles SS₂   2172 the] they B   2177 Complect] Complet SR
2183 wisily] wise S

Liquour is the conforte of this werke;   2185
Liquour gevith evidence to a clerke
Therbi to fastyn his Elementis,
And also to loose theym for som ententis;
Liquour conioynyth male with female wyfe,
And causith dede thingis to resorte to lyfe;   2190
Liquours clansith with theire ablucion;
Liquours to oure stone be chief nutricion.
with-owte liquours no mete is goode,
Liquours conveith alle Alimente & fode
To euery parte of mannys bodie,   2195
And so thei do with vs in alchymye.
Ye must considre the puryte
Of al youre liquours, and quantite,
And how thikke thei be, or thynne,
Or els therof shalle ye litill wynne.   2200
But not as phisicyans makith mencion,
For Elixer is a thing of a secunde intencion;
f. 50ᵛ   wherfore ye shal more wondir naturis fynd
In his worching then in al othir kynde.
Phisicyans say the thikker vryne be,   2205
The more it signyfieth humydite;
where thikke liquour with vs hath siccite,
And subtile liquour tokenyth humydite.
Many liquours be requysite
To oure stone for his appetite.   2210
In the boke of Turba Arisleus deposide
How ayre in watire was secrete incloside,
which bare vp erth with his Airly myght;
Pictagoras seid that was spoke with right.
Aristotil craftly his wordis sett he,   2215
Sayng, Cum habueris aquam ab aere.
Plato wrote ful sapiently,
And named it Stilla roris madii;

2185 *Small ornamental initial capital* L, *gold worn off*   2187 his Elementis]
this Ellement S, his Element S₂   2190 to resorte] tourne SS₂   2193 goode]
verie good SS₂   2194 Alimente] elementes BSS₂   2198 youre] *om.* B
2203 wondir] wonderfull SS₂, wondrous R   2205 thikker] more thicker
SS₂   2207-8 *om.* BSS₂, *in margin* R, *add. later* T   2209 *Small
ornamental initial capital* M   2210 his] our ESS₂   2211 deposide]
disposid SS₂   2212 secrete] secretlie SS₂R   2213 Airly] onelie SS₂

which was kyndly spoken for Alchymy.
But comon studientis in first philosophy   2220
Said Ayre condensid turned in to Rayne,
And watir Rarified becom ayre agayne.

f. 51ʳ Som seid how may was first seson & fayre
To take such watyr as is made of Ayre;
Som seid such watirs com hevyn fro   2225
Tille that the son entre in to scorpio;
Som seid alle liquours shuld be refusid
whiche frost infectid, shuld not be vsid;
The cause whi as tellith Auctours olde
Is that theire Acuyte is dullid with colde.   2230
Som philosophers said that ye shuld take
Milke for the liquour Elixer to make.
A nother sorte said after theire entent,
No liquour so goode for the complement
As watir of litarge, which wold not mys   2235
with water of Azogo to make lac virginis.
But democrite said best liquour to present
Elixer with-alle was water permanent,
whose naturalle vertue & propertie
was fyre to abide, & neuer to flee.   2240
Rupicissa seide that chief liquoure
was aqua vite Elixer to socoure,

f. 51ᵛ For she was spiritual, and wolde revyue
Dedde thingis fro deth to lyve;
She was quynt essence the v thinge,   2245
wherof Aristotille bi his writynge
In his boke of secretis seyth soo,
How that al perfeccion is in quinario.
Rupicissa callid it best liquoure of alle,
For it makith grose maters spiritualle.   2250
But of pictagoras ye may fynde
Oure aqua vite of a nother kynde;

2219 was] *om.* BS   2221 turned] *om.* ESS₂   2222 Rarified] raised SS₂
2224 is] *om.* BT   2225 com] came BR   2227 seid] said that SS₂
2228 shuld] & shold SS₂   2230 that theire Acuyte] because ther actyvitie SS₂
2231 philosophers] philisophers A   ye] he B, *om.* SS₂   2233 said] *om.* R
2235 As watir] As was ESS₂   2236 Azogo] Azoc S   2237 liquour]
water R   2245 was] *om.* BT   v] whiche SS₂, which *crossed through,*
vth *above with caret* S₃

He saide it was viuificans in this sentence:
Fac fugiens fixum, et fixum fugiens;
For in such wise with stronge coaccion,   2255
Fix maters were made of light liquefaccion.
A nother sorte said no liquour was a-bove
The liquour which congirs most desire & love;
Therfore such liquours were best fownde
Nye to Ilandis, & to suche grownde   2260
which the Occean see hath compaste a-bowte,
For there suche liquours be sonest fett owte.

f. 52ʳ Of a nother liquour wise men telle,
which is freshere then water of the welle;
Freshire liquour there is noon in taste,   2265
yet it wil nevir consume ne waste;
Thof it be occupied evirmore,
It wil nevir be lasse in store;
which Democrite named for his entent,
Lux vmbra carens, watir most orient.   2270
Hermes seid no liquor so necessarie
As was watire of crude Mercurie;
For he shal stonde, seid that noble clerke,
For the water within owre werke.
Now lerne ye which for this sciens haue sought,   2275
Bi al these liquours oure stone must be wroght.
Liquour is a thing moveable,
Of fletinge substance and vnstable;
Alle such thingis folowyn the moone
More than stondinge kyndes doone;   2280
And that apperith to a clerke
In wirchyng of the white werke.

f. 52ᵛ Liquours washen and make clene
Both extremytees & the meene.
God made liquour for man his vse   2285
To clense fowle thingis in euery hows;

2253 saide] saide yt S₃   2255-6 om. SS₂   2257 sorte] om. B
2258 most desire & love] must desyr loue SS₂   2267-8 om. SS₂
2268 Erasure [? of ne] after lasse.   2274 the] our ESS₂R   within
owre] with our ES₂, without S   2277 Small ornamental initial capital L
2279 folowyn] foloyng E   Erasure of one letter after folowyn   2280
kyndes] thinges BSS₂R   2282 white] subtill BT

Liquour bringith with-owten dowte
Hidde thingis in bodies owte,
As lawnders witnes evidentlie
when of Askis thei makith their lye;   2290
Liquour confortith the rotis of graas,
And of trees such as drye was;
For liquours of nature wille restore
Humours that were lost bifore;
Liquours departith qualitees a-sondyre,   2295
Substance resoluynge in attoms with wondire;
Liquours also bryngith in to oon
Many thingis to be one stone;
Liquour helpith to fluxe and to flowe
Many thingis; & lerne ye may nowe   2300
How liquour is in many maners fownde
Owte of thingis that be on grownde.

f. 53ʳ   Som bi cuttynge, as terebentyne,
Som with pressinge, as sydyre and wyne;
Som with grynding, as oyle is hadde,   2305
Som with stilling, as watirs be made;
Som with brennyng, as Colofonye,
And som with watire, as women make lye;
Som be otherwise broght a-bowte,
And bi natural worching fett owte;   2310
As vryne, swete, mylk, and al-so blode,
And rewnyng which for chese is good;
Bi as many maners & mo bi oon
we sech licours for owre stone.
Euery of the fornamyd wille cleve   2315
To that thei towche, and somdele leve;
But Quycsyluere, al be h[e] is fletyng,
yet he wil nevir cleve to a thing
But to metal of oone kind or odyre,
For there he fyndith sustir or brodyre;   2320

2287–92 *om.* SS₂   2293 of nature] *om.* SS₂   restore] againe restore SS₂
2297–2300 *om.* SS₂   2298 *om.* B (*one ruled line left blank*)   2301 many]
om. SS₂   2303 terebentyne] Turpentyne R   2306 watirs] maters E
2309–12 *om.* SS₂   2310 fett] lett E   2312 rewnyng]
Runnete R   2317 al be h[e] is] al be his AES₃, all by his B, though it
be SS₂, albeit it is R

Medlyng with subtyle erth doith him lett
To cleve to thingis such as he mett.

f. 53ᵛ Alle the seid liquours which rehersid be
Conteyne iiij Elementis as wel as he;
As mylke conteynyth whey, buttur, & chese,   2325
So doon truly eueryche of alle these;
which iiij may be departed a-twynn,
And efte conioynede to make yow wynn.
But moch more craftly thei be here soght
Then chese & buttur & whey be wroght,   2330
And drawe nere to symplicite
Then chese, buttur, or whey may be.
Of alle liquors which be in oure stone,
None is callid simple but watir allone.
Of euery liquour which to oure stone shal go,   2335
ye must know complexion & degre also;
And then with liquours ye may a-bate
The principal agent from his estate,
If he permanent and abidinge be
In any poynt of superfluyte.   2340
As if the Regnyng qualite be drynes,
ye may a-mende it with humour of moystnes,

f. 54ʳ Now more now las as ye se nede,
And so in alle qualitees procede;
And in such wise ordire at youre wille   2345
The principal agent your purpose to fulfille;
with knowlich of diuersite, Contrariete, & accorde,
ye may chose which qualite shal be lorde.
Your liquours be ordeyned to adde & to subtraye,
And to make equalite bi wisdome of assaye.   2350
But trust not that any thing may be
Hote & moiste both in oon degre,
For alle that trustith ij qualitees to be so,
Shal be deceyvid where-euyr thei go.

2321 subtyle] subtiltie S   2322 he] be E   2324 as wel as he] as ye
shall se SS₂   2326 om. ESS₂ (caret in right margin E)   2327 a-
twynn] atwayne ESR   2329-30 om. SS₂   2331 but let vs goo more
ner thinges of symplecytie SS₂   2338 from] for B   estate] state E
2339 he] the BT   abidinge] bidynge S₃   2341 As of the raignynges
qualites drynes SS₂   2347 accorde] discorde SS₂   2349-50 om. SS₂
2353-60 om. SS₂

Comon scolis to techinge be not trewe,   2355
leve that opynyon & lerne that of newe;
Alle olde men in that were ovirseyne
To set in oon degre any qualite[s] tweyne,
Els thei seid so that scolers shulde not fynde
The secrete mixtions of Elementalle kynde.   2360
Therfore who can not his graduacions,
May not be perfite in oure operacions;

f. 54ᵛ   For in trew nombre god made euery thinge,
with-owte tru nombre no man truly may singe;
who failith of his nombre, failith of his songe;   2365
who failith with vs, most do nature wronge.
Considre also the naturis of the meen
when it is in the thrid degre made clene.
The purire that youre meenys be,
The more perfeccion therof ye shalle se.   2370
The meenys reteyne a grete parte
Of the vertu[e]s of this arte;
For the principalle may not gefe influence
To the fynal ende, nethir he refluence
vn-to his principille withowte socoure and ayde   2375
Of meenys conteynyng thextremytes forsaide.
For like as bi meen of a treble spirytt
The sowle of man is to his bodie knytt.
Of whiche iij spiritis one is callid vitalle,
The second is callid the spirite naturalle,   2380
The thrid spirite is spirite anymalle;
And where thei dwelle now lerne ye shalle:

f. 55ʳ   The spirite vitalle in þe herte dothe dwelle;
The spirite natural, as olde auctours telle,
To dwel in the lyver is therof fayne;   2385
But spirite animal dwellith in the brayne.
And as longe as these spiritis three
Contynew in man in theire prosperite,
So longe the sowle with-owte al stryfe
wil dwel with the bodie in prosperous lyfe.   2390

2357 ovirseyne] euer seene E   2358 degre] gree S₃   qualite[s]] qualite A;
is *inserted above*   2361 Therfore who] he also that SS₂   2364 truly]
om. SS₂   2367 *Small ornamental initial capital* C   2372 vertu[e]s] vertuous A   2374 he] the BE   he refluence] her
effluence S₃

But when these spiritis in man may not abide,
The sowle forthwith departith at that tyde.
For the subtile soule, pure & immortalle,
with the grose bodye may nevir dwel withalle,
He is so hevy & she so light and clene,   2395
were not the subtilnes of these spiritis meene.
Therfore in oure werk, as auctours techith vs,
There must be Corpus, anima, & spiritus.
Also in oure werke ye shalle so fynde
That oure meenys must accorde in euery kynde;   2400
Of Both extremytees with wisdom sowght,
Els al our werke shuld turne clere to noght.

f. 55ᵛ   For prudent nature may not bi worching
Make complement of appetite of a thing,
And so passe bitwen extremytees,   2405
But if she first passe bi alle degrees.
Of euery meene this is trouth vnfeyned,
wherfore nature many meenes ordeigned.
Now after al this to lerne ye haue nede
Of vij circulacions of elementis for your spede,   2410
According to nombre of þe planetis sevyne,
which no man knowith but he haue grace fro hevyne.
Olde philosophers, men of grete engyne,
Said of circulacions how þere shulde be ix.
It is the suryr to do bi theire aduyse,   2415
Nethirles vij may your werkis suffise,
Bi Inuencions late fownde of newe
of latir philosophers whos werkis be trew.
But for circulacions of Elementis,
Som clerkis ween to haue theire ententis   2420
when thei fro fyre ordeyne to descende
To Ayre, thei ween to not offende

f. 56ʳ   If thei to watire do then procede,
And thens to erth when thei se neede;
And in such wise bi ordire falle   2425
Fro the hyest to the lowist of alle.

2393–6 *om.* SS₂   2394 with] *om.* R   2400 in] with S₃   2401–8 *om.*
SS₂   2402 clere] *om.* BT   2409 *Small ornamental initial capital* N
2412 but] except SS₂   2413 philosophers] philisophers AS₃   2418 philo-
sophers] philisophers AS₃   2419–32 *om.* SS₂

Upon these wordis thei take theire grounde,
That Aer est cibus ignis fownde.
But trust me that such circulacion
Is but oonly a Rectificacion,   2430
Bettir serving for seperacion
And for correccion then for transmutacion.
But the trowthe is that appetite of fyre
Hath to worche in erth his chiefe desyre,
As vppon his chiefe fode materialle.   2435
For fyre with erth hath moste concorde of alle,
Bicause þat siccite is the lyme of hete,
But Ayer of hir kynde is moste wete.
Yett fyre with-oute Ayer worchith nott,
For facys of elementis be knytt with a knott   2440
Of god his hande, þat thei may not departe
Bi noon engyne ne crafte of mannys arte;

f. 56ᵛ   As in plumpis ye haue exemple fayre,
where heuy watyre arisith aftir Ayre;
wherof no cause resonable ye shal fynde   2445
But connexion of facis of Elemental kynde.
But our circulacion is from fyre an hye,
which endith with watir his moste contrary.
A nothir circulacion bigynnyth with Ayre,
Ending with his contrarie clene erth & fayre;   2450
From fyre to erth, fro thens to watire clene,
Fro thens to Ayre, then fro thens bi a meen
Passing to erth, then efte sonys to fyre;
To such circulacions þe rede werk hath desire.
Other circulacions be bettir for the white,   2455
That be reherside for hir appetite.
Euery circulacion hath his propre seson,
As hir lightnes accordith with reson,
For as one planete is more ponderous
Then is an other, & slower in his cours,   2460

2430 but oonly] nott only but E   2433 But] But yet SS₂   appetite]
appetyte ys ESS₂   2436 moste concorde] concordance BTR   2437–8 om.
SS₂   2437 lyme] tyme B   2441–6 om. SS₂   2441 god his]
godes BER   2443 plumpis] the plumpes B, pumpes R   2446 Ele-
mental] elementes E   2447 fyre] om. ESS₂   2458 lightnes] highnes
SS₂   accordith] accordinge S

So som circulacion which clerkis seekis
Must for his tyme haue fully xxx wekis.

f. 57^r Othire Circulacions shal of tyme haue lasse,
As oon planete is lighter then a nothir was.
But þe tyme of oon with another wil amownt   2465
To xxvi wekis, provide bi accompte,
After alle Grose werkis made bi-fore-honde,
And aftir al circumstancis had we vndirstonde.
Ignorance herof deceyuyth many a man,
Cawsyng theym to cese where wise men bigan;   2470
Comon peple which for þis science haue soght
ween in xl dayes how it myght be wroght;
Thei know not how nature & þingis of arte
Haue a propre tyme assigned for theire parte;
As it apperith by this symylitude: 2475
The Elefante, for she is grete and Rude,
Goith with voole yeris fulli tweyne,
And fyfty yeris ar þat vole gendre agayne.
Anaxagoras seid in his consideracion
That metallis had for theire generacion   2480
A Ml. yeris, wherfore him luste to say,
Respecte þere-of oure werke is but oon day.

f. 57^v Alle-so ye most worch bi good aduyse
when ye see erthe a-boue watyre aryse;
For as watir berith erth which we go on,   2485
So wil it do in worching of oure stone.
Wherfore welle springis with strokis softe
Soberly make ye most in tymes ofte,
wherbi watir may sobirly flowe,
For violent fluxis be perilous as nowe.   2490
More ovir it helpith in Alchymy
To know vij watirs effectually,
which be copied with many a man
while thei be comon, sech them as ye can.
Desire not this boke to shew thingis alle,   2495
For this boke is but an Ordynalle.

2463 of tyme] ofte tyme S   2464 is lighter] be Lyghter S   2467–78 om.
SS₂   2472 how] om. S₃   2473 know] om. E   not] nowe B
2478 yeris] yeres cum R   2482 Respecte] in respect R   2484 aryse]
ryse SS₂   2491 *Small ornamental initial capital* M   2492 vij watirs]
the seaven matters R   2495–6 om. SS₂   2496 is] om. B

Bi those watirs men ween in mynd
Al fawtis to amend of metalle kynd.
Alle-so thei ween of the Elementis fowre
The effectis to wynne bi theire socowre.   2500
For thei suppose with confidence vnfeyned
That alle vertu[e]s requisite in theym be conteyned;

MS. SLOANE 1873

f. 69ᵛ   Some to mollifie metallis harde wrogth,
And some to hardyn metallis that be softe;
Some to purifie, Some to make malliable,   2505
Euery accordynge to that he was able.
Such liquours to knowe it is profite & goode,
How be it thei may not to our stoon be foode.
Noble auctours men of glorious fame
Callide oure stone Microcosmos bi his name,   2510
For his composicion is with-owten dowte
Like to this worlde in which we walke abowte.
Of hete of colde, of moyste & of drye,
Of harde of softe, of ligth & hevye,
Off rowghe, of smoth, & of thyngis stable,   2515
Medlide with thyngis fletynge & moveable,
Of all kyndis contrarie brogth to oon accorde,
Knytt by ye doctrine of god oure blesside lorde;
Wherbie of metallis is made transmutacion
Not only in colour, but transubstanciacion.   2520
In which ye haue nede to knowe this thynge,
How all the virtues of the elemente transmutynge
f. 70ʳ   Vpon the transmutide moste haue full dominacion
Bifore that the substance be in transmutacion;
And all parties transmutide moste figurede be   2525
In the element transmutyng, impressid by degree,
So that the iijde thynge elementide of them all
Off such condicions euermore be shall

2497 watirs] om. SS₂   2498 of] in R   2502 vertu[e]s] vertuus A
2503–2622 missing in A   2503 Elaborate initial capital S   2503–6 om.
SS₂   2507 profite] profitable SS₂   2510 Microcosmos] Micocrosmos
S₃BES₂   2511 composicion] complexion E   2513 moyste] moisture B
2514 &] om. SS₂   2515 rowghe] e heavy and large to cover some other letter
of smoth] & smothe R   &] om. SS₂   2517 kyndis] thinges S   contrarie]
om. ESS₂   2521 ye] we R   2523 the] om. B   2524 in]
of SS₂   2525 And] to B

That it trewly haue, it may be no nodire,
But hir substance of yat one, & hir virtues of yat   2530
  odir.
A chylde at his natyuyte can ete his mete & crye,
Our stone at his natyuyte will colour largilye;
In thre yeres after a childe can speke & goo,
Then is our stone more colorynge allso.
Oon vpon a Ml. his tyncture trewly is   2535
Of clene washen metall, I am trewe witnys.
Fastly beleve it & fully in your thogth,
It makith as good siluere as of ye myne is wrogth.
And allso our stone will augment & encrese
In quantite & in qualite & therof nevyre cese;   2540
And therfore his growyng & augmentacion
Is likned to man in wexinge & creacion.

f. 70ᵛ Nethirles one poynt of trowth I will reporte
Which to som men may be discomforte.
At the firste makyng of oure stone,   2545
That tyme for wynnynge loke for none.
If ye then cese I vndirstonde,
Ye shall depart with lesynge honde,
The costis be so grete before,
Expendid & set vppon the scoore.   2550
But at the first augmente of alle,
Which tyme our stone departe ye shalle
In parties tweyne full equallye,
With subtile balance & not with Eye;
One for rede, that other for the white,   2555
To maynteyne both for youre delite;
Then wynnyng first begynnyth to aryse.
But aftyrwarde if ye be wyse,
At euery augment contynuallye
Profite shall growe comodiouslye,   2560

2530 hir . . . hir] the . . . the R   virtues] virtuous S₃   yat odir] thother S
2536 washen] wassheng B, wasshed E, washe SS₂   2538 as good] om. as R
2540 & in] and ESS₂R   2541 augmentacion] his augmentacion BR
2542 to] vnto ER   2544 discomforte] to discomforteESS₂   2548 with]
with the SS₂   2551 at] all SS₂   2552 departe ye] departyd
be SS₂   2553 equallye] egallye B   2555 that other] & that
other E, and another SS₂   for the white] om. the S₂R   2557 aryse]
rise BR

In this oure white worke allone,
As well as in the Rubie stone.

f. 71ʳ   Therof sayd Maria, suster of aaron:
Life is shorte & science is full longe.
Nethirles it gretelye retardith age   2565
When it is endid bi stronge corage.
But some that haue be taght trulye
Haue forsake theire werke lewdlye,
When theire grete labours haue be paste,
For thei knew not how, at the laste,   2570
Growith the profite and the wynnynge
Which thei wold haue at the begynnynge.
Therfore I fynde that it is nede
The trowthe to tell when ye shuld spede;
For when I am paste and owte of mynde,   2575
This my witnys shall reste behynde;
For which cause I do not spare
Of this arte the trowth to declare
As moch as I darre that I be not shent
For brekynge of god his commaundement.   2580
This wyse endith all owre white werke
Shewid sufficiently for an able clerke.

f. 71ᵛ   Aftire all this vpon a daye
I herde my noble Mastire saye
How that many men, pacient & wyse,   2585
Fownde oure white stone with excercise,
Aftire that thei were trewly tagth,
With grete labour that stone thei cawgth;
But fewe, saide he, or scantly oone
In xv. kyngdoms hadde oure rede stoone.   2590
And with that worde he caste his Eye,
Lokynge on me full stedfastlye.
Of his wordis he sawe me woo;
I sayde: alas what shall I doo?

2561 oure] *om.* ESS₂   2562 Rubie] read R   2563 Therof] Wherof BSR,
wherfore ES₂   Maria] Maria the B, *om.* S   2564 full] *om.* BR
2565–6 *om.* SS₂   2569 labours] laborours S₃   2571 the profite and]
om. SS₂   2573 Therfore] I therfore B, wherfore E   2580 god his]
goddes BSS₂R   2581 owre] your SS₂   2582 sufficiently] sufficient SS₂
2583 *2-line space for capital; small* a *guide letter*   2589 fewe] fewye B
2592 Lokynge] & lookyd R   on] vpone SS₂   2593 me] my SS₂

For above all erthlye thynge   2595
I mooste desire & love connynge;
And for the rede stone is preseruatife,
Moste precious thynge to length my life,
The rede stone, saide I, is levire to me
Then all were Golde that I wolde so to be.   2600
He saide I was to yonge of age,
Off bodye lustye, and likly to owtrage,
f. 72ʳ   Scantly of the age of xxviijt yeres,
He said philosophers had no such compeers.
This wofull awnsere then he made to me: 2605
Till ye be eldire, he said, it may not be.
Alas good Mastire, Remembre, saide I,
How be it my bodye be ligth & lustye,
Prove & assay, & ye shall fynde
Age sufficient with-in my mynde.   2610
He hilde his wordis full still that tide,
And so longtyme he didde abyde.
After this sodenly in wondire wyse
He temptide me aftir ye philosophers gyse;
Which to reherce it were to longe,   2615
And to shewe how I shulde do wronge;
For that most be kepte secrete
For them which shall with this science meete.
Yet at the laste with leysere & with space,
I wanne his loue, bi helpe of god his grace;   2620
So that I had with grace the trewe doctryne
Off confeccion of the rede Medicyne;

B.M. MS. ADD. 10302

f. 66ʳ   whome to seche it availith ryght noght
Til the white medicyne be fully wroght.
Also both medicyns in theire begynnyng   2625
Haue one maner of vessel & of worching,

2596 mooste] must S₂   2598 to length] prolongyng S, prolong S₂
2599 is] am S   levire to me] mor desyred of me SS₂   2601 He saide]
then saied he ESS₂   2604 philosophers] philisophers S₃; add. the SS₂
2605 awnsere] om. BT   2606 om. E   2608 How be it] all thoughe
SS₂   2611 that] at yt R   2613 wondire] wonders B, wordes R
2614 me] om. B   philosophers] philisophers S₃   2617–18 om. SS₂
2618 shall] om. B   this] the R   S₂ ends in effect   2620 god his] godes
BESR   2621 the trewe] and trewe S   2623 A recommences

C 9205   G

As wel for the white as for the redde,
Til alle quyke thingis be made dedde;
Then vessels and forme of operacion
Shal change in matier figure & graduacion.   2630
But my hert quakith, my hond is tremeling,
when I write of this most selcowth þing.
Hermes broght forth a tru sentence & blont,
Said, ignis et azogo tibi sufficiunt.
Thexpositor of hermes & of aristotille ioynte   2635
In that ioynt werke shewid a strange poynte;
He seid that Albertus magnus the blake frere,
Nothir frere Bacon Minour his compere,
Hadde not of oure red stone consideracione,
Him to encrece in multiplicacione;   2640
Thexpositor knew it sufficiently,
And my master tawght me trewly;

f. 66ᵛ   Alle be it that I made neuyr assay
Of the redde werke before this day.
The cavse apperith in this boke before,   2645
when y was robbid, then I wold nomore.
Nethirles I haue put me so ferre in preese
That secrete trowth to shew I kan not cese,
Rehercinge such as were gretly to bolde
So grete secretis to shew as thei tolde.   2650
Thei seide with-in centris of incomplete white
was hidde oure red stone of most delite;
which may be with strength & kind of fyre
Made to apere right as we desyre.
Pandophilus in turba seide: mente secura   2655
Et eius vmbra in vera tinctura.
Maria confermede it in fide oculata,
Quod in ipsa albedine est rubedo occultata.
The boke laudabile sanctum, made bi hermes,
Of the rede werke spekith in this verse: 2660

2628 quyke] the quycke ES   2630 matier] matters B, maner s   graduacion]
generacion BT   2632 most] om. BT   2634 Said] when he said S₃
2635 Thexpositor] Thexposicyoure S   2636 that] om. BT   strange]
hard R   2640 om. ES   2641 knew] Knowith S₃   2643 that]
though S   2646 Erasure of one letter after then   2651 incomplete]
a complete S₃   2652 stone] om. S   2653 & kind] om. BT   2660 verse]
wise S

Candida tunc rubeo iacet vxor nupta marito;
That is to say, if ye take hede therto,

f. 67ʳ Then is the faire white woman
Mariede to the rodie mane;
vndirstonding therof if ye wolde gete,   2665
when oure white stone shal suffre hete,
And rest in fyre as rede as blode,
Then is the mariage perfite and gode;
And ye may trewli knowe that tyme
How the semynale sede masculyne   2670
Hath wroght & wonn the victorie
Vpon the menstruallis worthily;
And wel convertide them to his kynde,
As bi experience ye shalle fynde
Passinge the substance of Embrion;   2675
For then complete is made oure stone;
whome wise men saide that ye shulde feede
with his owne venome when it is nede.
Then ride or go where ye delite,
For alle your costis he wille yow quyte.   2680
Thus endith the subtile werk with al hire store,
It nede not, I may not, I wille shewe no more.

MS. SLOANE 1873

f. 74ʳ   Capitulum vj

[T]owarde the maters of concordance,
Considere there be no variance
Bitwene such thyngis as shuld accorde,   2685
For of variance may growe discorde,
Wherbie your werkis mygth be loste
With all your labours & all your coste.
He that will take our werke in honde,
V. Concordis he moste vndirstonde.   2690
The first concorde is nede to merke,

2662 to] *om.* B   2663 the faire] *om.* S   2664 rodie] redd R
2667 rest] roste S   2668 perfite] profitable S   2670 semynale]
feminale BT   2680 quyte] acquyte B   2681 with al hire] of all our s
2682 A *ends*   2683 *3-line space for capital; no guide letter*   2686 of] a E
2690 Concordis] concordances BR   2691 concorde] *om.* B

Whethir his mynde accorde with the werke
Which shall be lorde to pay for all,
Ells all your lab[o]ur destroye he shall;
The ijde. concorde is nedfull to kenn   2695
Bitwen this crafte & hirr werkmen;
The iijde. shall well serve your ententis,
When werke concordith with Instrumentis;
The iiijth. concorde most well be sowgth
With ye place where it shall be wrogth;   2700
For trewly it is no litill grace
To fynde a perfite worchynge place;
f. 74ᵛ   The vth is of concorde & of love
Bitwen your werkis & the spere above;
Of these v. concordis reherce we shall   2705
Bigynnynge with the firste of all.
For the firste ye shall well fynde
That full fewe lordis be stable of mynde;
Thei be hastie, the werke is longe,
Thei wolde haue yowe do nature wronge;   2710
Some now be onwarde as hasty as fyre,
Halfe yere herafter thei haue no desire;
And some in a weke, it is no nay,
Will change theire mynde, & some in a day;
And for oon monthe haue full byleve,   2715
The nexte month thei will ye arte repreve.
It were moch bettir for such to cese
Then for this arte to put theym in preese.
Late such like botirflyes wandir & passe,
And lerne this latyne both more & lasse,   2720
Folowinge the sentence of this holy letter:
Attingens a fine vsque ad finem fortiter & disponens
      omnia suaviter;
f. 75ʳ   That is, procede myghtly to the ende
Fro the begynnynge, magre the fende,

2692 the] his ES   2694 he] ye BESR   2695 nedfull] nede E, maid S
to kenn] to knowe S, to been R   2696 werkmen] worke men nowe S
2698 concordith] accordeth R   2703 and of] and SR   2706 om.
E   2709 Thei] for they S   2712 Halfe yere] half a yere SR
herafter] after E   2715 haue full byleve] ye art beleve S   2716 ye
arte] it S   2719 such like] syche E   2722 &] om. BESR   2724 magre]
mawger of ES   the fende] thie ffrinde

All thyngis disposinge in the meen space   2725
With grete suauyte that comyth of grace.
All shorte wittide men & mutable,
Such most nedis be variable;
And some do euery man bileve,
Such credence dothe theire cofirs greve;   2730
To euery new tale to them tolde
Thei gyve credence and leve the olde;
But som lordis be stable of witte,
Such be apte to fynyshe itt;
Euery such lorde or mastir of this werke,   2735
Be he lay-man or be he clerke,
Be he ryche man, knyght, abbott, or lorde,
He hath with this arte grete concorde.
The seconde concorde with this arte is
When ye can fynde apte mynystris.   2740
No mynystre is apte to this entent
But he sobre be, wise, & diligent,

f. 75ᵛ   Trewe, and wachlew, and allso tymorous,
Close of tonge, of bodie not viciouse,
Clenly of hondis, in towchynge curiouse,   2745
Not disobedient, neither presumptuouse;
Such Servantis may your werkis of charge
Mynystre, & save from all owtrage.
But trust not that ij. suche servantis or three
May sufficient for youre werke be;   2750
Iff youre matier be of quantite resonable,
Then .viij. such servantis be convenable;
But vppon litill quantite fynde ye shalle
Foure men able to performe alle.
That oon halfe of theym moste wurch,   2755
While yat other slepith, or goon to church;
For of this arte ye shall not haue your pray,
But it be mynystride aswell nyght as day

2725 thyngis] *om.* S, thing R   2727–8 *om.* S   2729 And] *om.* S
2731 new] *om.* S   2733 But] and B   2737 knyght] *om.* S
abbott] bysshop ES   2739 *2-line space for capital; small* t *guide letter*
2743 allso] *om.* B   2744 not] t *inserted above with caret*   2745 curiouse]
not curiouse R   2747 may] *om.* B, myne S   2749 that] to that ES
2751 quantite] qualite B   2756 church] kerke B   2758 nyght as day]
by nyght as by daye E   2758 as] *inserted above with caret*

Contynually, except the holi sonday allone,
From evynsonge bigon, til evesong efte be done.   2760
And while thei werke thei moste nedis eschew
All rebawdry, els thei shall fynde this trew,

f. 76ʳ   That such myshappe shall theym befall
Thei shall destroye parte of theire werke or all.
Therfore all the mynystris most be men,   2765
Othir thei most be all wommen;
Sett theym not occupied oon with odire,
Thofe some to yow be sustire or brodire.
Yett they most have some good disporte
Theire grete labours to recomforte;   2770
Then no thynge shall bettir avance
Your werkis then shall this concordance.
The thridd concorde to many is full derke,
To ordeyn Instrumentis accordyng to ye werke.
As euery Chapiter hath dyuerse ententis,   2775
So hath thei dyuerse Instrumentis;
Both in matere, and allso in shappe,
In concorde that no thynge myshappe.
As werke of diuision & separacion
Haue small vessels for their operacion;   2780
But vessels brode for humectacion,
And somdell brode for Circulacion;

f. 76ᵛ   But longe vessellis to precipitacion,
Both shorte & longe serue sublimacion;
But narow vessels & iiij. ynchis hye   2785
Serve Correccion most proprelye.
Of vessels som be made of ledde,
And some of cley, both quykke & dedd.
Dedd clay is callide such a thynge
As hath soeffrede grete Roostynge;   2790
Such medlide in powdire with good rawe cley,
Will fyre abide & not go awey.
But many cleyes will leepe in fyre,
Such for vessell do not desire.

2760 efte] *om.* BS   2762 els] or elles S   2764 Thei] that B, as R
werke] *om.* S   2768 or] and BES   2772 shall] *om.* B   2773 *One-*
line space for capital; small t *guide letter*   2780 small] finall B   2783 to]
for ER   2793 will] doo R   2794 for] In E

Othir vessels be made of stone,   2795
For fyre sufficient, but fewe or noon
Amonge werkmen as yet is fownde
In any contray of english grownde
Which of watire no thynge drynke shall,
And yet abide drye fyre with all.   2800
Such stonys large for owr entente
Were a precious Instrumente.

f. 77^r All other vessells be made of glasse,
That spirituall maters shuld not owte passe.
Of ashis of verne in this londe euerych on   2805
Be made, but els where thei be of stone.
Of oure glassis the bettir kynde
The mornynge stuffe ye shall it fynde,
Which was ashis the nygth bifore,
Stondynge in hete all nygth & more.   2810
The hardir stuffe is callide freton,
Off crippynge of othir glassis it com;
Tyncture with anelynge of Glaciers
Will not perse hym as thei reherse.
By these doctryne chese or refuse,   2815
Take which ye will vnto your vse.
But for figuris of vessell kynde,
Euery man folowith his awne mynde.
The best fassion is, ye may be sewre,
She yat beste concordith with vessell of nature;   2820
And figure yat beste concordith with quantite,
And with all circumstance, to mater best is she.

f. 77^v And this shewith well albertus magnus
In his boke de Mineralibus.
Herof a secrete discloside was   2825
By my good mastir to more & lasse,
Saiynge: Si deus non dedisset nobis vas
Nichil dedisset, and that is glasse.

2796 but] *om.* R   2801 large] Larde S   2805 *After* londe, ey *under-lined and crossed through*   2806 but . . . stone] or else where be made of stone E   2810 in hete all nygth] all neight in heat S   2812 crip-pynge] cryspyng E, the clipping S   glassis] glas BE   2815 these] this BR, chef S   2818 awne] *om.* ES   2822 with] to S   2825 discloside] c *written over original* l   2827 dedisset] dedisti E

Instrumentis nedefull there be more,
As be fornacis ordeynede therfore.   2830
Olde men ymagynede for this arte
A speciall fornace for euery parte;
Euerych dyuysynge after his owne thogth,
But many fornacis of them be nogth;
Some were to brode, & some to longe   2835
Many of them dide nature wronge.
Therfore some fornacis may be well vside,
But many of them moste be refuside;
For thei were made but bi aduyse
Of them that semyde & were not wise.   2840
The most commendable fassion of them all
In this boke porturide fynde ye shall.

f. 78ʳ   Oon fornace bi me is fownde of newe
Such as olde men nevir knewe;
Whose secrete powere with studye sowgth,   2845
And with grete coste was deerly bogth;
In hym will be at oon tyme wrogth
Lx. werkis, and cost rigth nogth
More then it shulde for one werke or tweyn,
Therfore profitable it is certeyn.   2850
Lx. degrees dyuerse ye may geete
For Lx. werkis, & euerych of dyuerse hete,
Within that fornace to serve your desire;
And all thei servide with oone litill fyre
Which of a fote square only shalbe,   2855
Yet euery of the lx. asmoch space as he.
Many purposis ye may therbye fulfill,
For here ye shall have hete aftir your will.
Of this Instrument all men may not be sure,
Therfore it is not formede in picture.   2860
A nothir fornace will serve iij. score
Glassis trewlye, & yet for more;

2829 *One-line space for capital; guide letter* I   2830 ordeynede] mad R
2835 some] some wer S   to] *om.* E   2837 well] *om.* S   2840 &
were not] nothyng ES   2841 commendable fassion] commendacion ES
2842 porturide] portraicted B, portryd S, portrayte R   2843 is] ye S
2845 sowgth] I sowght E   2846 deerly] dedly E   2847-8 *om.* B
2848 Lx.] threescore R   2851 Lx.] threescore R   2852 Lx.]
threescore R   2853 your] at your S   2858 hete] fire B   aftir] at S
2862 yet] *om.* B

f. 78ᵛ Euerych of them stondynge in like hete,
As bi the picture doctryne ye may gete.
An other fornace for this operacion 2865
By me was fownde bi ymaginacion;
Nobilly servynge for separacion
Of dyuydentis, and for altificacion,
And for disiunccion callid dyuysion,
And for Correccion callid ablucyon; 2870
It will for some thyngis serve desiccacion,
It servith full well for preparacion;
So for vj. thyngis it servith well,
And yet for all at oons as I can tell.
This is a newe thynge which shall not be 2875
Sett owte in picture for all men to see.
A nothir fornace in picture be shall
More full of perils then othire fornessis all;
Made for magnesia, wherof bolde men had dowte
To tuych with handis a pore lynyne clowte 2880
Which in ye myddill therof vnbrennyde stode,
For drede of flammys brennyng ferce of wode.
f. 79ʳ Which subtile fornace I deuyside allso,
In which I fownde many wonders mo
Then is convenient at this seson to tell, 2885
Whos graduacion is dowtefull and casuell;
Wherin Magnesia, matere of grete coste,
Moste quikly be servede or sodenly be loste;
Of whose graduacion yf ye will not mysse,
Considre youre stoppellis and lerne well this, 2890
The more is the stoppell, the lasse is the hete;
Bi manyfolde stoppellis degrees ye may gete.
Who knowith the power, ye worchyng and kynde
Of euery fornace he may well ye trouth fynde;
And he which therof dwellith in ignorance, 2895
All his werkis fallith vppon chaunce.
No man is sure to haue his entent
With-owte ful concorde of arte with Instrument.

2866 om. E   2867 Nobilly] notable R   2871 serve] serue for BR
2873 well] full well S   2878 fornessis all] fornace all B, pictures be all S
2879 for] of B   2881 therof] om. S   2882 ferce of wode] of fors woode
R   2888 be loste] lost E   2895 he] om. E   2896 fallith] ffaillithe S
2898 of arte with Instrument] with arte & Instrument E, of art and Instrument S

Many mo Instrumentis occupied ye shall see
Then in this chapiter now rehersid bee,   2900
Which ye most ordeyne bi gode & sadde aduyse,
And prove them biforehande oft, if ye be wyse.

f. 79ᵛ   The iiijth concorde is full notable
Bitwene this arte & placis convenable.
Some placis most nede be euermore drie,   2905
Close from airys no wyse wyndye;
Som most be derke or dym of lyght,
In which sonbemys noon may light;
But for som placis the trouth so is
Thei can not haue to moche brightnes;   2910
Som placis most nedly be moyst & colde,
For some werkis, as auctours tolde.
But in oure werkis in euery place
Wynde will hurte in euery case.
Therfore for euery werke in seson   2915
Ye moste ordeyne placis bi reson.
Philosophers saide bi theire engyne
How it shulde be wroght within lokkis ix.
Astrologiers seide it was a grace
To fynde a chosen worchinge place.   2920
For many thyngis will wondirs do
In some placis, and elswere not so;
f. 80ʳ   But contrarie wondris be of one thynge
In contrary contries wroght withoute leysyng;
Wherof noon other cawse may appere   2925
But only contrarie placis of the speere,
Where-to placis contrary of the grownde
To them concordant & obedient be fownde.
Herof grete evidence & witnes full clere
In the Magnete stone opynly doth appere,   2930
Whose north poynt drawith towarde in yis cuntrey,
Which vndir ye sowth sterre dryvith nedillis awey.

2900 now] *om.* S   bee] shalbe ES   2902 if] *om.* B   2903 concorde]
om. B   2903 *2-line space for capital; small* t *guide letter*   2905 euermore]
allwaie S   2912 tolde] haue told B   2917 Philisophers S₃   2920 worchinge
place] work in plaice S   2923–4 *om.* S   2923 wondris] wordes B   2924 con-
tries] contraries S₃R   2927 where-to] And wherto S   2928] be]
& E   2930 opynly] playnlye R   2931 in] *om.* R   yis] his ES
2932 dryvith] draweth R   nedillis] *om.* S

Wherfore wyse men which for this arte soght
Fownde som placis concorde, & som to be noght.
Trewly such placis where lechery is vsyde 2935
Moste for this arte vttirly be refuside.
The vth. concorde is knowen well of clerkis,
Betwene ye spere of hevyn & our subtill werkis.
No thyng in erth hath more symplicitie
Then the elementis of owr stone will bee; 2940
Wherfore, thei beynge in werkis of generacion,
Haue most obedience to constellacion.

f. 80ᵛ Wherof concorde most kyndly convenyent
Ys a directe & fyrie ascendent;
Beyng sygne common for these operacions, 2945
For the multitude of there Iteracions.
Fortune your ascendent with his lorde allso,
Kepynge aspectis of shrewys them fro;
And if thei most let, or nedely enfecte
Cause them to looke with a tryne aspecte. 2950
For the white werke make fortunate ye moone;
For ye lorde of ye iiijth howse likewyse be it done;
For this is thesaurum absconditum of olde clerkis,
So of ye vjth. howse for servantz of ye werkis.
Save all them well from grete Impedymentis, 2955
As it is in picture, or like ye same ententis,
Enlas then your nativitie pretende Infeccion
In contraryetie to this election.
The virtew of ye mover of ye orbe ys formall,
The virtew of ye viijth spere is here Instrumentall, 2960
With his signis & figuris & parties aspectuall;
The planet virtue is propre & speciall;

f. 81ʳ The virtew of Elementis is here Materiall,
The virtew infuside resultith of them all.
The firste is like to a werkman his mynde, 2965
The ijde. like to his hande ye shall fynde;

2933 arte] science R   2934 concorde] om. E, concordant R   2937 con-
corde] om. S   2938 subtill] om. ES   2941 generacion] governaunce E
2944 fyrie] a ffaire S   2946 Iteracions] operacyons S   2949–50 om. S
2950 them] om. B   2951 fortunate] tu inserted above with caret
2952 ye lorde of] om. ES   2953 olde] om. S   2959 mover] mother S
ye orbe] worlde B   2960 viijth] iii B   2962 planet] plaines S,
planetes R   2964 of] om. S   2965 like] om. S

The iijde. is like to a good Instrumente;
The remenant like a thyng wrogth to your entent.
Make all ye premyssis with other well accorde,
Then shall your meritis make yow a grete lorde.   2970
These wysis Elixer of whom we make mencyon
Ys gendrid, a thyng of a secunde intencion.
Trust not Geomancye, that supersticious arte,
For god made reason which yer is sett a-parte;
Trust not to all astrologyeris, I say why,   2975
For that arte is as secrete as alchymye.
That other is disprovide, & playnly forbodde
By holy sayntis of the church of gode.
Trust not, ne love not Nigromancye,
For it is appropriede to the devill to lye;   2980
Trust to this doctrine, sett herin yowr desyris,
And now lerne ye regymentis of your fyris.

Capitulum 7

f. 81ᵛ   A Perfite Maister ye may hym trowe
Which knowith his hetis hye & lowe.
Nothyng may lett more your desires   2985
Then ignorance of hetis of youre fyres.
Of many auctours writen ye may see:
Totum consistit in ignis regimine.
Wherfore in all chapiters ye most so procede
That hete worche not more ne lasse then nede;   2990
Wherin many of Gebere his cokis
Deceyvid be, thofe thei be wise in bokis.
Such hete wherwith pigge or gose is scallid,
In this arte decoccion it is callid;
For mynerall meenys servith such hete,   2995
And to make oure litarge to geve swete.
Such hete as drieth lawnde kerchows faire,
In xxxti. operacions servith for oure Aier;

2971 These wysis] this wise is B, This wise S, This wise the R   2973 super-
sticious] superfluous B   2975 all] om. E   2977 disprovide] deproved S
2980 appropried to] appropriate to ER a propertie for S   2983 trowe]
call I trowe S   2983 3-line space for capital; small a guide letter
2993 scallid] scalded BESR   2996 Hand pointing in left margin

But for dyuysions ye most vse such hete
As cokis makith when thei roste grose mete;   3000
The same hete with cercle fire
For seperacions of dyuydentis we desire;
f. 82ʳ But for Circulacion of Elementis,
Ignis candens observith youre ententis,
Which fire most euer be coequall   3005
In euery mynute, and yet perpetuall;
For it may nevir abate ne encrece,
And yett that fire may nevir cese.
Study wysely and loke abowte
Such a fire trewly to fynde owte;   3010
And in that fire no moyster may be
Which hande may feell or eye may see.
Ignis humidus, a nothir fire allso
Is, and yett it semyth oppositum in adiecto.
Such hete disseverith at certeyne tydes   3015
Maters clevynge to vessellis sides.
Many mo thyngis that hete may wynne,
It makith ofte thikke maters thynne.
A philosopher mystily spake of this hete,
And saide the hiest degre therof to gete   3020
Shall cause and gendre such egall siccite
As of drye hete shall be in the first degre.
f. 82ᵛ A nothir fire is fire of desiccacion
For maters which be inbibide with humectacion;
A nothir fire is fire of conservacion,   3025
For all drye thyngis of this operacion;
For magnesia is fire of effusion,
Full of perils and full of illusion,
Not only perils which to ye worke may fall,
But such allso the mastire which hurte shall;   3030
Ageyn which ons receyvede is no bote;
Ordeyne therfore to fech breth fro your fote,

3001 cercle] a circle BER, a rounde cyrcle S   3004 observith youre]
serveth our R   3009 loke] look well R   3010 fynde] look S
3014 adiecto] obiecto BS   3018 makith . . . thynne] makith thycke
matters thynne S   3019 philosopher] philisopher S₃   mystily spake]
spak mich S   3020 gete] heat R   3021 egall] equall BR, om. S
3024 with] for B   3027 For] om. S   3030 which] om. B

Provyde for mowth, for Eres, Eyes, & nose,
For it is worse then x. tymes the pose.
Men herby have fownde peynys sore,   3035
Bi-cause thei had not this warnynge bifore.
Ignis corrodens servith in this arte
Elementa propinqua wisely to departe.
Of oon poynte of excesse all your werke is shent,
And oon poynte to litill is insufficient;   3040
Who can be sure to fynde his trewe degre,
Magister magnus in igne shall he be;

f. 83ʳ It is the hardyr to know trewly his myght,
There is no triall for it but our Eye sygth.
Therfore all men faile in his presence,   3045
Hir hete is lernede with cost of experience.
Of this hete in speciall Anaxagoras said thuse:
Nemo prima fronte reperitur discretus.
An othir hete is of mygthy coaccion,
For myneralls that be of harde liquefaccion;   3050
This hete can not be to stronge,
Be he contynued nevir so longe.
An othir is hete of calcinacion,
For fowle metallis for theire preparacion,
Which may not brenne, ne do theym mylte,   3055
For so all they may soone be spylte.
The xij. is hete for to sublyme
All the spiritis of the myne;
The laste hete of these goith for all,
When to proieccion our stone shall fall.   3060
Vse makith mastrye, yer is no more to sayne
But he yat failith most nede bigyn ageyne.

f. 83ᵛ Now haue I tagth you euiry thynge bi name
As men tech othir the way to walsynghame;
Of euiry village, watire, bryge, and hyll,   3065
Wherby wise men theire Iournay may fulfill;

3037 *Hand pointing in left margin*   3040 insufficient] sufficient S
3041 fynde] *om.* B   3041 his] h *inserted above with caret*   3044 Eye]
om. ES   3047 in] *om.* B   in speciall Anaxagoras] Anaxagoras inspecy-
allie S   3049 hete is] is hete BES, heate is heate R   3056 all] *om.* S
3057 xij. is hete] xij hete is hete E   3060 proieccion] subiecyone S
3065 bryge] byrge S₃

So may clerkis bi this doctryne fynde
This science well if thei be clere of mynde.
All othir may fynde herby hym selfe a fole
To dele therwith which litill can of scole;   3070
For this is thende of wordly connynge;
Where to atteyne can nothir pope ne kynge
Bi theire honours, ne by theire grete councell,
But only bi vertue & grace, as autours tell.
This precious stone will not be fownde ne wrogth,   3075
But if he be rigth devowtly sowgth.
The autours fornamede, with this boke of myne,
Shewith of alchymye all the doctryne,
If ye complecte theire sentencis all
Not bi opinyon, but aftire this ordynall;   3080
For in this ordynall, I sett yow from all dowte,
Is no thynge sett wronge, nothir on poynt lafte owte.
f. 84ʳ   The dayes were yat this doctryne & grownde
Hadd pleasid me more then a thowsande pownde;
Thre hundrede li. was not for my desire   3085
As wolde haue bene this chapiter of ye fyre.
And Mervaile not lordis, ne ye frendis all,
Whi so noble science as all men this arte call
Is here sett owte in englishe blonte & rude,
For this is so made to teche a multitude   3090
Of rude peple which delyn with these werkis,
Ten thowsande lay men ageyn two able clerkis;
Wherby yerly grete riches in this londe
Is lewdly lost, as wise men vndirstonde;
And many men of every degree   3095
Yerly be brogth in grete pouerte.
Cese lay-men, cese, be not in foly evire,
Lewdnes to cese is bettir late then nevyre.

3067 bi] om. B   3069 All] anie R   herby] om. S   3070 To medill
with yis science which litle can therof skoll S   3071 wordly] euery
wordlie S   3072 pope] bisshopp BR, prince S   3076 But if] But
BES   except it be by godly meanes out sought R   3079 complecte]
complete ES, gather vppe R   3080 aftire] by S   3082 Is] That ther
is S   3083 grownde] this grounde B   3085 li.] om. B   3088 as]
is as B   3089 owte] forthe S   3090 made] done R   3092 ageyn]
e clumsily altered from a   3092 two] ten BESR   3093 grete riches]
om. S   3094 is great riches loste as I perceive & vnderstonde S

All that have pleasure in this boke to rede,
Pray for my sowle, & for all quykke & dede.   3100
In the yere of Crist Ml. CCCC. sevynty & sevyne
This werke bigane, honour to Gode of hevyne.

Explicit. deo gracias.

3100 for all] all B   3102 of] in B

GLOSSARY

Vocalic y *is treated as* i; *initial vocalic* v *is treated as* u.

abate *v. intr.* decline 3007; *tr.* reduce, lessen 2337.

abhominable *a. & adv.* unendurable, unnatural 2081; *adv.* 2103.

abiding *a.* enduring, persistent 2339.

ablucion *n.* washing, cleansing 1619, 2191, 2870.

above *adv.* in heaven 86, 261; *prep.* superior to 2257.

abowte *adv. & prep.* from all points of view 809; alle ~, in all respects 877; go ~, proceed 130; bring ~, see **bring**; *prep.* throughout 1401.

acceptide *pp.* received 226.

accidentalle *a.* not essential, occurring only as a fortuitous quality 1746.

accompte *n.* counting, working out 2466.

accorde *n.* agreement 1470; *pl.* harmonies 1661, 1666.

accorde *v.* acquiesce, 563; agree 1705.

according(e *a.* suitable 2506, 2774; agreeable 2021.

acquyte *v.* fulfil 1920.

acte *n.* accomplishment 556.

actyuyte *n.* activity, operative ability 1481.

actyve *a.* productive of effect, active 1475; *pl.* actyuys 1477.

actualle *a.* real, existential 1669.

actually *adv.* in fact, in reality 422, 1715.

acuyte *n.* penetrative or dissolving power 2230.

adamant *n.* the load-stone 1801.

addresse *v.* direct, apply 19.

aduyse *n.* counsel, instruction 411, 2415, 2839.

affermys *v. pr. pl.* assert 1729.

after, aftir *adv.* afterwards 835, 981.

afterwarde *adv.* afterwards 335.

agayne, ageyn(e *adv.* once more 724, 896, etc.; in reply 840; *prep.* against 738, 801.

age *n.* age 2603; old age 235, 1073.

agent *n.* operative quality 1750, 1753, etc.

ayde *v. intr.* be of use, be effectual 249.

aire, aier, ayere *n.* the element of air 375, 390, 2998, etc.; *pl.* airys, draughts 2906.

airly *a.* essential to the element air 2213.

alchymy(e *n.* alchemy 5, 54, 127, 292, etc.

alchymystre *n.* alchemist 133.

aliment(e *n.* food, sustenance 1719, 2194.

alle be it *conj.* although 867.

almis *n. pl.* for ~, as a charity 1103.

aloes *n.* alloes 2002.

als *adv.* as well, also 892.

altificacion *n.* distilling or subliming 2868.

amatiste *n.* amethyst 1813.

ambiciosnes, ambyciousnes *n.* ambition 193, 1035.

ambre *n.* amber 1997.

amende *v.* correct, 1428, 2342; improve 1810; *pp.* amendid 1810.

amownt *v.* ~ to, add up to 2465.

anelynge *ger.* annealing 2813.

angwish(e *n.* pain 1047, 1373.

animal(le *a.* see **spirit**.

antymonye *n.* antimony 1058.

aparte *adv.* aside 2974; see **set**.

aperage *n.* ? complete manifestation 1133.

apostata *n.* apostate, one who has left a religious order 550, 619.

apotecarys, poticaris *n. pl.* apothecaries 377, 1311.

appere, *v. intr.* appear, be evident 136, 369, 453, 466, 873, 1503, etc.; *3 pr. sg.* apperith 1503, aperith 369; *pt.* aperide 873.

appetite *n.* natural propensity of a substance 2210, 2433; desire 20, 377, 738, 2158.

applye *v.* apply (a text to a situation) 1246.

apprehende *v.* join with, adhere to 1787.

appropriede *a.* suited, fitting 2980.

apte *a.* fitting, suitable 401, 993, 2740, 2741; prepared, ready 1446; likely 2734.

apte *v.* prepare 1121.

ar *conj.* before 304.

arabies *n. pl.* Arabians 149.

archymastrie *n.* supreme accomplishment, supreme mastery 181.

arere *adv.* in arrears, behindhand 763.

arise *v.* arise, come about, develop 693, 1692, 2444; *3 pr. sg.* **arisith** 693, 2444, *pr. pl.* **aryse** 1692.

arismetically *adv.* arithmetically 1655.

armonye *n.* harmony 1667.

arsenek *n.* arsenic 1058.

arte *n.* craft, skill (always refers to alchemy) 74, 228, 443, etc.

artificers *n. pl.* craftsmen 39.

artificiall *a.* not natural or inherent; hete ~, extraneous heat (from a furnace, etc.) 1698.

ascendent *n.* The astrological sign, house, planet, just above the eastern horizon 2944.

askis, ashis *n. pl.* ashes 2290, 2805, 2809.

aspect *n.* Relative position of one planet to another; **trine** ~, the angular distance of 120° 2950; *pl.* influences 2948.

aspectuall *a.* pertaining to the aspect of a planet 2961.

assay *v.* test, prove 65, 1054, 2609; *pp.* **assaied** 1054.

assay(e, asay *n.* attempt, trial, proof, 600, 761, 828, 2350; **make** ~, put to proof 2085, 2643.

assawte *n.* attack 771, 801.

assigned *pp.* ordained, specified 2474˙

astrologyeris *n. pl.* astrologers 2975.

attendance *n.* observation, attention 2045.

attoms *n. pl.* atoms 2296.

atwynn *adv.* into parts 1447.

auctor *n.* author, writer, authority 69, 359, 1083, etc.

augment *v. intr.* increase, multiply 2539; *tr.* 1327.

augmentacion *n.* increase, growth 2541.

augmente *n.* multiplication, increase 2551.

auncient, auncien *a.* ancient, 499, 2107.

avance, avaunce *v. tr.* help on, further, make to progress 161, 848, 1564, 2181, 2771; *3 pr. sg.* **auauncith, auawncith** 161, 1564.

aventure *n.* good fortune 734.

avise *v. refl.* recollect (oneself), consider 345.

avoid(e *v.* get rid of 99, 1306; escape from, evade 1368; *pp.* **avoydide** 1368.

awaite *n.* watch 325; **lay in** ~, lay in wait, ambushed 977.

awaite *v.* attend 881; watch 749.

azogo *n.* Azoth, an alchemical name for 'mercury', the first principle of metals 2634; **watir of** ~, another periphrasis for 'mercury' 2236.

azure *n.* azure 1847.

baynys *n. pl.* baths 1744.

balance *n.* weighing scales 2554.

bare *a.* empty 320, 1320; ~ **of hue**, with faded colours 93.

becom *v. 3 pt. sg.* became 2222.

bedis *n. pl.* prayers, ? beads 1074.

begyn, bigyn(ne *v. intr.* begin 186, 706, 811, 896; *tr.* 6, 816, 2760; (with inf.) 546, 559; *3 pt. sg.* **began** 546, **bigan(ne** 186, 811, *pp.* **bigon** 2760.

behind(e *adv.* to come, remaining 913; in arrears 1321.

beholde *a.* under an obligation 1409.

beleve, bileve *v.* believe 32, 687, 900, 1337.

bemys *n.* sunbeams 398; see also **sonebemys**.

bere *v.* bear, carry 351, 469, 1145; support 2213, 2485; generate 1623; give birth to 1396, 1398; ~ **awaye** steal 351; ~ **forth** convey 1987; *3 pr. sg.* **berith** 469; *3 pt. sg.* **bare** 2213; *pp.* **born(e** 1396, 1398.

berille *n.* beryl 1793, 1798.

besy *a.* busy, occupied 1042.

GLOSSARY

besogthe *v. 3 pt. pl.* besought 1086.
beste *n.* beast 362, 375, 492.
bezoars *n. pl.* stones used as antidotes against poison, bezoars 2078.
bidith *v. 3 pr. sg.* endures 1130.
bifalle *v. intr.* happen, occur 899, 1387; (with dat. of disadvantage) 902; *3 pt. sg.* **befille, bifille** 899, 1387.
bifore *adv.* earlier, before 974.
biforehonde *adv.* sooner 1300, 2467.
bifor(e)tyme *adv.* previously 94, 1806.
bild(e *v.* build 301, 617.
byleve *n.* belief 2715.
birefte *v. 3 pt. sg.* (with dat. of disadvantage) stole from 906.
bityng *a.* sharp, biting 2113, 2148.
bitter *a.* sharp, bitter 736, 2104, 2115.
bittyrnys *n.* sharpness, bitterness 2136.
blak(e *a.* black 1518, 1522, etc., ~ **frere** Dominican friar 2637.
bla(u)ncher *n.* a whitening agent, a silvering agent 113, 1061.
blessid *pp.* praised 989.
blessid(e *a.* holy, sacred 117, 144, 251, 266; happy, fortunate 481, 483, 786, 1324.
blewe *a.* blue 1839; **pl. blewis** 1845.
blyve *a.* quickly 1619.
blode *n.* blood 225, 1066; **grete of** ~, of noble descent 25.
bloke *n.* block 1005.
blont(e *a.* straightforward, unpolished 2633, 3089.
bodi(e *n.* substance, piece of matter 1499, 1811; **squyer for the** ~, squire attending personally (on a king) 921.
boylle *v.* boil up, boil over 1267.
bolde *a.* confident 1425, 1479, 1491; rash, presumptuous 718, 2649.
bonde *n.* band, troop 958; *pl.* **bondis** links, bonds, connections 874.
borders *n. pl.* ornamental trimming, edging 453.
botirflyes *n. pl.* butterflies 2719.
brasse *n.* brass 383, 438, 678.
breke *v. intr.* discontinue, stop 647; *tr.* break, crack 303; disunite 418; break (one's word etc.) 851, 943.

brenne *v. intr.* burn 1197, 3055; *pp.* **brent** burnt, calcined 1503.
brennyng *a.* hot, fierce 28.
brennyng *ger.* burning 2307.
breth *n.* air (from a bellows) 3032.
brigge, bryge *n.* bridge 633, 640, 662, 3065.
bright, briȝt *a.* bright 451, 1132, 1153.
brightnys *n.* brightness 1613.
bring *v.* bring 519, 925, 978, 1133; ~ **abowte** effect, produce 302, 416, 650, 2309; ~ (**in**) to reduce to (a certain state) 76, 338; ~ **in** to **oon** unite 2297; ~ **owte** make manifest 2287; *3 pr. sg.* **bringith** 2287; *pr. pl.* **bringith** 519, 2297; *pt.* **broght** 925, 978, 987; *pp.* **broght** 76, 2309. **broȝt** 416, **broȝthe** 1133.
brode *a.* broad 2781, 2782.
broder, brodire *n.* colleague, fellow-member of a brotherhood 841, 855, 1093; brother 2768; complementary substance, partner 1204.
brown(e *a.* brown, dark 1132, 1135.
bubbil *v.* boil vigorously 1267.
bubbilyng *ger.* boiling 1270.
buttir, buttur *n.* butter 1268, 2325, 2332.

calce vive *n.* quick-lime 1059.
calcidonye *n.* chalcedony 1815.
calcinacion *n.* calcination, oxidization 3053.
calle *v.* name, designate 144, 197, 361, 470, 505; ~ **for** ask for, demand 524, 1296; ~ **upon**, demand (to do sth.) 783; ~ **to minde** recall, remember 805; *3 pr. sg.* **callith** 524; *pr. pl.* **calle** 805; *pt.* **callid** 1143, 1161, **callide** 263; *pp.* **callid** 144, 197, 470, 1455, **callide** 361.
camfere *n.* camphor 2029.
can *v.* know 501, 824, 882; know how to (do sth.) 115, 144; be able to (do sth.) 304, 1346; *pt.* **cowde** 304, 824.
canon, chanon *n.* canon 966, 968, 1163.
carbuncle *n.* carbuncle 663, 666.

care *n.* trouble 781, 2180.

case *n.* situation 371.

cast(e *v.* cast, throw, throw away 954; ~ away 266; ~ owte suggest, insinuate 797; ~ eye (loke) give a hard look 936, 2591; ~ vole (of a mare) miscarry 2020; caste in care brought into distress 781; *pt.* caste 936, 2591, cast 954; *pp.* caste 781.

casuell *a.* fortuitous 2886.

cause *n.* cause, reason 10, 102, 104, 238, 804, 938; ~ efficient see efficient; clowdy causis obscure reasons, recondite explanations 72.

cause *v.* cause, produce 64, 162, 754; make (*sb.* do sth.) 1361, 1436; make (sth. to be the case) 333; *pr. pl.* causith 64.

cawght *v. pt.* acquired, achieved 2588; *pp.* cawght 544.

cercle *a.* circular 3001.

certeyn(e *a. & adv.* sure, assured 396, 742; made ~ assured 1092; in ~ assuredly 1325, 1957; as *adv.* surely, certainly 964.

certeynte *n.* certainty, certitude 815, 817.

cese *v. intr.* stop, desist 35, 327, 1233, 3096; give up 281; *tr.* put an end to 1026, 1073, 3098; ~ of stop discussing 1437; *pr. pl.* cesyn 281.

chance, chaunce *n.* event, contingency 899, 1324, 2013; luck, fortune 307; fallith vppon ~ depend on chance 2896.

change, chaunge *n.* exchange 1383, 1386; *pl.* changis transmutations 257.

change, chaunge *v.* alter 170, 658; ~ mynde (desire) 727, 732, 2714.

charge *n.* expense 122, 2747; responsibility 991; importance 1077; no ~ therof no matter for that 1077; take litille ~ pay small heed 288; turne to ~ become (my) responsibility, make (me) guilty 1181.

charnelle *n.* charnel house 1902.

cheffare *n.* business activity 340.

chere *n.* facial expression 837, 998, 1007.

chose *v.* select 2099; *pp.* chosen choice, excellent 1136, 2920.

circulacion *n.* passing a body through a series of changes (from solid to liquid to gas or vice versa) by heating and cooling 2410, 2414, 2782, 3003.

circumstance(s *n. pl.* concomitant conditions of an alchemical process 809, 1323, 1339.

citrinacions *n. pl.* reagents for yellowing a metal to make it appear gold 113, 1061.

citryne *a.* orange, yellow 1536, 1855, 1872.

clarifie *v.* purify 1274.

cley, clay *n.* clay 1146, 2793; rawe (quykke) ~ unbaked clay 2788, 2791; dedd ~ baked clay 2788, 2789.

clense *v.* cleanse, purify 1619, 2191, 2286; *3 pr. sg.* clansith 1619; *pr. pl.* clansith 2191.

clensinge *ger.* purifying 1257.

clere *a. & adv.* bright, unsullied 1499, 1500, 1524, 1777; perspicacious, intelligent 707, 1185; complete 508; as *adv.* completely 2402.

clerke *n.* learned man, scholar 3, 49, 152; secretary 927; parish ~ 34.

clernys *n.* brightness 1780.

cleve *v.* adhere, cleave 2315, 2318; *pr. ppl.* clevynge 3016.

close *a.* closed up 389, 2906; secretive, silent 826, 2744.

clowdy *a.* obscure 72.

clowte *n.* cloth 2880.

coaccion *n.* activity, working 1615, 2255, 3049.

coagulacion *n.* coagulation 1747.

coequall *a.* equal 3005.

colde *n.* one of the four primary qualities, coldness 404, 1455, 1505, 1792; in hete and ~, in all operations 717.

cole *n.* coal 2019.

colofonye *n.* resin from distilled turpentine, colophony 2307.

colorid *pp.* gilded 112.

colorynge *a.* able to transmute (to gold or silver) 2534.

colour(e *n.* colour 825, 1494, 1498; excuse, reason 37; colours of the rose, red and white, i.e. the alchemical process 825.

com *v.* come 551, 675, 843, 853, 2225; ~ by acquire 734, 965, 1032, 1442; ~ forth appear 422; *pr. pl.* com 2225, come 853; *pt.* came 551, 965; *pp.* come 675, 843.

combynde *v.* combine 1281.

combust(e *a.* burnt 1781, 1818.

combustion *n.* burning 1782.

comforte, conforte *n.* encouragement 342, 844; consolation 1078; pleasure, relaxation 1371.

comforte, conforte *v.* strengthen, nourish 1834, 2067, 2291.

comynalte *n.* the common people 1028.

commendable *a.* recommended 2841.

commixted *pp.* blended 1723.

com(m)ixtion *n.* blending, mingling 1783, 1873; adulteration 1342.

com(m)on, com(m)yn, comone *a.* ordinary, everyday 29, 57; public, shared by all 635, 954; familiar 1509; easily found, frequent 2494; ~ speche unadorned language 58; sygne ~, universal sign 2945.

commons *n. pl.* the people, those lower in rank than the knightly classes, 1022.

comodiouslye *adv.* suitably, proportionately 2560.

compactid *pp.* dense 1519.

compas *v.* attempt 350; *pp.* compaste abowte surrounded 2261.

compere, compeer *n.* partner 2604, 2638.

complect(e) *v.* compile, assemble 2177, 3079.

complement *n.* that which completes, complement 1380, 2234; make ~ of complete, satisfy 2404.

complexion *n.* blend of the four primary qualities, constitution 1714, 2126.

componentes *n.* component parts 1202, 1586.

composicion *n.* the joining of different components, process of composition 1572; unified structure of components 418, 1201; mixture 1553, 1554; of litill ~ of little complexity, uncomplicated in structure 1888.

compown *v.* compound, 1456, 1598, 1905; *pp.* compownyde blended 2163.

concell(e *n.* advice 6; wisdom 3073; advisor, counsellor 729; kepe ~ keep secret 572, 886.

concepcion *n.* origin, cause 2125.

conclusyon *n.* achievement 12; argument 687.

concordance *n.* natural similarity, sympathy 1283, 2683; grammatical concord 1644; *pl.* concordance 1644.

concordant *a.* sympathetic, agreeable 2928.

concorde *n.* sympathy, agreement 159, 2690, 2691, 2738; grammatical concord 1638, 1639; attraction 2436; as *adj.* sympathetic, concordant 2934.

concordith *v. 3 pr. sg.* is suited to 2698.

condensid(e *pp.* condensed, liquefied, contracted 1863, 1864, 2221.

condicion *n.* character, trait of character 830, 1036; property, characteristic 2528.

confeccion *n.* making, preparation 2622.

confermede *v. 3 pt. sg.* corroborated 2657.

confession *n.* profession, declaration 695.

confidence *n.* trust 691, 802; squyere in ~ confidential squire 929; have ~ in trust 947.

confusion *n.* ruin; fall to ~ come to nothing 614.

congelid *pp.* frozen 404.

congirs *n. pl.* conger eels 2258.

congregate *a.* collected together 1822.

conioyne *v.* unite 1596, 2189.

coniunccion *n.* the process of uniting elements 1584, 1635, 2085; union 259.

connexion *n.* connection, adhesion 2130, 2446.

connyng *a.* learned 514.

connyng(e *n.* knowledge, science, learning 85, 347, 484, 1172.

conservacion *n.* preservation 3025.

conservid *pp.* preserved, kept from impurities 2048.

consideracion(e *n.* observation 2479; have ∼ of concern oneself with 2639.

considre *v.* take into account 294, 809, 1063; ponder 16; consideringe in view of 267, 1927.

constant *a.* steadfast, 532; stable, rigid 1721.

constellacion *n.* stellar influence 2942.

constrayne *v.* compel 95; *pr. p.* constreynyng making thick, condensing 1520.

consume *v.* dry up 1068, 2266.

conterfett, contrefet *v. intr.* make an inferior imitation 1314; *tr.* make (imitation precious metal) 112.

contynualle *a.* ceaseless 1372.

contynually(e *adv.* one after the other 865, 2559; unceasingly 2759.

contynuance *n.* continued operation 1266.

contynue, contynew(e *v.* remain, endure, persist 42, 45, 647, 733, 2388.

contrary(e *a.* opposite 1031, 2923; of opposite tendency or influence 373, 2924; incompatible 1641; opposed, displeasing 701, 2023; as *n.* contraries incompatible properties 1469.

contrariete, contrarietie *n.* opposition 2347, 2958.

contrey, contray, cuntrey *n.* neighbourhood, region 636, 2798, 2924, 2931.

convenable, covenable *a.* suitable, 2084, 2752, 2904.

convenient *a.* suitable, appropriate 366, 2943; beneficial 914.

conveniently(e *adv.* appropriately 263, 1638; customarily 1157.

conversion *n.* change, transformation 78, 1760.

converte *v.* transform 1759, 2673.

convertibilite *n.* changeableness, adaptability 1931.

convided *pp.* summoned, invited 289.

copyr *n.* copper 256, 459.

corage *n.* determination 2566; addresse ∼ direct (one's) interest 19.

correccion *n.* purification from adulterants 2432, 2786, 2870.

corrosyfe *a.* corrosive; ∼ watirs, acids 424.

corrumpeth *v. 3 pr. sg.* becomes corrupt, rots 2046.

corrupcion *n.* rusting (of metal) 369; in ∼, corrupt, decomposed 2009.

cost(e *n.* outlay of money, expense 66, 190, 895, 1047; did ∼ incurred expenses 279.

costelewe *a.* expensive 1250.

cours *n.* orbit 2460.

coveride *v. 3 pt. pl.* concealed, disguised 1189.

covert *n.*, write undir ∼ write ambiguously, write with a hidden meaning 70.

covetyce, covetise *n.* covetousness 28, 334, 525; a covetous person 332, 338.

craft(e *n.* art, skill, craft 30, 32, 1483, 1565; the product of a craft, something made by a practical art 604, 676; guile 1002.

craftily, craftly *adv.* skilfully 1116, 1680, 2165, 2215.

creacion *n.* making, generation 1712, 2542.

create *a.* created, finished 1726.

creaturis *n. pl.* parts of creation, creatures, substances 1716, 1717.

credence *n.* belief 40; credulity 2730; geve ∼ to believe, trust 98, 2732.

crippynge *ger.* crushing 2812.

cristall *n.* crystal 1793, 1795.

crowfote *n.* buttercup 1055.

crowne *n.* head, crown of the head 303; were a ∼ be a king 858.

crude *a.* unrefined raw 2272.

cure *n.* task, responsibility 255.

curiouse *a.* careful 2745.

curyously *adv.* artistically, beautifully 56.

darre *v.* dare 342, 1208, 2579.

deceyte, disceyte *n*, fraud, deception 326, 750, 879, 978; *pl.* deceytis, deceptis 7, 100, 341.

declynyng *a.* of an element: changing, tending (towards another element) 1795.

declynyth *v. 3 pr. sg.* tends 1797.

decoccion *n.* heating, cooking 1858, 2994.

dedd(e, dede *a.* reduced to calx, rendered inactive 2244, 2628; of clay: roasted 2788, 2789; dead 713.

defawte *n.* mistake 772, 1343.

defilede *pp.* spoiled, destroyed 135.

degre(e *n.* one of four grades of intensity of a quality 1690, 1713, 2127, 2145; a vaguer measure of heat 1700, 2851; rank 22; **in every ~**, in all respects 1014.

degression *n.* error 696.

dele *v.* be occupied with (a work) 33, 3091; *3 pr. pl.* **delyn** 3091.

delycious *a.* beautiful 744.

delyte *n.* desire; **have ~ to** have desire for 702, 2157; **set your ~** fix your mind (to do sth.) 1339.

delyte *v.* wish (to know sth.) 1981.

departe *v. intr.* go off, leave 281, 522, 608, 2392; become separated 2441; *tr.* divide, separate 1226, 1447, 2295; *3 pr. pl.* **departith** 2295.

deposide *v. 3 pt. sg.* declared, testified 2211.

dere *adv.* dearly 841; *comp.* **derere** at a higher price 1844.

derk(e *a.* obscure, mysterious 62, 873, 2773; dull in colour, opaque 1779, 1783, 1798; *comp.* **derker** 1798.

derkli *adv.* obscurely, mysteriously 1673.

derknes *n.* opaqueness, dullness 1521, 1800.

desicaccion *n.* the process of drying 2871, 3023.

desire *n.* wish 576, 598, 923; object, goal 1040; **have ~ to** wish for 28; **sett desyris in** fix (one's) wish on 2981.

desire *v.* wish for 13, 456; **~ after** wish for 26.

despite *n.* malice; **for ~** maliciously 90.

destruccione *n.* destruction 370, 754; **in ~** in ruin 2010.

devise *n.* opinion 1559.

dewly *adv.* correctly 1723.

dyapason *n.* musical interval of an octave 1663.

diapente *n.* musical interval of a fifth 1664.

diaphanyte *n.* transparency 1156.

diatesseron *n.* musical interval of a fourth 1664.

dye, deye *v.* die 968, 987, 999, 1011.

dietarie *n.* method of adding substances to a mixture during an operation, diet, regimen 1241.

digerent *a.* effecting digestion 1740.

digestere *n.* that which effects digestion 1739.

digestible *a.* to be digested 1741.

digestion *n.* change through heating, digestion 1707, 1708, 1857; a degree or stage in the process of heating 1691.

dignite(e *n.* distinction, rank 221, 226; inherent worth, value 1813; **of ~** honoured, distinguished 21.

directe *a.* not retrograde, moving from east to west 2944.

directly *adv.* in a straight line 398.

discerne *v.* distinguish, recognize 2042, 2094; **~ of** judge of, determine 1878, 1948.

discomforte *n.* discouragement 2544.

discorde *n.* opposition, antipathy 525, 1280.

discovered(e *pp.* disclosed, revealed 577, 1180.

discrete *a.* intelligent 489.

disiunccion *n.* separation of a substance into its elements or qualities 2869.

disporte *n.* amusement, recreation 2769; foolish activity 681.

dispose *v.* ordain, make provision 1895; direct, regulate 2725; get (oneself) ready, 862; *pp.* inclined 343; of matter: having potentiality, tending to a condition 399.

disposicioun *n.* character, disposition 829.

disprovide *pp.* disapproved of, disallowed 2977.

dissolucion *n.* solution; **made ~** dissolved 424.

diversite *n.* difference, distinction, 385, 709, 872, 794.

dyvydentis *n. pl.* materials to be divided or broken down 2868, 3002.

dyvysible *a.* **mater ~,** materials to

be broken up into components
1230.

division *n.* separation into component parts 1907, 2779, 2869.

do *v.* effect (sth.), accomplish 366,
1421, 2921; act, operate, do 624,
1350, 1354, 1367, 2594; ~ cost
incur expense 279; ~ the deede
721; ~ vertue achieve good end
751; ~ office perform (its) function
1308; fowle done ill done 962;
~ the same 475; *with inf.* ~
make have (sth.) made 1140, ~
mylte cause (sth.) to melt 3055;
*with inf. as equivalent of a simple
verb* 95, 149, 262, 505, 1587, 1787,
2321; *with inf. to form negative* 194,
386, 2577; *neg. imper.* 1265; *as
substitute for another verb* 718, 1685,
2280; *for emphasis* 382; *inf.* do 624,
721, 751, 2577; *3 pr. sg.* doith 95,
262, 516, doithe 718, doth 336,
dothe 2383; *pr. pl.* do 382, 1354,
2011, 2012, 2366, doyn 149, doon
1592, 1685, 1833, doone 2280,
doith 1675; *pt. sg.* dide 571, 984,
1590, did 475; *pt. pl.* dide 505,
2836, did 278, 1587, dit 386; *pp.*
do 1367, 1421, doon 366, done 962.

doctour *n.* learned man, philosopher
268, 276, 1228.

doctryne *n.* teaching, instruction 8,
97, 381; information 2170.

dominacion *n.* control 2523.

dotage *n.* folly 633, 684.

dote *v.* grow foolish 546.

dowce *a.* one of the nine tastes, sweet
to the taste 2115.

dowcet, dowsett *a.* same as dowce
2118, 2128; pleasant to the ear
1430.

dowsegyre *a.* bitter-sweet 2164.

dowte *n.* doubt 415, 798; fear 245,
810, 2879; puzzle, mystery 873,
1083; take no ~ have no doubt,
rest assured 878; for love or for ~
out of love or fear 810.

dowte *v.* fear 793, 1089, 2167; doubt
820.

draw(e *v.* attract 2931; *intr.* ~ to
(towarde) approach 417, 1282, 1424;
~ toward conform to, tend to
1915.

dredful(le *a.* terrible, 140; solemn 220.

dredfullie *adv.* fearfully 244.

dresse *v.* make, prepare 1311.

drye *n.* dryness, one of the four elemental qualities 1573.

drynes, drynys *n. same as* drye
1455, 1484.

drinke *v.* absorb liquid 1239, 2799.

dronklew *a.* drunken 889.

dullid *v. pt.* stupefied 72; *pp.* blunted
2230.

dwelle *v.* live 27, 508; exist, have
seat or centre 2382; remain 2895.

effecte *n.* essence, gist 132; power,
efficacy 1454; result 1662; **in** ~
in fact 208.

effectually(e *adv.* as a result 2124;
effectively, well 2492; in fact
251.

efficient *a.* **cause** ~, efficient cause
393, 1525.

effusion *n.* fire of ~, fire for the
process of adding or pouring on
liquid 3027.

efte-sonys *adv.* a second time 2453.

egall *a.* equal 3021.

egally *adv.* with ingredients in equal
proportions 1906.

eye-ledis *n. pl.* eyelids 1953.

election *n.* choice of an astrologically
favourable occasion 2958.

element *n.* one of the four elements,
earth, air, fire, water 1448, 1452,
1596, 1609; regnyng ~ *same as*
regnyng qualite 1944.

elemental(le *a.* ~ **kynde** element
2360, 2446.

elementatife *a.* inorganic 431.

elementide *pp.* compounded, composed 2527.

elixer(e *n.* transmuting substance,
the philosophers' stone, elixir 149,
1176, 1200; **white** ~ stone for
transmuting into silver 1391, 1633;
redde ~ for gold 1391; ~ **of lyfe**
medicine for preserving life 905.

embrion *n.* embryo 2675.

encrece, encrese *v. intr.* grow
larger, develop 386, 414, 2539; *tr.*
make grow, multiply 328, 426.

encrese *n.* advantage, furtherance
1266.

ende *n.* border, boundary 1397; conclusion 783, 2374; in ~ of every myle every mile 568.

endynge *ger.* conclusion 698; ~ day finish, cessation 524.

endite *v.* write 56.

enforme *v.* direct 1209.

engyne *n.* contrivance, device 439, 1332, 2442; craft, accomplishment 51, 776, 1568; intelligence, ingenuity 2077, 2413; *pl.* ingynys 1332.

enlas *conj.* unless 2957.

entent(e, intent *n.* wish, desire 123, 195, 616, 1015, 1928; scheme, plan of operations 1915, 2233; purpose 653, 1207; to ~ according to plan, effectively 1595.

erth(e *n.* the element earth 1608, 1823; a kind of solid substance 1132; the ground, above ~ above ground 368, 369, 372; under ~ buried, dead 1150.

erthy *a.* having qualities of the element earth 1826.

erthly(e *a.* resembling earth 1605; having qualities of the element earth 1818; of this world 2595.

eschew(e *v.* avoid 7, 108, 777, 2761.

ese, ease *n.* convenience 635; wealth 1022.

estate *n.* rank of society 26; (royal) authority 581; condition (of dominance) 2338.

ete *v.* eat 1733; combine with or absorb a substance 1239, 1243; *pr. pl.* eten 1733.

every, eviry *a. & pron.* every 17, 280; everyone 2506.

everych(e *pron.* everyone 452, 1091.

evermore, evyrmore *adv.* always 105, 1045, 1477; continually 1035.

evidence *n.* indication, evidence 1683, 2186, 2929.

evidentlie *adv.* plainly 2289.

evil(le *a.* corrupt 2008, 2015; wicked 239.

examynacions *n.* inspections, tests 114.

exceding *a.* transcending, too lofty 1942.

excellent *a.* exceptional 248; the best, very good 464; excessive 1792.

excitid *pp.* stimulated 1699.

exemple *n.* a specimen, instance 447, 2443; a moral tale, exemplum 548; bi ~ by analogy 1510.

exercise *n.* practice, experience 2586.

expansid *pp.* spread out 1734.

experience, experiens *n.* skill, 1338; knowledge from experience 1570; practical experience 3046.

expositor *n.* interpreter, commentator 2635, 2641.

extende *v.* expand 1603.

extendibilite *n.* ability to expand 1611.

extendible *a.* far-spreading, able to spread 1970.

extremite *n.* highest degree (of a quality) 1275, 2284; point of opposition 1528, 1807; evil, excess 196; in ~ at the highest point, at the crisis, 1837.

faade *v.* waste away, disappear 2070.

fable, fabul *n.* lie, old wives' tale 283, 596.

face *n.* face 92, 2143; edge, surface 2440, 2446; ~ to ~ personally, in person 850.

faders *n. pl.* sages, alchemical writers 144, 263, 1143.

fayl(l)e *n.* mistake, error 154, 724; make (committ) a ~ perpetrate an error, make a mistake 1288, 1336.

faile *v. intr.* go wrong, make a mistake 712, 714, 717, 2366; *tr.* let (sb.) down 1002, 1072; ~ of miss (one's object) 280, 2365.

fayne *a.* desirous, eager 735, 995, 2385; content, resigned 1139.

faire *a.* persuasive, specious 75, 337; good, effective 389, 2443; light, bright 1153, 1785; beautiful 875; *comp.* fairere 1841.

falle *v. intr.* come to pass, be the case, happen 795, 1411, 1909; be realized 1023; decline, disappear 1618; ~ behinde lag, fail 103; ~ in drede become fearful 655; ~ to nogthe (confusion) come to nothing 614, 1062; ~ vppon happen to (sb.) 915; ~ vppon chaunce be at the mercy of chance 2896; *pr. pl.*

fallith 2896; *pt. sg.* **fille** 655, 915, 1062; *pp.* **falle** 1411.

fals(e *a.* treacherous, lying 8, 94, 310, 353; guileful 326; counterfeit, fake 112, 115; erroneous 97, 1052; unreal, illusory 11, 688; wicked 201; ∼ **fownd** exposed as erroneous, exploded 284.

fantasie *n.* delusion 543, 733.

fassion *n.* shape, design 2819, 2841.

fast *adv.* strongly 524; *comp.* **faster** sooner 1990.

fastyn *v.* join (elements) in a stable compound 2187.

fastly *adv.* firmly 2537.

favour *n.* inclination 493.

fawte *v.* lack (sth.) 178, 214, 578, 1152.

fawtis *n. pl.* faults, defects 2498.

fech(e *v.* bring, fetch 314, 457; draw (breath) 3032; produce 2262, 2310; *3 pr. sg.* **fecchith** 314; *pp.* **fett** 1309, 2262, 2310, **fet** 457.

feende, fende *n.* the devil 784, 787, 2724.

feld(e, feell *v.* feel 1695, 2096, 3012.

feldyng *ger.* feeling, sensation 432.

felows *n. pl.* companions, colleagues 468, 1092.

fensith *v. 3 pr. sg.* ward off (adversity) 194.

ferforth *adv.* far forward 1208.

fer(re *adv.* far 103, 305, 981, 1942.

fevirly *a.* feverish; ∼ **hete** the heat of a fever 1743.

figure *n.* representation, image 1868; shape 2630; constellation 2961.

figurede *pp.* represented 2525.

filyde *pp.* defiled 1298.

find(e *v.* discover, bring to light 74, 172, 185, 874, 2417; gain, acquire 6, 10, 48, 279, 474; observe, find by inspection 368, 393, 435, 831, 1126; prove, expose, ascertain 205, 284; attain (an object) 122, 253, 714, 1043; come across (sth.) 79, 167, 554; meet with (sb.), locate 234, 993; experience 153; ∼ **owte** locate 819, 1402, discover 620; **is fownde** is available in nature 2301; *pt.* **fownde** 48, 79, 279, 714, 831, 993, 1043, **fownd** 474; *pp.* **fownde** 153, 185, 1126, 2301, **fownd** 284.

fyne *a.* pure, free from alloy or adulteration 256, 446, 1863, 2090.

fynyd *pp.* clarified, purified 2091.

fire *n.* the element of fire 390, 1598, 1610, 1611, 1621, 1650; *fig.* desire, lust 27; a furnace 164, 883, 2982; degree of heat 1068, 1130; a fire producing a certain temperature 3005, 3008, 3013, 3023; **in** ∼ **in** the furnace, in process of manufacture 597; **laborere in** ∼ worker at the furnace 1039.

fyrie *a.* fiery, burning (applied to the signs of Aries, Leo, and Sagittarius) 2944.

firste *a.* ∼ **and laste** throughout, perpetually 1198; ∼ **philosophie**, see **philosophie**.

firthist *sup. adv.* furthest.

fixacion *n.* depriving of volatility or fluidity 1607.

fix(e *a.* non-volatile 1467, 1608, 1642, 2256.

fixid *pp.* firmly set 536.

fle(e *v.* retreat 1735; evaporate 2240; ∼ **fro** shun 97.

fletyng(e *a.* fluid, liquid 1282, 2278, 2317, 2516; impermanent, transient 1403.

flow(e *v.* be fluid or volatile, melt, 1467, 1642, 2299; of water: to run 955, 2489.

flowre *n.* flower 378; *fig.* excellency 16, excellent result 1231.

fluxe *v.* be liquid or volatile 2299.

fluxis *n. pl.* gushings out 2490.

fode, foode *n.* substances added to the materials of the stone during alchemical operations 1244, 1250, 2508; something consumed by an element 2435.

foialte *n.* fidelity, fealty 139; **breke** ∼ break (one's) oath 851.

folowe *v.* be controlled by 2279; come next in order to 1813; ensue 840; observe 2721; *pr. ppl. as adj.* subsequent 540, 1038; *pr. pl.* **folowyn** 2279.

forbood, forbodde *pp.* forbidden 268, 2977.

foreyn *n.* a privy 954.

formall *a.* formal (cause) 2959.

forme *n.* beauty 178; method, design

2629; ~ **substancialle** essential form constituting the specific substance of something, differentiating it from other genera 1747.

formed *pp.* given form, actualized 1682; created 400; drawn 2860.

fornace *n.* furnace 2832; *pl.* **fornacis** 2830, **fornessis** 2878.

forsake *v.* renounce 196, 511; give up 2568; *pp.* forsake 2568.

fortunate *a.* **make** ~ arrange that (a planet) be in a favourable position 2951.

fortune *v.* prosper (sth.); ~ **ascendent** select a fortunate ascendant to begin operations 2947.

fossis *n. pl.* ruts 407.

fowle *a.* dirty 152, 256, 1279; evil 962; *sup.* **fowlist** 1273.

fre *a.* not of servile status 503; unhindered 1975; **fremasons** skilled masons 34.

freton *n.* broken glass, fretten 2811.

frore *pp.* frozen 410, 1478, 1798.

fume *n.* a vapour, smoke 1809, 1985, 1986.

fume *v. intr.* become vapour, vaporize 1067; ~ **awai**, burn up (sth.) 40.

fumygalle *a.* productive of vapour 1996.

fumose *a.* vapoury, gaseous 2094.

fumosite *n.* fume, vaporous exhalation 1822, 2007.

gendre, gendire *v. intr.* come into being 1514; *tr.* produce, generate 1784, 2972, 3021, bring forth offspring 2478.

generacion *n.* development of the 'stone' 1446, 1604, 1606, 1711, 1912; production, development 401, 2480.

generalle *a.* **in** ~ as a rule 2091, in general terms 1117.

gentille *a.* graceful, beautiful 1882.

gete, geete *v.* obtain 581, 1881, 2851, 2864.

geve, gefe *v.* give 1473, 1492, 2373, 2996; *1 pr. sg.* **geve** 138, **gife** 342; *3 pr. sg.* **gevith** 857, 1683, 2186; *pr. pl.* **geve** 98, **gyve** 2732, **gife** 38; *2 pt. sg.* **gave** 991; *3 pt. sg.* **gave** 970, 971, 980; *pp.* **govyn** 189, 262.

gyde *n.* direction, information 1588.

gyde *v.* direct, control 109, 165, 1018, 1680, 1918.

gyse *n.* way, manner 1647, 2614.

gisse *v.* suppose, know 739, 1866.

glasiers, glaciers *n. pl.* glaziers 35, 2813.

gleire *n.* the white of an egg 2153.

go, goo *v.* walk 2485, 2533; move, run on 955, 1182; proceed in a natural process 1678; exist, be alive 283, 685, 2354; advance in a course of action 1336, 1966; die, pass 713, 994; of time: pass 603, 675, 1037, 1076; ~ **abowte** come in sequence 130; ~ **awey** disintegrate 2792; ~ **for all** be worth all the rest 3059; ~ **with vole** carry young, be pregnant 2477; **ride or** ~ ride or walk 235, 2679; ~ **to church** 2756; with little or no semantic content: ~ **and lerne** 1450; *3 pr. sg.* **goith** 1182, 2477, 3059; *pr. pl.* **go** 130, 283, 1336, 1678, 1966, 2354, 2485, **goo** 685, **goon** 2756; *pt. sg.* **went** 607, 611; *pp.* **go** 675, 994, **goon** 603, **goone** 713, **gone** 1037, 1076.

goode *n.* money, property 26, 351, 680, 1046.

grabbis *n. pl.* crab-apples 2144.

graduacion *n.* division into degrees, adjustment, 2630, 2886; degrees of intensity of the four qualities in a mixture 1556, 1557; the tempering of a mixture according to these degrees 1572.

grawnte *pp.* granted, given 269.

gre(e *n.* same as **degre** 1552, 1816, 2135.

grefe *n.* pain 2074.

grene *a.* green 1538; fresh, unseasoned 1516; raw 2144; *pl. as n.* **grenys** green colours 1820.

grete *a.* great 5, 221, 725; important 246; notable, learned 49, 268; noble 25: *comp.* **grettir** 644.

greve *v. intr.* cause injury 888; *tr.* hinder 235, 313; damage 2730; *pr. pl.* **grevis** 888.

grose *a.* dense, heavy 1513, 2250; ~ **mete**, strong meat, esp. beef

3000; ~ **werk**, ~ **werkis**, preliminary work, purifying and preparation of materials 151, 1205,
1273, 1332, 2467.

grosnes *n.* density 2042.

grow(e *v.* be generated, be produced
380, 388, 461; come into being
344, 635, 1020; become 1035;
develop 1498; increase 2571; *pp.*
growe 1020, **grow** 461.

grownd(e, grounde *n.* fundamental
theory, basic theory 80, 553, 1044,
2177; premiss 2427; basic material
1219; territory 1138; soil, subsoil
401; **above** ~ not underground
402; **under** ~ below the ground
367; **upon the** ~ in the world
206.

growndede, groundid *pp.* ? forming a ground or basic material 1134,
1222.

grue *a.* Greek 1169.

hadd-y-wist *n.* repining over what
might have been, (= had I known)
2179.

half *n.* in ~ **a leche** something of a
physician 629.

haloe *v.* make holy 250.

handcrafte *n.* craft, handicraft 1334,
1482.

handlyng *ger.* in in ~, to the
touch 1154.

hanfulle *n.* handful 488.

happe *v. intr.* happen (to do sth.)
303; fall to the lot of (sb.) 712;
occur, 975.

hard(e *a.* difficult 812, 1394, 3050;
tough, solid 1575, 2514; ~ **frore**
frozen hard 1798; ~ **wrogth**,
made hard 2503; *comp.* **hardir**
2811, 3043.

hardide *pp.* made hard, hardened
405.

hastely, hastly *adv.* soon, quickly
240, 339, 862, 2064.

have *v.* have, possess 137, 432, 794;
keep 86; cause (sb. to do sth.) 963;
force (sb.) 985; put into effect
2468; ~ **in mynde** keep in
remembrance 914; ~ **me excuside**
forgive me 1727; *3 pr. sg.* **hath** 248,
262, 1653, **hathe** 769, 787; *pr. pl.*

have 1184, 1312, 1481, 1541, 2712,
hath 860, 1411, 1991, 2776; *pt. sg.*
hadde 137, 544, 577, 1367, 2590,
hadd 239, **had** 794, 1051, 1986;
pt. pl. **hadd** 1391, 3084, **had** 1186,
2604, 2879, 3036; *pp.* **had** 914,
2468.

hede *n.* attention; **take** ~ **to**, attend
to 1227, 1362.

hedlye *adv.* rashly 1229.

heere *n.* hair 1057.

heyre *n.* heir 853, 855, 994; **recipient**
674.

helpe *v.* give aid to 191, 960; make
possible (to do sth.) 564, 1121;
help (sb. to do sth.) 472; contribute
1178; ~ **forth** help along 1943;
pr. pl. **helpith(e** 1121, 1178; *pt.
pl.* **holpe** 472.

herbis *n. pl.* vegetation, plants 419,
1623; medicinal herbs 1053, 1879.

hert(e *n.* feelings, spirits 42, 1050;
conscience 938; **hevy** ~ sad
feelings 837, 897.

hete *n.* heat, one of the four primary
qualities 1455, 1475, 1480, 2437;
a degree of heat 2984, 2986; a fire
2810; **artificialle** ~ heat supplied
from outside a substance 1698;
naturalle ~ the heat inherent in
a substance 1693, 1697, 1833.

hevy(e *a.* heavy, weighty 1575, 2395,
2444; sad, depressed 1006; ~
smylle, offensive smell, rank smell
1959, 2004, 2011; ~ **hert** 837,
897.

hevyn(e *n.* heaven 137, 2412; the
sky 272.

hevynly, hevenly *a.* of the sky;
~ **hewe** blue 1840, 1850; ~ **speer**
the sidereal heavens 160, 397.

hyde *v.* conceal, obscure 74, 1587;
pp. as adj. hidden, occult 1309,
2288; *pt. pl.* **hidde** 74; *pp.* **hydde**
1309, 2288.

hy(e *a.* high, lofty 378, 1160; **an** ~
up high 2447; ~ **degree** noble
rank 22; ~ **tyme** fully time 1074;
of ~ **price** expensive 1147.

hight *n.* height; **in** ~ high up 639.

hight *v. pt. sg.* was called 917.

hire *v.* hear 700, 728, *pt. sg.* **herde**
2584, **herd** 1293; *pp.* **herd** 587.

GLOSSARY

hyringe *ger.* sense of hearing 1978.
holdith *v. 3 pr. sg.* keeps, preserves 423; *pt. sg.* **helde** 591, **hilde** 2611 maintained.
honde, hande *n.* hand 887; **at ∼** available 1025; **with lesynge ∼** out at pocket 2548; **goddis handis, god his ∼** God's power 258, 2441; **have in ∼** have in operation, have to deal with 1774; **take in ∼** undertake 1444, 2689.
hoste *n.* group 1770.
hote *a.* hot, describing the primary quality of heat 1880, 2132, 2352; the primary quality heat 2127.
hows(e *n.* house 2286; one of twelve equal divisions of the heavens at any time 2952, 2954.
howsholde *n. in ∼* **man** domestic servant 1351, 1365.
hue, hewe *n.* colour 93, 1840.
humectacion *n.* wetting, soaking 2781, 3024.
humydite *n.* an excess of the quality moistness, or of the phlegmatic humour, 2155, 2206, 2208.
humour *n.* humour, one of the four chief bodily fluids—choler, blood, phlegm, and black bile 1721, 1726, 2046; by analogy applied to quicksilver 1858; any liquid or juice 2294, 2342.
hurt(e *n.* injury, damage 344, 890.
hurt(e *v.* cause trouble to, injure 892, 952, 1004; *pt. sg.* **hurt** 892.
hurtyng *a.* injurious 2061.

ylle *a.* unpleasant, evil 2102.
illusion *n.* deceptive appearance, deceit 11, 688; hidden danger 3028.
il-willid *a.* malicious 884.
ymaginacion *n.* invention, the power of envisioning something 2866.
ymagynede *v. pt.* envisioned, designed 2831; *pp.* **ymagined** 633.
impressid *pp.* imprinted, stamped 2526.
inbibide *pp.* supplied with fluid, soaked 3024.
incensid *pp.* made hot 1806.
inclyne *v.* have an inclination (towards sb.) 834.

incloside *pp.* shut in, hidden in 2031, 2212.
incomplete *a.* unfinished, i.e. not having undergone a complete process, not mature 2651.
infeccion *n.* injurious effect 2957.
infecte, enfecte *v.* spoil, corrupt 2228, 2949; *pp. as adj.* contaminated 1257.
influence *n.* transference of power or virtue 1682, 2373.
infuside *pp.* given by stellar influence 2964; imbued 1822.
instrumentall *a.* instrumental cause 2960.
instrumente *n.* a piece of apparatus 2698, 2774, 2776, 2802; means, method 1640.
intellectuall(e *a.* attainable only by mind, conceivable, not tangible 1670, 1694.
intencion *n.* meaning, purpose 1246; **secunde ∼** subsequent process, more subtle proceedure 2202.
intent see **entent(e.**
invencions *n. pl.* discoveries 2417.
inward *a. & adv.* internal 1886; **∼ hete,** same as **naturall hete** 1693, 1724; *as adv.* inwards 1735.
ypate *n.* lowest-pitched string in a Greek tetrachord 1665.
ypaton *n.* lowest of the three Greek tetrachords 1665.
ire *n.* iron 438, 455, 457.

iape *n. in no ∼* no child's play 1763.
iape *v.* play tricks, fool about 889.
ioyn(e *v.* unite (qualities), compound, 1594, 1647, 1652; link up (ideas) 1216; cf. **conioyne.**
ioynte *n.* combination, compound 1226.
ioynt(e *a. & adv.* combined 2636; *as adv.* together 2635.
iupardie *n.* hazard 243.

kele *v.* grow cold 408.
kenn *v.* know 2695.
kepe *v.* preserve, guard, watch over 959, 967, 992; withhold, prevent 2948; retain unused 2005; *pt.* **kepte** 826, 959, 967; *pp.* **kepte** 99: 2005.

kidels *n. pl.* barriers in a stream for catching fish 2026.

kynd(e *n.* nature 306; individual nature, species, type 430, 436, 1054; a substance 258, 1127, 1129, 2280; bi (of) ~ by nature 254, 367, 525, 1130.

kyndly *a. & adv.* natural, appropriate 152; *as adv.* appropriately, suitably 2219.

king(e *n.* king 25, 925, 949; dominant element 1892.

knyghthode *n.* the knightly class 1028.

knytt *pp.* joined, linked 2130, 2378, 2440, 2518.

know *v.* know (sth.) 52, 106, 1148, 2937; perceive, be made aware of 600, 684; be familiar with (sb.) 974; recognize, distinguish 8, 310; ~ of find out about 829; *pt. sg.* knewe 589; *pt. pl.* knew 1044; *pp.* know 824, 974, knowen 2937.

knowlich, knowlige *n.* knowledge 104, 161, 1594, 2043.

labour *v.* strive, work hard 748; work at (a task) 1290; *phr.* ~ to try to persuade (sb.), work on 580, 827.

lac virginis *n.* a synonym for mercury 2236.

lay *n.* complaint 1073.

lay-man *n.* someone not a cleric, uneducated person 2, 275, 683, 1289.

lake *n.* ditch, drain 954.

large *a. & adv.* generous 85; *as adv.* freely 1182.

largily(e, larglie *adv.* openly 139, 1206; plentifully 2532.

las(se *a. comp.* less 384, 406, 934, 1960.

late *v.* allow, let 622, 1003, 1366, 1437.

late *adv.* lately, recently 250, 541, 2417.

latir *a. comp.* more recent 2418.

laureolle *n.* the juice of the bay tree 1889.

laxatife *n.* laxative 1889.

leche *n.* physician, healer 629.

ledd(e, lede *n.* lead 383, 465, 1538, 2787.

lede, leede *v.* direct 803; drag about 1018.

ledy *a.* leaden 1825.

leepe *v.* crack, burst 2793.

leere *v.* learn 9, 231, 275.

leest *a. sup.* least 31, 206, 290.

leys *v.* lose; *pr. pl.* leys 66, lesith 374; *pt.* loste(e 522, 676, 1012, 1015; *pp. as n.* lost what is lost 1047.

leyser(e *n.* length of time, leisure 190, 760, 1912.

leyserlye *adv.* slowly 1244.

lekanos *n.* the third note in a Greek tetrachord 1665.

lengire *adv. comp.* for any longer time, further 291, 836.

length *v. tr.* lengthen 2598.

lern(e *v.* learn (sth., to do sth.) 101, 310, 490, 866; *pp. as adj.* instructed, learned 312, 707.

lesyng(e, leysyng *n.* a lie 327, 441, 470; 2924.

lesynge *a.* losing; with ~ honde out of pocket 2548.

lett *v. intr.* hinder 749; *tr.* 313, 748, 2321.

lettre, letter *n.* missive, epistle 837, 863, 1673; a letter of the alphabet 453; a text, quotation 2721; *pl.* litteris 453, 1673.

leve *v.* leave behind 894, 2316; abandon 474, 1566, 2732; leave (sth. in a certain state) 1835; ~ behynde leave for posterity 233, 556; ~ owt omit, exclude 29, 1377; *intr.* ~ of cease, give up 47; *pt.* left(e 474, 894, 1377; *pp.* left 47, laft(e 29, 1566.

levire *a. comp.* dearer, more precious 2599.

lewde, lewed *a.* ignorant, unlearned 50, 592, 593, 694, 1052.

lewdly(e *adv.* ignorantly 687, 2568.

liberalle *a.* liberal 506.

liberte(e, libertie *n.* the status of a free man, freedom 504, 508; permission 972; freedom from work, relaxation 1369.

lye *n.* lye, an alkaline solution from wood ashes or other vegetable ashes 1860, 2308.

ligge *v.* lie 1390, 1736; ~ in a-wayte,

lie in ambush 977; *pt.* lay 977, 1390; *pp.* layne 1829.

light, ligth *a.* easy 634, 1616; nimble, 2608; of little weight, 1575, 2395.

light *v.* enter, alight 2908.

likinge *a.* pleasing 1856.

lyme *n.* lime 1478; *fig.* something which entraps 2437; ~ **stonys** 1504.

liquefaccion *n.* liquefaction, melting 1616, 2256, 3050.

liquor(e, licour *n.* a liquid, fluid 1766, 2185, 2191, 2249, 2314.

list *v.* wish (to do sth.) 291, 1881; *impers. pt. sg.* **luste** 2481.

litarge *n.* litharge, one of the two proximate materials of the 'stone' 1134, 1198, 1204, 1605, 1632; **water of** ~ ? a liquid resulting from mixing litharge in an acid 2235.

lyvydite *n.* pallidness 1831.

lokkis *n. pl.* locks 2918.

lond(e *n.* an area of ground 583; kingdom 551, 648, 944; **in towne and** ~ in town and country, everywhere 773; ~ **of god (light)** the Holy Land 1420.

longith *v. 3 pr. sg.* in ~ **for** concerns, pertains to 1252.

loore *n.* teaching 1672.

loose *v.* undo, untie, separate (elements) from a compound 2188.

lorde *n.* a lord 25, 582; God 696; Christ 989, 995; someone in charge 2693, 2708; a dominant element 1706; *astrol.* a planet in his 'house', i.e. the sign or part of the heavens where the planet is most powerful 2947, 2952; ~ **god (ihesu)** 165, 200, 995; **oure** ~ 261, 266, 959.

lowde *a.* talkative, boastful 823.

low(e *a.* low, close to the earth, earthy, 160, 1160; *sup.* **lowist** 2426.

lowly *adv.* humbly 988.

lowlye *a.* humble 270.

lunarye *n.* the fern moonwort 1056.

lune *n.* silver 1109.

lust *n.* wish, desire 536.

lusty(e *a.* healthy, vigorous 1051, 2602, 2608.

luxurious *a.* sensual 2158.

magnesia *n.* one of the two proximate ingredients of the 'stone' 1159, 1168, 1204, 1295, 1545, 1546, 1803, 1930, 2879, 2887.

magnete-stone *n.* loadstone 2930.

magre *prep.* in spite of 2724.

make *v.* manufacture, produce, make 115, 203, 661, 1142, 2224; build (a bridge) 634, carry out (a search, journey, trial) 18, 960, 2643, write (a book) 2, paint (a picture) 300; cause, force (sb. to do sth.) 41, 46, 232, 2328; cause (sth. to be in a certain condition) 174, 320; ordain (that sth. be the case) 117; ~ **no store** not hesitate, make no bones 103; **use makith mastrye** 3061; *pr. pl.* **make** 115, **makith** 320; *pt.* **made** 2643; *pp.* **made** 2, 634, 2224.

malgams *n. pl.* amalgams 1061.

malliable *a.* malleable 2505.

maner *n.* in **what** ~ what kind of 142, 588; **in** ~ in attitude 497; *pl.* **maners** customs, morals 230, 806, 1428.

manyfolde *a.* many and various 830, 2892; many 837; **bi** ~, by many times 1843.

marcasite *n.* in **our chosen** ~ one of the two proximate materials of the 'stone' 1136; *pl.* **marchasites** pyrites 1060.

mariage *n.* perfect union of opposite principles to form the philosophers' stone 2668.

mastir(e, maister *n.* master, teacher 216, 807, 820; alchemist 61, 718, 740, 2983; *pl.* **mastres** predominant knowledge 1687.

mastrie, maistrie *n.* craft, skill 181; mastery, control 1501, 3061; supreme achievement 1328; **for a** ~ excellently 467.

mater(e, matier *n.* substance, material 399, 410, 678, 888, 2630; constituent of the 'stone' 1108; topic, theme 166; affair 594; ~ **of oure stone** 148, 1038, 1112.

material(le *a.* constituent 1122; pertaining to matter (as opposed to form) 1748; made of matter 2435; the material cause 2963.

me *pron.* people in general 84.

mechanycalle *a. in* **arte** ~ handicraft 1334.

meddille, medle *v.* mingle, mix 50, 888, 912, 1963, 2516.

medicyn(e *n.* the philosophers' stone (considered as a medicine for metals) 440, 445, 951, 1327; medicament 1564, 1566; **red** ~ the red 'stone' 919.

medlyng *ger.* mingling 2321.

meen(e *adj.* intermediate, intervening 1240, 1537, 1539, 1784, 2112.

meete *v. intr.* encounter 334; join together 1469; *tr.* come in contact with 2322; *3 pr. sg.* **mett**; *pp.* **mett** 334.

mekille *a.* great 671, 984, 1368.

mene, meene *n.* a substance representing an intermediate stage between natural material and the finished work 1276, 1277, 1307, 2452; material used to make the 'stone', *in* **mineralle meenys** 1114, 1274, 2995; an intermediary 579; **bi** ~ **of** by means of 633.

menstruallis *n. pl.* the female element in the union of two components of the stone, sophic mercury 2672.

mercurie *n.* one of the components of metals, and of the 'stone'; not ordinary mercury 1108, 1111; **crude** ~, quicksilver 2272.

merdis *n. pl.* dung 1057.

mesure *n.* proportion 1577; moderation 196.

metal(le *n.* metal 112, 356, 382, 413; ~ **kynd** metallic nature 2498.

mezereon *n.* a small shrub, *Daphne mezereon* 1055.

microcosmos *n.* microcosm 1718, 2510.

mightly *adv.* strongly 1722, 2723.

mylt(e *v. intr.* melt 1618, 3055.

mynd(e *n.* mind, soul, character 121, 285, 471, 528; intention, purpose (esp. *pl.*) 111, 571, 608, 686, 731; attention, interest 333; remembrance 104, 168, 914, 2575.

myne *n.* a mine 52, 457, 2078; as a collective term for minerals 1331, 1567.

minerall *n.* a mineral substance 376, 1060.

mineral(le *a. in* **meenys** ~ mineral components of the 'stone'; 1114, 1274, 1295; **vertu** ~ occult force developing minerals in the earth 394.

mynystre *n.* an operative, attendant 1347, 2740, 2741.

ministre *v.* attend to, look after 1120, 2758.

myrre *n.* myrrh 1997.

mysliking *a.* displeasing, unpleasant 2002.

mysse *n. in* **withowte** ~ certainly 1826.

mys(se *v. intr.* fail 2022, 2235, 2889.

mystily *adv.* obscurely 3019.

mixte *pp.* compounded 1818, 1891.

mixtions *n. pl.* mixtures, recipes for mixtures 2360.

moch(e *a.* much 285, 511; many 18, 76, 1385.

mocione *n.* proposal 811.

moist(e *a. & n.* damp, 2911; describing the primary quality of wetness 1505, 1513, 2352; *as n.* the primary quality of wetness 1573, 2127.

moystnes *n.* moisture 2342.

moystour, moisture, moyster *n.* the primary quality of wetness 1455, 1476, 1752; dampness 3011.

mollifie *v.* soften 2503.

mo(o *a.* more 69, 236, 521, 686, 1410.

more *a. & adv. comp.* larger 384, 409; more 737, 861; ~ **and lasse**, great and small, everyone; *as adv.* farther 864; further, 1797.

mortagon *n.* a kind of lily, *Lilius martagon* 1056.

mortified *pp.* of a metal: altered in form, calcined, corroded 1620.

most *n.* the greatest part 80.

most(e, moost(e *a. & adv. sup.* greatest 1528, 2448; *as adv.* most, very 220, 471, 762.

most(e, must(e *v.* must 218, 222, 237, 312, 509.

move *v.* affect, stir, urge, provoke 32, 793, 838, 1894; *pr. pl.* **movith** 32.

moveable *a.* mobile, changeable 1609, 2277, 2516.

mover *n. in ~ of ye orbe* primum mobile 2959.

multiplicacion *n.* increase in quantity 402; increase (of the elixir) in potency 1603, 2640.

multipli(e *v. intr.* increase in quantity 356, 359, 382, 386, 429; develop, grow 412; make gold 349; *tr.* make (gold etc.) increase in quantity 330.

multiplier(e *n.* fraudulent goldmaker 12, 336, 340, 433, 441; an element capable of producing increase in quantity 1629.

multiplying *ger.* increase, growth 416, 419, 1621, 1622; gold-making 443; *~ of our stone* increase in power and size of the Elixir 1630.

muse *v.* ponder 559, 1665.

mutable *a.* changeable, fickle 2727.

narde *n.* nard 1997.

nativite, nativitie *n.* horoscope 1399, 2957; birth, moment of production 2531, 2532.

natural(le *a.* natural 78, suited to a specific nature 380; **hete ~**, **~ hete**, see **hete**; **magik ~** 479; **spirite ~**, see **spirit(t.**

nature *n.* nature in general 358, 710, 2403; the particular nature or characteristics of an individual or species 373, 2022, 2293; a substance (of a particular nature) 160, 1220, 1331, 1648, 2367.

necligent *a.* negligent 883.

nede *n. & a.* lack, want, necessity 191, 813; **no ~** no reason, no cause 808; **he hathe ~** he must 108; *as adj.* necessary 849.

nede *adv.* of necessity 218.

nede *v.* have need (to do sth.) 529, 820; *impers.* **it ~** there is need 1375, 2682; **hym nedethe** he must 120; *3 pr. sg.* **nede** 1375, 2682, **nedethe** 120, **nedith** 1329.

ned(e)ly *adv.* of necessity, necessarily 222, 1306, 2949.

nedis *adv.* of necessity 852, 2728.

nere *a. comp.* nearer 468.

nere *adv.* narrowly, closely, 838; densely 1818; *comp.* **nere** closer 2331.

new *a.* fresh, new, novel 728, 732; **of (the) ~** newly, recently 643, 2417, 2843; **~ and ~**, continually, without fail 1623.

nyce, nyse *a.* foolish 50, 146, 652, 693.

ny(e *a. & adv.* close, close to 976, 1386, 1888; *as adv.* nearly 986.

nigromancye *n.* necromancy 2979.

nyhenes *n.* closeness 225.

nobilly *adv.* splendidly, well 2867.

noght(e, nogth(e *n.* nothing, nought 48, 278, 1062, 2848.

nombre *n.* proportion, numeration of proportional parts 1577, 1580, 1581, 1656; rhythm, metre, 2363, 2364, 2365.

norshide *v. 3 pt. sg.* fostered, nourished 541.

nutricion *n.* nutriment 2192.

obedience, obediens *n.* monastic rule 618; **have ~ to** be influenced by 1681, 1991, 2942.

obedient *a. in ~ to**, influenced by 1983, 2928.

obscuryte *n.* darkness 1814.

observith *v. 3 pr. sg.* preserves, fulfills 3004.

occean *n.* the ocean 2261.

occupied *pp.* used, in use 2267, 2899; employed 2767.

odour(e *n.* odour, scent 1766, 1960.

offende *v.* be incompatible with (sth.), disturb 1788; upset natural process 2422.

oyle *n.* oil 1268, 2305.

olde *a.* old 455; of ancient times, *in ~ faders* (men) the ancient sages 79, 144, 2831; *comp.* **eldire** 2606; *sup.* **eldist** 1407.

onychine *n.* onyx 1544.

onyd *pp.* joined, united 420.

onward(e *a.* advanced, ahead 1300; impetuous 2711.

operacion *n.* experiment, process, course of work 1062, 2362, 2629, 2780.

operatyfe *a.* active, acting 1484.

opinion *n.* theory, belief (opposed to proven knowledge) 485, 732, 2033.

opposid *pp.* opposite 1723.
oppresse *v. intr.* cause hardship 194; *tr.* persecute 1017; obfuscate, cloud 1780; *pr. pl.* **oppressith** 1780.
orbe *n.* in **mover of the ~** the primum mobile 2959.
ordeyne, ordeigne *v.* order, arrange, prescribe, dispose 156, 379, 500, 1187, 2349, 2408, 3032; arrange to have, make 654, 2774.
ordinalle *n.* ordinal, an ecclesiastical calendar showing the day-by-day liturgy for the Church year 127 129, 1379, 2496.
ordir(e, ordre *n.* proper arrangement, order 126, 252; **owte of ~** in disarray 1212; **bi ~** in sequence 2425.
ordire, ordre *v.* set in order 1216; arrange 2345.
ordirlye *adv.* in order 132.
organallis *n. pl.* organs 2093, 2095.
orient *a.* bright as morning 1839, 2270.
ornate *a.* embellished 1648.
othir(e, other, odir(e *a.* other 203, 658, 823, 1094, 1119.
outward *a.* from an external source 1698, 1732; on the outside 1880; extraneous 122.
ovir *adv.* excessively; **~ bolde** rash 885; **~ hastelie** too quickly 1243; **~ sharpe** very bitter 2104; **~ stronge** too strong 2105; **~ swifte** premature 39; **~ white** too pale 2154.
ovirealle *adv.* everywhere 1024.
ovirseyne, oversayne *pp.* read through 176; mistaken, deluded 2357.
ovyrtake *v.* understand 512.
owtrage *n.* desecration 287, 992.
owtrage *v.* desecrate 2602.

payne, peyne *n.* distress, sorrow, hardship 700, 703, 723; trouble, difficulty 64, 146, 741; **take ~** take the trouble 1140.
parabols *n. pl.* allegorical or symbolical utterances 63.
paralisie *n.* paralysis 2076.
parte *n.* portion, part 796, 1119; **for the most ~** mostly 324; **have no ~** have no share, have no

influence 118, 227; **of the deville his ~** from the devil 756.
passe *v.* move, go 2405, 2406; go away 2719; **~ out** escape, emanate 1930, 2804; *pp.* **past(e** fulfilled 716, 2569; dead, passed away 603, 986, 2575.
passinge *pr. p.* surpassing 2675.
passion *n.* change, the being acted on 1748.
passive *a.* non-active 1476; *as n.* 1481, 1723.
penetratife *a.* penetrating 1969, 2062.
perceive *v.* understand, realize, recognize 403, 1215, 1440, 1511; *pr. pl.* **perceyvyn** 403.
perfeccion *n.* maturity, completion 1692, 1726; flawlessness 2248, 2370; something flawless (i.e. the 'stone') 1236.
perfit(e, parfite *a.* perfect, complete 392, 458, 2668; thorough 1240; fully skilled 2362.
perfitly *adv.* fully, completely 211, 1720.
permanent *a.* remaining stable, permanent 2238, 2339.
permyscible *a.* able to be well mixed 1612.
perse *v.* penetrate 1465, 2064; affect, have an effect on 838.
persone *n.* personality; **in your ~** you yourself 845.
perspectyfe *a.* in **science ~** science of optics 1683.
perspicuate *a.* transparent 1785.
perspicuatly *adv.* clearly, transparently 1863.
perspicuyte *n.* transparency 1155, 1789, 1848.
philosophers *n. pl.* alchemists 440, 2413.
philosophie *n.* knowledge 53, 183; natural philosophy, science 867, 1509; **comon (firste) ~** natural philosophy 312, 1441, 1509, 1883, 2220.
phisik(e *n.* the science of medicine 478, 1562; **~ of mynys** science of perfecting metals, 1567.
planet *n.* planet 271, 2411; *gen. sg.* **planet** 2962.

plate *n.* silver (or gold) plate 115, 328.

plesance *n.* pleasure 550.

plese *v.* please 332, 636, 1998; ~ their ententis, satisfy their desires 1928; *pr. pl.* plesith 1998.

plumpis *n. pl.* pumps 2443.

point(e *n.* piece of knowledge 306, 1091, 1225, 2636; a very small amount 3039, 3040; point (of a needle) 2931.

poyses *n. pl.* poems 63.

pollible *a.* polishable 1867.

ponder, pondire *n.* weight 1576, 1580, 1585; *pl.* pondres 1585.

ponderose, ponderous *a.* important 177; heavy 2459.

pontike *a.* rather sour, astringent 2121.

popyngayes *n. pl.* parrots, 2100.

portreture *n.* drawing 300.

porturide *pp.* pictured, drawn 2842.

pose *n.* cold in the head 3034.

poticaris, see **apotecarys**.

poware, power *n.* power, efficacy 1737, 1758.

practice *n.* practical work, practical operation 65, 103, 1102, 1346, 1487; practical experience 716.

practice *v.* engage in practical work 1042.

pray(e *n.* desired object 326, 1180, 1210, 2757.

precipitacion *n.* taking out of solution 2783.

premyssis *n. pl.* preliminary plans, preparations 2969.

preparacion(e *n.* preliminary operations 1445, 2872, 3054.

prese *n. in* putt in ~ bestir (oneself), take pains 4, 36, 1259.

present *n.* the present time 785; gift 520; the affair in hand 247.

preservatife *a.* preserving life 2597.

prestehode *n.* the clergy 1028.

presume *v.* be overconfident 285.

presumyng *a.* presumptuous 720.

pretende *v.* portend, presage 2957.

prime *a.* primary 1474, 1493.

principalle *a. & n.* most powerful, predominant 1914; ~ agent dominant quality 1750, 1753, 1757; *as n.* dominant quality 1770, 1914; primary material 2373, 2375.

privacion *n.* lack, deprivation 1521, 2162.

private *n.* removed, lacking 1522.

privite *n.* secret knowledge 172.

profe *n.* proof 483, 489; *pl. provis* 830.

profett, profite *n.* something useful, profit 520, 2507.

profitable *a.* useful 1602, 2082, advantageous, money-saving 2850.

profite *v.* be of use to 1004.

proieccion *n.* transmutation by casting the 'powder' on to molten metal 3060.

prompte *a.* ready 1102.

propertie, propurtie *n.* individual characteristic 1161, 1307, 1489, 2239.

propinquyte *n.* close relationship, similarity 437.

proporcion *n.* ratio (of one element to another) 1560, 1588, 1591, 1668, 1932; musical ratio of pitches of notes 1667; accuracy of temper in a compound 1064.

proporcionally *adv.* in due ratio 1656.

propre *a.* peculiar, individual, own 102, 1730, 1877, 2962.

proprelye *adv.* appropriately 2786.

prosperite *n.* well-being 2388.

prosperous *a.* healthy 2390.

prove, preve *v.* demonstrate, show, prove 205, 211, 414, 846, 2466; test, check 318, 828; ~ your entent check your plan; *3 pr. sg.* previth 414; *pp.* provid(e 211, 846, 205.

providence *n.* care, caution 722.

puncte *n.* instant 775.

purchase *v.* buy 583, 586; gain, acquire 528, 1030.

pure *a.* unadulterated, unalloyed 458, 768, 1220, 1987; clear, intelligible 873; *comp.* purire 2369.

pursue, pursew(e *v.* search, seek, sue 291, 532; follow 126, 644; ~ for seek for 309, 668.

put *v. in* ~ in prese, see prese; be put away be discharged from service 1363; *pr. pl.* puttith 4; *pp.* put 1363.

putrefaccion *n.* rotting, decomposition 361, 365.

putrefie, putrifie *v. intr.* rot, decompose 2015, 2040, 2050.

quadripartite *n.* a work in four books, or in four parts 477.

qualite *n.* used for **elemente** 2341.

qualitees *n. pl.* the four primary factors heat, cold, moistness, dryness, constituting the four elements 1475, 1476, 1493, 2021, 2096, 2295.

queynt *a.* strange, odd 297.

quenching *ger.* extinguishing, dousing 2020.

quykke, quyck, quike *a.* alive, volatile 1520; immediate 1360; immediately intelligible 171; retaining natural properties 2628, 2788.

quyknys *n.* life 1708.

quyksilver *n.* mercury 1199, 1854, 2317; sophic mercury, considered a major constituent of metals 1851.

quynt(e essence *n.* the fifth element 907, 2245.

quyte *v.* repay 2680.

rage, raage *v. intr.* act wildly 1063; have an over-great effect 1772.

rayle *v.* assert vehemently 329; ~ **abowte** wander about 619.

rangyng *pr. p.* travelling, wandering 550.

rarified *pp.* expanded, thinned 222.

rawe *a.* raw 1280; ~ **cley**, unbaked clay 2791.

rebate *v.* restrain, reduce 1903, 2158.

receptis, receytis *n. pl.* recipes, formulae 90, 99, 100, 554, 1052.

reche *v.* attain to, succeed in 142, 215, 1591.

recomforte *v.* provide relief from, aid recovery from 2770.

recreacion *n.* relief, encouragement 1105.

rectificacion *n.* purification (by a distilling process) 2430.

red(d)e, reede *a.* red 459, 1532; ~ **werk**, the operations producing the red 'stone' 2644 ~ **stone (medycine)** the red elixir transmuting metals to gold 919, 2590.

reddolent *a.* fragrant 1963.

refluence *n.* reflux, reaction 2374.

refuge *n.* something reliable 2058.

refuse *v.* reject 221, 1601, 2227.

regymentis *n. pl.* governance, control 164, 2982.

regnyng *a. in* ~ **element (qualite)** dominant quality 1944, 2341.

regnyth *v.* 3 *pr. sg.* flourishes 1024, 1811.

reherse *v.* tell, recount 1162, 1438, 1466, 2323, 2814; repeat (sb.), quote 2649; go through 2456.

relesse *v.* relax 1371.

remanent *n. & a.* the remainder, the others 1196, 1376; *as adj.* remaining 1759.

remitt *v.* consign, dismiss 308.

renewe *v.* repeat 1748.

repaire *v.* go 376.

repeyre *v.* strengthen, renew 799.

reporte *n. in* make ~ decide 2167.

repugnance *n.* incompatibility, opposition 1906.

resolve *v.* loosen, disintegrate 1973, 2007, 2296.

resonable *a.* according to reason 595, 876; fair, moderate 2751.

reson(e, resoun *n.* an argument, ground for belief 75, 387, 391; the faculty of reason 803, 900.

resorte *v.* move, go 1833; *fig.* 1635; return 2190; have recourse to 84, 569, 2168.

respecte *n.* regard, consideration 2173; ~ **of** in respect of, compared with 2482.

reste *v.* remain, remain undestroyed 2576, 2667; ~ **in** depend on 1569; ~ **upon** hang over 244.

reteyne *v.* keep back, retard 1990; contain 2371.

rew *n. in* **bi** ~ **in** sequence 1756.

rewnyng *n.* rennet 2312.

ryalle *n.* the Rose Noble or Ryal, a gold coin worth ten shillings 933.

right *n. in* **of** ~ by rights 120, 444; **with** ~ correctly 2214.

right, rigth, ri3t *adv.* very 43, 821; absolutely 2848.

rightful *a.* having a right, true 243; righteous 537.

rodi(e *a.* reddish brown, red 1132, 1135; ~ **man** red man, the masculine principle in the alchemical marriage, sophic sulphur 2664.

roffe *n.* roof 484.

rombled *v. pt. pl.* wandered 1045.

rubie *a.* red as a ruby 1809; ~ **stone** the 'red stone' 2562.

rude *a.* unrefined, uneducated 3089, 3091; rough, crude 391; great, large 2476.

rufe *a.* brownish red 1536.

sadde *a.* serious, sober 2901; *comp.* sadder, duller 1845.

sai(ne, sei(ne *v.* say 911, 1168, 3061; *3 pr. sg.* seithe 758, 1100; *pr. pl.* say 209, sei 199, sayes 500, says 359; *pt.* saide 573; seide 427.

salandyne *n.* celandine, probably the common celandine 1055.

sal armonyak(e *n.* sal-ammoniac 1113, 1193.

saltish(e *a.* tasting of salt 2113, 2134.

sapour *n.* the sense of taste 1766, 2053, 2057, 2082; taste, flavour 1977; ~ **pontike** 2121, ~ **styptike** 2122.

save *a.* safe 818.

scallid *pp.* scalded 2993.

scamony *n.* scammony, a kind of resin 1889.

scantly *adv.* scarcely, 2589, 2603.

scoffe *n.* taunt 48.

scoore *n.* **in vppon the** ~ **on the** tally, on credit 2550.

seche *v.* seek, investigate 5, 378; *pr. pl.* seche 113, 315 sechene 704, sechithe 790, seekis 2461; *pt.* sought, sowght 474, 1045, soght 869; *pp.* sowght 188, soght(e 277, 2329, sowgth(e 1080, 2699.

sechers *n. pl.* seekers 311.

secrete *n.* something secret, hidden 9, 908, 1179.

secrete *a. & adv.* secret 183; taciturn 823; *sup.* secretiste 306; *as adv.* in an occult way 2212.

secte *n.* those of a particular theory or persuasion 207.

se(e *v.* see 2, 783; *pr. pl.* see 66, seeis 1876; *pt.* sawe 999; *pp.* sayne 145, 566, seyne 699, 1141.

seek *a.* ill, sick 2180.

selcouth *a.* strange, marvellous, rare 172, 217, 2632.

seld *a.* few, rare 1696.

selfe *a.* selfsame 2014.

sende *v.* send 216; *pp.* **sende** 158.

sensityfe *a.* having sensation, sensitive 430.

sentence *n.* meaning, 171, 177, 454; aphorism, saw 357, 789; judgement, threat 243; **geve** ~, make a decision 1492.

seperable *a.* separate 2083.

seperacion *n.* analysis by resolving into the four elements 2779, 2867, 3002; purifying, extraction 2431.

seperate *a.* separated from impurities, extracted, purified 1133.

serve *v.* be of service for, be effective for 957, 2038, 2853, 2871; provide for 2854; worship 918; be an operative in (an alchemical operation) 2071; ~ **for** effect 2431, 2872.

service *n.* service 346, 969; religious services 130; **do your** ~ effect your plan 1127.

seson *n.* a particular period of time; **at this** ~ now 1190; **in (good)** ~ in good time, quickly 48, 1260, 1421; **that** ~ at that time 730, 899.

set *v.* fix, place (the mind, a feeling etc.) 333, 535, 555, 616, 1339; arrange, dispose, establish 798, 1212, 1241, 1579, 1690, 2215; ~ **adowne** destroy 241; ~ **afyre** 1516; ~ **aparte (asyde)** disregard 518, 2974; ~ **out** display, publish, 129, 132, 3089; *pt.* set(t 616, 1241; *pp.* sett 111, 333.

seth *conj.* since, because 1457.

seve *n.* sieve 314.

sewe *v.* petition, ask 1359.

shap(p)e *n.* shape 451, 1341, 2777.

sharpe *a.* pungent (in taste) 2110, 2118, 2138.

shent *pp.* punished, ruined 7579.

shew *v. intr.* appear, be apparent 1992; *tr.* tell of, deal with 737, 1038, 2582; reveal 96, 348, 1084; demonstrate 387, 1762; adduce (arguments) 75; communicate 594.

shorte wittide *a.* unable to concentrate, scatter-brained 2727.

shrewde *a.* evil, wicked 608.

shrewys *n. pl.* malignant planets 2948.

siccite *n.* dryness 1721, 1799, 2207, 2437, 3021.

sydyre *n.* cider 2304.

signe *n.* symptom, evidence 1765; 2051; constellation 2945, 2961.

sympire, sympre *v.* simmer 1265, 1268.

simple *a.* uncompounded 1220, 1679.

simplicite, symplicitie *n.* lack of complexity in composition 417, 1888, 2939.

sympring *ger.* simmering 1264.

singuler *a.* unique 184.

sisely *adv.* competently, thoroughly 1244.

skylle *n.* knowledge 1311; reason, cause 2031.

slyde *v.* slip, descend 110.

slymye *a.* viscous 1815.

slow *a.* tardy, behindhand 762.

slowfulle *a.* slothful 1101.

smaragde *n.* emerald 1817.

smylle *n.* odour, smell, stench 1959, 2004, 2025, 2035.

smylle *v. intr.* give off a smell 2005, 2032; *tr.* to smell 1958, 1965; ~ **to** sniff at 2019.

smyllyng *ger.* the sense of smell 1943, 1947, 2093.

smytt *pp.* stricken 2076.

smokish *a.* like smoke 1973.

snofe *n.* burnt end of candlewick 2020.

socoure *n.* support, assistance 1262, 1453; basis, ? cause 2028.

socoure *v.* support 2242.

soeffre *v. intr.* be patient 591; *tr.* endure 1408; experience, undergo the action of 1477, 2790; allow 1911.

solace *n.* comfort 844, 1020; support 579.

soleyne *a.* solemn, sacred 61; reserved 828.

solide *a.* hardened, solid 1721, 2064.

sondyfere *n.* sandiver, glass gall 1059.

soote *a.* sweet 1879, 1950.

sophisticate *a.* fallacious 1652.

sowre *a.* sour 2103, 2110.

sowrish(e *a.* rather sour 2121, 2149.

space *n.* lapse of time, time 190, 211, 849, 969, 2725.

spare *v.* leave immune, spare 319; shirk (labour) 1319, 2577.

sparkille *n.* small spark 1626, 1628.

speciall(e *a.* particular, individual 1762, 1790, 2962; **in** ~ in detail 1343, especially 3047.

specious *a.* beautiful 1305, 1796.

speculacion *n.* theory 1488.

speke *v.* talk, speak 648, 850; *pp.* **spoke** 2214, **spoken** 2219.

spende *v.* spend 560, 1046; *pp.* **spendide** 1051.

spere *n.* the planetary and sidereal heavens considered as a unit 160, 397, 2704; one of the nine spheres of heaven 2960.

spille *v. intr.* be spoilt 2003; *tr.* ruin, destroy 240, 719, 962, 3056.

spirit(t *n.* volatile substance 3058; a tenuous material able to penetrate solids 2377; ~ **animalle** principle of sensation and voluntary motion 2381, 2386; ~ **naturalle** principle of the individual's character 2380, 2384; ~ **vitalle** principle of life 2379, 2383.

spiritual(l *a.* volatile, fluid 1968, 2243, 2804.

staynours *n. pl.* makers of stained glass 35.

stele *v. 3 pt. pl.* stole 894.

stilling *ger.* distilling 2306.

stynch(e *n.* stink 2007, 2012, 2013, 2018.

stiple *n.* steeple 301.

stiptike *a.* harsh in taste 2122.

stonde *v.* be in a certain position 2881; ~ **bi** depend on 1786; ~ **for** constitute 2273; *3 pt. sg.* **stode** 2881.

stondinge *a.* stable 2280.

stone *n.* a hard solid non-metallic, non-combustible substance, a stone 1129, 1130, 1131, 1175; **oure** ~ the philosophers' 'stone' 148, 744, 1038, 1080; **adamant** ~, **carbuncle** ~ 663, 1801.

stoppell *n.* stopper 2890, 2891, 2892.

store *n.* quantity 919, 2268; **kepe in** ~, keep secret 1223; **make no** ~, make no bones, make no objection 1103.

stownde *n.* space of time 931.

straite *a.* strict 828.

straitly *adv.* strictly 229.

stronge *a.* violent 2076; powerful 2006; *comp.* **strenger** fiercer 1736.

suauyte *n.* gentleness, calm 2726.

subiecte *n.* something placed below 1933.

sublimacion *n.* sublimation 2784.

sublyme *v.* sublime 3057.

substance *n.* material 1070, 1496, 1694, 2046, 2126, 2675.

substancial(le *a.* forming a substance 1726; **forme ~,** substantial form, distinct essence 1747.

subtile *a.* thin, tenuous, rare 1132, 1862, 2063, 2393; intellectually subtle, refined 54, 1656, 1754; delicate 2554; crafty 730; **~ werk,** the more skilled and demanding part of the alchemist's work 155, 1382, 1438.

subtilnes *n.* rarity, tenuousness 2042, 2396.

subtraye *v.* subtract 2349.

succendid(e *pp.* set on fire, burnt 1809, 1823.

suerte, sewertie *n.* assurance 555, 792, 2092, 2098.

sulphur(e *n.* sulphur 1197, 2002; ? sophic sulphur 1112; **~ of kynde** natural sulphur 1193.

summe *n.* end, conclusion 1463.

superduced *pp.* added 1805.

superegression *n.* going too far 1272.

surcharge *n.* excess 1064.

suspendide *pp.* counteracted 1824.

swage *v.* reduce, tone down 1771.

swete *n.* exudation, exhalation 1240, 1974, 2996.

take *v.* seize, take 909, 953, 979; use 1110, 1113; **~ downe** knock down 304; **~ for** consider as 629; **~ charge** take notice 288; **~ dowte** be doubtful 878; **~ fortune** accept (one's) luck 307; **~ ground** base (itself, an argument) 1219, 2427; **~ swete** go through a process of dehumidification 1240; **~ thought** worry 671; *pt.* **toke** 671, 677, 979; *pp.* **take** 629, 953.

talagis *n. pl.* levies, tallages 1026.

taste, taaste *v.* taste 2144, **~ of** experience 736.

tawny *a.* brown 1821.

tech(e *v.* teach 141, 151; *pt.* **taghte** 810, **tagthe** 1088, 1091, **tawghte** 796; *pp.* **taght** 210, **tagth** 2587, **taught** 695, **tawgthe** 706.

telle *v.* tell 44; *pr. pl.* **tellith** 2229; *pp.* **told** 886, 939.

temperate *a.* moderate, of medium quality 2000.

terebentyne *n.* turpentine 2303.

termynat(e *a.* bounded, having a boundary 1821, 1866, 1869.

termynede, termynyd *pp.* same as **terminate,** 1500, 1778, 1862.

terrestreite *n.* earthiness 1781, 1846.

thik(ke *a.* dense 1517, 1519, 1827, 2199.

think(e *v.* believe, opine 561, 596, 1959; **me think** it seems to me 990; *pt.* **thoght** 561, 835, 952.

thyn(n)e *a.* rare 1988, 2199.

thof(e *conj.* although 249, 637.

thoght(e, thoʒt *n.* thought 257; anxiety 665, 671.

thrifte *n.* money, property, savings 40, 676.

tyncture *n.* colour 38; the process of colouring 2813; 'colouring', i.e. transmutation of base metals 182, 1607, 1649; ability to transmute 2535.

tiraunys *n. pl.* overbearing or unruly men 976.

titanos *n.* a name for magnesia 1162.

toties *n. pl.* tutiae, or tutties, zinc oxide 1060.

transmutacion *n.* change in quality (of base metal to silver or gold) 2432, 2519, 2524.

transmutide *pp.* transmuted 435, 2523, 2525.

tregedie *n.* trickery 343.

tremeling *pr. p.* trembling 2631.

tryne *a.* **in ~ aspecte** an angle of 120 degrees between two heavenly bodies 2950.

trouth, trowithe *n.* truth 96, 847.

turne *v. intr.* **in ~ to (into)** become 278, 2402; **~ to charge** render (one) subject to a penalty 1181; *tr.* change 606; *pp.* **tornyde** 278, **turned** 606.

twynkelinge *ger.* sparkling 1803.

unce *n.* an ounce 428, 1137, 1146, 1157.

unctuous *a.* one of the nine tastes, fatty, greasy 2110, 2118, 2131.

undersowre *a.* one of the nine tastes, a little sour 2115.

understond(e *v.* know, understand 150, 552, 943, 1021; *pt.* **undirstode** 1094; *pp.* **understond** 867.

undirwhite *a.* off-white, pallid 1543.

unformyd *pp.* unformed, in an elemental state 1679.

unknow(e *pp.* unknown 14, 1166; 1695.

unorderide *pp.* set out of order, confused 131.

unsaverye, unsavory *a.* tasteless, insipid 2123, 2162.

unstable *a.* fluid, not fixed 2278.

unthryfe *v. intr.* lose money 46.

unwroȝt *pp.* not formed into a substance, in an elemental state 1679.

uryne, ureyne *n.* urine 1057, 1550.

use *n.* practice, experience 3061; habit 1317; employment 658.

use *v. intr.* be accustomed 889, 1832; *tr.* employ, make use of 58, 441, 722, 1602, 1728.

utmoste *a. sup.* outermost 1499.

utterid *pp.* revealed, betrayed 942.

vapoure *n.* mist, gas 1805.

variance *n.* difference, variation 1816, 2684, 2686.

vegetatife *a.* characteristic of vegetable life, vegetable 430, 1890.

veyne, vayne *n.* a vein (of metal) 384, 408, 413.

venenous *adv.* poisonously, sharply 2105.

venome *a.* acid 2678.

verbayn *n.* vervain 1056.

verray *a.* true, genuine 841, 1073, 2012.

vertually *adv.* intrinsically 2031, potentially 421.

vertu(e, vertew *n.* power, property 394, 1604, 2239; virtue, moral good 213, 228, 751; a good habit 230, 248, 802; good habits in general 1436.

vertuous, vertuys *a.* virtuous 806; conducive to virtue 206.

vessell *n.* container, glass 389, 2783, 2794.

vicious *a.* evil 1029, 1032, 1893; impure 1306.

vyle *a.* cheap 1143, dirty, unpleasant 1306; *sup.* **viliste**, least noble 1601.

virtualle *a.* possessing intrinsic efficacy; ∼ **hete** natural heat 1740.

vitalle *a.* supporting life at the vegetable level 2379; **spirite** ∼ see **spirit(t.**

vitrialle *n.* a metal sulphate, usually copper or iron sulphate 1059.

voide *v. intr.* disappear, escape 1196; *tr.* get rid of, remove 192, 193, 946, 1349, 2106.

vole, voole *n.* foal (of a mare), offspring (of the elephant) 2020, 2477, 2478.

wacch *n.* staying awake 1249.

wachlew *a.* wakeful 2743.

wanhope *n.* despair 800.

wash *v.* wash, cleanse 2283, 2536; *pr. pl.* **washen** 2283; *pp.* **washen** 2536.

water, watir(e *n.* water 314, 404, 1478, 2308; body of water, stream 3065; tears 1000; the element water 1597, 1610, 2423, 2444; a special fluid 2492, 2497; ? alcoholic liquid 2306.

water flowris *n. pl.* flowers growing in water 378.

watirly *a.* of the element water 1805, 1826.

ween(e *v.* believe, opine, think mistakenly 249, 290, 544, 870, 2420, 2422, 2497; *pr. pl.* **ween(e** 870, 2420, 2422, **wenyth** 290.

welnere *adv.* almost 1158, 1229, 1830.

wenynge *ger.* thinking, believing 487.

werish *a.* one of the nine tastes, tasteless 2113, 2123, 2152.

werk(e, worke *n.* work, piece of work, undertaking 6, 50, 255, 637, 928; project 587; task 509; operation 33, 719; **grosse** ∼, **subtile** ∼, see **grosse, subtile**; **white** ∼ the operations producing the white elixir 1128, 2951; **this** ∼ alchemy 474.

wexe *v.* increase 1628.

wexinge *ger.* growing 2542.

white *a.* white 1135; ~ **stone**, the elixir for silver 1192, 2586; ~ **werk**, the process for obtaining this 1128.

wille *n.* desire, wish 377, 563, 1008; **at (aftir) your** ~ as you wish 2345, 2858; **do your** ~ 998; **have** ~ have one's wish 239, have an intention 1312.

wil(le *v.* desire, wish 246, 309, 963; *pt.* wolde 963.

willing *pr. p.* wishing, intending 552.

wyn(ne *v. intr.* attain one's object 1448; *tr.* gain, acquire 5, 326, 560, 2200, 2620; effect 3017; succeed 1200; attain to, achieve 228, 705, 815, 1002, 1040; ~ **victorie** 2671; *pt.* wanne 2620; *pp.* wonn 2671.

wynnynge *ger.* profit 2546.

wise *n.* manner 59, 136, 1013; *pl.* wisys 749, 1335, 2971.

wise *a.* clever, capable, intelligent 133, 294, 1128; informed, alert 345; *comp.* wisere 791.

wite *v.* know, discover 588, 659, 740; *pt.* wiste 659.

witt *n.* mental power, intelligence 286, 707, 779; mind 213.

witty *a.* intelligent 891, 1347.

wondir(e, wondre *a.* wondrous, wonderful 162, 297, 1034, 1172, 2203, 2613.

wone, woone *a.* dull, wan 1538, 1825.

woode *a.* mad 679.

worche, werch *v. intr.* do work, perform operations 722, 1066, 1228; *tr.* do 106, 2847; make, effect 102, 190, 258, 2700; ~ **illusion** effect a deceit 12; *pr. pl.* worch 12, worchyn 1228; *pt.* wroȝt 258; *pp.* wroght 102, 190, wrogth 2700, 2847.

worching, wirching *ger.* operation, working 710, 1678, 1882, 2282; ~ **place** work-place 2702; **in** ~ in process 2060.

wordly *a.* worldly 13, 509.

wors *a. comp.* worse 1036; **for better ne for** ~ in any circumstances 169; *sup.* worste 880.

wrech *n.* evil, wretchedness 245.

wreke *n.* violence; *in* do ~ 1582.

write *v.* write 55, 89, 548; *pt.* wrote 71, 77, 621, 840; *pp.* write 1150, writen 99, 689, wrete 757.

INDEX OF NAMES AND WORKS

Albert, Albertus Magnus 1330, 1592, 1631, 2637, 2823–4. Now St. Albert. He deals with alchemy in Books iii and iv of his *De Mineralibus*, and considered transmutation possible. However, he was influenced by the genuine works of Avicenna as well as the spurious *De Anima*, and his own observations led him to believe that most alchemical gold and silver were false. An alchemical work attributed to him, *Libellus de Alchimia*, has been edited by Virginia Heines, 1958.

Alchymus 470. A mythical king, alleged to be the founder of alchemy. He is so presented in a letter of Thomas of Bologna to Bernard of Treves (Thorndike, iii. 33).

Anaxagoras 77, 1100, 1291, 1583, 1593, 1760, 2479, 3047. One of the speakers in the *Turba Philosophorum*, speeches 3 and 54. I have not traced Norton's references to him or to the work **Conversion(s Naturalle** 78, 1761.

Arisleus 2211. This name in Latin versions of the *Turba Philosophorum* is shown by Ruska in his edition to be a corruption via Arabic spelling and Latin transliteration of the Greek name, Archelaos. He is given the fifth speech in the work.

Aristotil(le 70, 81, 1485, 1905, 2215, 2246. The pseudo-Aristotle, author of the *Secreta Secretorum* (**Boke of Secretis**), from which extracts are taken, 1905 ff., 2216; see the text in R. Steele, *Opera hactenus inedita Rogeri Baconi*, fasc. v, p. 115.

Arnalde, Arnolde 1099, 1217, 1251. Arnald of Villanova (a. 1250–1311), physician to James II of Aragon and Pope Boniface VIII. Several alchemical works are attributed to him, the most famous being *Rosarium Philosophorum*. (See Thorndike, ii. 842–73, Sarton, *Introduction to the History of Science*, ii. 893–900.)
The book **Multipharie** does not seem to be by him.

Avicenna, Avycenn 67, 1235. The famous philosopher. The most important spurious alchemical work attributed to him is the *De Anima* or *Porta Elementorum*, called by Norton **Porta** (1235). For his unfavourable view of alchemy see Introduction, p. lix.

Bacon, Bakon 69, 625, 1225, 1233, 1587, 1592, 1672, 1673, 2638. One of the first Englishmen to interest himself in alchemy. He refers to it in his *Opus Maius* (*c.* 1266), and has sections on it in his *Opus Minus* (*c.* 1266) and *Opus Tertium* (*c.* 1267). He also wrote a commentary on the *Secreta Secretorum*, edited by Robert Steele. In addition a *Speculum Alchemiae* (in Zetzner, v. 844–61) and a *Tractatus Trium Verborum*, the three letters mentioned in 1673 (see Introduction, p. lxx) are attributed to him. (See Thorndike, ii. 616–91, and D. W. Singer, *Catalogue of Alchemical Manuscripts . . .*, Items 187–212.)

Boicius 1658. Boethius; for quotation from the *De Consolatione Philosophiae*, see iii, metra IX, 10.

Boke of Metyre 1634. Not traced.

Boke of Secretis see **Aristotil(le**.

Bryan 1041. Nothing further is known of him.

Bryse 1383. Hugh Brice, a goldsmith of London, appointed Clerk of the Mint, 2 February 1466, when the coinage was to be altered; sheriff of Middlesex

1475 and of London 1475–6. Presumably the Hugh Bryce who paid for the printing of Caxton's *Mirrour of the World* (1480).

Chawcer 1162. See *Canterbury Tales*, G 1456–7.

Conversion(s Naturalle 78, 1761. See **Anaxagoras.**

Dalton, Thomas 917 and frequently until 1005. Probably a real person. He had his red medicine from a Canon of Lichfield (966), and had been **Delves's** clerk (927). Since the Delves were a Staffordshire family it is natural to associate him with the diocese of Lichfield. The Cathedral archives were destroyed during the civil war, and so we have no evidence of his having been ordained there.

Delvis 926 and frequently to 1012. John Delves, beheaded after the Battle of Tewkesbury, 1471 (Stow, *Annales of England*, 1592, pp. 695–6). See Introduction, pp. xlix–l.

Democrite 68, 1086, 2237, 2269. Besides the pseudo-Democritus, author of the *Physika Kai Mystika*, the name occurs in the **Turba Philosophorum,** speech 6. D. W. Singer, *Catalogue of Alchemical Manuscripts* . . . , Item 8, lists a work attributed to him, printed in Zetzner, v. 78–83. I have not, however, succeeded in tracing any of Norton's references to him.

Gebere 67, 2991. Geber. A number of Latin works, dating probably from the end of the thirteenth century, under this name are available in an English translation by Richard Russell, 1678, reprinted by Holmyard in 1928. On the confusion of this name with Jabir ibn Hayyan, see von Lippmann, i. 362–3, ii. 89–92, iii. 69–70. The phrase 'Gebere his cokis' means ignorant alchemical experimenters like **Tonsile;** the same phrase is used by Ripley (Ashmole, *Theatrum Chemicum Britannicum*, p. 191).

Gilbert Kimere 1559. Died 1463. A Doctor of Medicine; Chancellor of Oxford 1431–4, 1446–53, Dean of Salisbury 1449–63.

Herbard(e Thomas, also **Herberd(e, Herbert** 922 and frequently to 1016. Brother of William Herbert, first Earl of Pembroke (see Introduction, pp. xlix–l).

Hermes 67, 470, 1937, 2271, 2633, 2659. Hermes Trismegistos, the Greek god identified with the Egyptian god Thoth. The legendary founder of alchemy. (See von Lippmann, *Ambix*, ii, no. 1 (June 1938), 21–5.) The poem **Laudabile Sanctum** (2659) is also attributed to Merlin. The most famous alchemical piece attributed to Hermes is the *Tabula Smaragdina*, quoted twice by Norton, *Ordinal* 1937, and 2063–4; a Latin version occurs in some versions of the *Secreta Secretorum*; it follows immediately the Norton citations referred to under **Aristotil(le,** and perhaps Norton read the text in this form.

Holton 1041. Nothing further is known of him.

Kalide 1433, 1435. Khalid ibn Yazid (635–704) apparently had books of Greek alchemy translated into Arabic, but no certain writings by him survive. He appears in the *Liber de Compositione Alchemiae*, translated *c.* 1144 by Robert of Chester. According to this he was visited by the alchemist Morienus Romanus **(Morien),** who successfully completed an alchemical demonstration for him and left secretly. Whereupon Khalid had a search made, found Morienus and brought him back. The body of the work mentioned consists of Khalid's questions and Morienus's answers. (See Thorndike, ii. 214–17; Holmyard, *Makers of Chemistry*, pp. 43–4.)

King Edward(e 921, 930. Edward IV.

Laudabile Sanctum 2659. A poem in Latin hexameters, also known as *Gemma Salutaris*. (See D. W. Singer, *Catalogue of Alchemical Manuscripts* . . . , Item 793. Also attributed to Merlin and Rhazes.) For the quotation (2661) see Zetzner, iii. 740.

Maria 2563, 2657. The probably real Mary the Jewess (see Introduction, p. liii) became in alchemical legend identified with Miriam, sister of Moses. For speculations associating the name with the Virgin Mary and one of Mohammed's wives 'Mary the Coptic Woman', see von Lippmann, ii. 142. The quotation in 2658 is not in any of Mary's speeches in the *Turba*. However, it is very like a passage in speech 69 by Fiorus (see Ruska, ed. *Turba*, p. 167).

Merlyn 68. See **Laudabile Sanctum**: for another work attributed to Merlin see D. W. Singer, *Catalogue of Alchemical Manuscripts* . . . , Item 373.

Morien 68, 1434, 1711. Morienus Romanus. For the legend see **Kalide**. The analogy of the generation of the stone and of man, 1711–12, appears in the *Liber de Compositione Alchemiae*, in Manget, i. 514.

Multipharie 1221. Probably the *Speculum Alchimiae* attributed to Roger Bacon, which imitates the opening of Paul's *Epistle to the Hebrews*: 'Multipharie multisque modis loquebantur olim philosophi . . .' (Zetzner, ii. 377–85).

Ortolane 68, 1450. Probably Martinus Ortholanus, author of *Practica Vera Alchemica*, and perhaps a *Clavis Sapientae Majoris*; he is implausibly identified by D. W. Singer with Joannes de Garlandia. (See D. W. Singer, *Catalogue of Alchemical Manuscripts* . . . , Item 32; Thorndike, iii. 176–90; John Ferguson, *Bibliotheca Chemica* (1906), i. 420–1, ii. 158.)

Pandophilus 2655. More commonly Pandolfus in Latin versions of the *Turba Philosophorum*, in which he has the fourth speech. The Latin tag quoted by Norton seems to be from this speech, cf. Waite's translation: 'But he who has tinged the venom of the wise out of the Sun and its shadow has arrived at the highest Arcanum' (p. 70). Ruska in his edition (p. 24) shows that the name is ultimately the Greek Empedocles; cf. **Arisleus**.

Philosophers Fest 757. Not traced. The quotation from it (758) occurs in a work of **Gebere** (Holmyard, ed., *The Works of Geber. Englished by Richard Russell, 1678*, p. 17), entitled 'Investigation or Search of Perfection'. An emendation of *Fest* to *Quest* is tempting but yields no better results from research.

Pictagoras 2214, 2251. Pythagoras, represented as chairman of the assembled sages in the *Turba Philosophorum*. It is the assembly, not only Pythagoras, who endorse the speech of **Pandophilus**. The quotation attributed to Pythagoras in 2254 I have not traced to any work bearing his name; it is a résumé of the whole alchemical opus, and is based on the *Emerald Table* (see Introduction, p. lxiii).

Plato 1161, 2217. See Skeat's note on the *Canterbury Tales*, G 1450. A pseudo-Platonic work, *Platonis Libri Quartorum cum commento Hebuhabes Hamed*, is printed in Zetzner, v. 101–85. I have not found the phrase 'stilla roris madii' in it.

Porta 1235. *Porta Elementorum*, a pseudonymous work. (See Introduction, p. lxix.)

Prophete 1245. The psalmist. The following Latin lines are from Ps. 64: 10, 106: 34, 35 (Vulgate).

Rasis 67, 1241. The famous chemist al-Razi, *c*. 850–925. Several Latin alchemical works are attributed to him, of which *De Salibus et Aluminibus* has been edited by R. Steele, *Isis*, xii (1929), 10–46. The quotation (1242) is from *Porta Elementorum* (see **Porta**).

Raymond(e, Raymunde Lully 69, 449, 625, 1558, 1592, 1672, 1674, 1713, 1762. A number of alchemical writings in the fourteenth century were attributed to Ramon Lull of Majorca, who, however, did not believe alchemical claims. The most important of these spurious works are the three parts of the *Testamentum*, the *Theoria*, *Practica*, and *Codicillus*, printed in Manget, i.

A legend of his having made gold for Edward III, under the patronage of an imaginary Abbot Cremer of Westminster is narrated in Michael Maier's *Tripus Aureus*, 1618. I have seen no other reference to the statues described in 447 ff.

Rupicissa 2241. Johannes de Rupescissa, a fourteenth-century Franciscan. His principal works concern the quintessence, and his *Liber Lucis* is printed in Manget, ii. 84–7. (See Thorndike, iii. 347–69, and Sarton, iii. 1572–4.)

Tonsile 1039 and frequently to 1175. Nothing is known of this possibly real contemporary of Norton. He is presented as an industrious but ignorant alchemical experimenter, one of 'Geber's cooks'.

Turba 2211, 2655. The *Turba Philosophorum*, consisting of a series of addresses given by great philosophers of the past to a kind of alchemical convention, under the chairmanship of Pythagoras. It has been edited by J. Ruska, 1931, and translated by A. E. Waite, 1896. For a brief account see Holmyard, *Alchemy*, pp. 80–4.

EARLY ENGLISH TEXT SOCIETY

LIST OF PUBLICATIONS
1864–1974

JUNE 1974

Orders from non-members of the Society should be placed with a bookseller Orders from booksellers for volumes in part 1 of this list should be sent to Oxford University Press, Ely House, 37 Dover Street, London W. 1. Orders from booksellers for volumes in part 2 of this list should be sent to the following addresses orders from the United States and Canada to Kraus Reprint Co., Route 100 Millwood, N.Y. 10546, U.S.A.; orders from Germany and Japan to Kraus Reprint Co., FL 9491 Nendeln, Liechtenstein, or Oxford University Press orders from Great Britain and all other countries to Oxford University Press Ely House, 37 Dover Street, London W. 1.

EARLY ENGLISH TEXT SOCIETY

The Early English Text Society was founded in 1864 by Frederick James Furnivall, with the help of Richard Morris, Walter Skeat and others, to bring the mass of unprinted Early English literature within the reach of students and to provide sound texts from which the New English Dictionary could quote. In 1867 an Extra Series was started of texts already printed but not in satisfactory or readily obtainable editions. In 1921 the Extra Series was discontinued and all publications were subsequently listed and numbered as part of the Original Series. In 1970 the first of a new Supplementary Series was published; unlike the Extra Series, volumes in this series will be issued only occasionally, as funds allow and as suitable texts become available.

In the first part of this list are shown the books published by the Society since 1938, Original Series 210 onwards and the Supplementary Series. A large number of the earlier books were reprinted by the Society in the period 1950 to 1970. In order to make the rest available, the Society has come to an agreement with the Kraus Reprint Co. who reprint as necessary the volumes in the Original Series 1–209 and in the Extra Series. In this way all the volumes published by the Society are once again in print.

Membership of the Society is open to libraries and to individuals interested in the study of medieval English literature. The subscription to the Society for 1975 is £5·00 (U.S. members $14.00, Canadian members Can. $14.00), due in advance on 1 January, and should be paid by cheque, postal order or money order made out to 'The Early English Text Society', and sent to Dr. Anne Hudson, Executive Secretary, Early English Text Society, Lady Margaret Hall, Oxford. Payment of this subscription entitles the member to receive the new book(s) in the Original Series for the year. The books in the Supplementary Series do not form part of the issue sent to members in return for the payment of their annual subscription, though they are available to members at a reduced price; a notice about each volume is sent to members in advance of publication.

Private members of the Society (but not libraries) may select in place of the annual issue past volumes from the Society's list chosen from the Original Series 210 to date or from the Supplementary Series. The value of such texts allowed against one annual subscription is £6·00, and all these transactions must be made through the Executive Secretary. Members of the Society may purchase copies of books O.S. 210 to date for their own use at a discount of 25% of the listed prices; private members (but not libraries) may purchase earlier publications at a similar discount. All such orders must be sent to the Executive Secretary.

Details of books, the cost of membership and its privileges, are revised from time to time. This list is brought up to date annually, and the current edition should be consulted.

June 1974

ORIGINAL SERIES 1938-1974

O.S. 210 **Sir Gawain and the Green Knight**, re-ed. I. Gollancz, with £1·50
introductory essays by Mabel Day and M. S. Serjeantson.
1940 (*for* 1938), *reprinted* 1966.

211 **The Dicts and Sayings of the Philosophers**: translations made £4·50
by Stephen Scrope, William Worcester and anonymous
translator, ed. C. F. Bühler. 1941 (*for* 1939), *reprinted* 1961.

212 **The Book of Margery Kempe**, Vol. I, Text (*all published*), ed. £4·25
S. B. Meech, with notes and appendices by S. B. Meech and
H. E. Allen. 1940 (*for* 1939), *reprinted* 1961.

213 **Ælfric's De Temporibus Anni**, ed. H. Henel. 1942 (*for* 1940), £2·50
reprinted 1970.

214 **Forty-Six Lives translated from Boccaccio's De Claris** £3·25
Mulieribus by Henry Parker, Lord Morley, ed. H. G. Wright.
1943 (*for* 1940), *reprinted* 1970.

215, 220 **Charles of Orleans: The English Poems**, Vol. I, ed. R. £3·75
Steele (1941), Vol. II, ed. R. Steele and Mabel Day (1946 *for*
1944); *reprinted as one volume with bibliographical supplement*
1970.

216 **The Latin Text of the Ancrene Riwle**, from Merton College £2·70
MS. 44 and British Museum MS. Cotton Vitellius E. vii, ed.
C. D'Evelyn. 1944 (*for* 1941), *reprinted* 1957.

217 **The Book of Vices and Virtues**: A Fourteenth-Century English £4·50
Translation of the *Somme le Roi* of Lorens d'Orléans, ed.
W. Nelson Francis. 1942, *reprinted* 1968.

218 **The Cloud of Unknowing and The Book of Privy Counselling**; £3·00
ed. Phyllis Hodgson. 1944 (*for* 1943), *corrected reprint* 1973.

219 **The French Text of the Ancrene Riwle**, British Museum MS. £3·25
Cotton Vitellius F. vii, ed. J. A. Herbert. 1944 (*for* 1943),
reprinted 1967.

220 **Charles of Orleans: The English Poems**, Vol. II; *see above*
O.S. 215.

221 **The Romance of Sir Degrevant**, ed. L. F. Casson. 1949 (*for* £3·00
1944), *reprinted* 1970.

222 **The Lyfe of Syr Thomas More, by Ro. Ba.**, ed. E. V. Hitch- £3·75
cock and P. E. Hallett, with notes and appendices by A. W.
Reed. 1950 (*for* 1945), *reprinted* 1974.

223 **The Tretyse of Loue**, ed. J. H. Fisher. 1951 (*for* 1945), £2·50
reprinted 1970.

224 **Athelston: a Middle English Romance**, ed. A. McI. Trounce. £2·50
1951 (*for* 1946), *reprinted* 1957.

225 **The English Text of the Ancrene Riwle**, British Museum MS. £3·00
Cotton Nero A. xiv, ed. Mabel Day. 1952 (*for* 1946), *reprinted* 1957.

226 **Respublica**: an interlude for Christmas 1553 attributed to £1·80
Nicholas Udall, re-ed. W. W. Greg. 1952 (*for* 1946),
reprinted 1969.

O.S. 227   **Kyng Alisaunder,** Vol. I, Text, ed. G. V. Smithers. 1952 *(for*   £4·50
1947), *reprinted* 1961.

228   **The Metrical Life of St. Robert of Knaresborough,** together   £2·50
with the other Middle English pieces in British Museum MS.
Egerton 3143, ed. Joyce Bazire. 1953 *(for* 1947), *reprinted*
1968.

229   **The English Text of the Ancrene Riwle,** Gonville and Caius   £2·10
College MS. 234/120, ed. R. M. Wilson with an introduction
by N. R. Ker. 1954 *(for* 1948), *reprinted* 1957.

230   **The Life of St. George by Alexander Barclay,** ed. W. Nelson.   £2·40
1955 *(for* 1948), *reprinted* 1960.

231   **Deonise Hid Diuinite** and other treatises related to *The Cloud*   £3·00
of Unknowing, ed. Phyllis Hodgson. 1955 *(for* 1949), *reprinted*
with corrections 1958.

232   **The English Text of the Ancrene Riwle,** British Museum MS.   £1·80
Royal 8 C. i, ed. A. C. Baugh. 1956 *(for* 1949), *reprinted*
1959.

233   **The Bibliotheca Historica of Diodorus Siculus translated by**   £4·80
John Skelton, Vol. I, Text, ed. F. M. Salter and H. L. R.
Edwards. 1956 *(for* 1950), *reprinted* 1968.

234   **Paris and Vienne translated from the French and printed by**   £2·50
William Caxton, ed. MacEdward Leach. 1957 *(for* 1951),
reprinted 1970.

235   **The South English Legendary,** Corpus Christi College   £3·75
Cambridge MS. 145 and British Museum MS. Harley 2277,
with variants from Bodley MS. Ashmole 43 and British
Museum MS. Cotton Julius D. ix, ed. C. D'Evelyn and A. J.
Mill. Vol. I, Text, 1959 *(for* 1957), *reprinted* 1967.

236   **The South English Legendary,** Vol. II, Text, ed. C. D'Evelyn   £3·75
and A. J. Mill. 1956 *(for* 1952), *reprinted* 1967.

237   **Kyng Alisaunder,** Vol. II, Introduction, commentary and   £3·00
glossary, ed. G. V. Smithers. 1957 *(for* 1953), *reprinted with*
corrections 1969.

238   **The Phonetic Writings of Robert Robinson,** ed. E. J. Dobson.   £1·80
1957 *(for* 1953), *reprinted* 1968.

239   **The Bibliotheca Historica of Diodorus Siculus translated by**   £1·80
John Skelton, Vol. II, Introduction, notes and glossary, ed.
F. M. Salter and H. L. R. Edwards. 1957 *(for* 1954), *re-*
printed 1971.

240   **The French Text of the Ancrene Riwle,** Trinity College Cam-   £3·25
bridge MS. R. 14. 7, with variants from Paris Bibliothèque
Nationale MS. fonds fr. 6276 and Bodley MS. 90, ed. W. H.
Trethewey. 1958 *(for* 1954), *reprinted* 1971.

241   **Þe Wohunge of Ure Lauerd** and other pieces, ed. W. Meredith   £2·70
Thompson. 1958 *(for* 1955), *reprinted with corrections* 1970.

242   **The Salisbury Psalter,** ed. Celia Sisam and Kenneth Sisam.   £5·40
1959 *(for* 1955–6), *reprinted* 1969.

243   **The Life and Death of Cardinal Wolsey by George Cavendish,**   £2·70
ed. R. S. Sylvester. 1959 *(for* 1957), *reprinted* 1961.

244   **The South English Legendary,** Vol. III, Introduction and   £1·80
glossary, ed. C. D'Evelyn. 1959 *(for* 1957), *reprinted* 1969.

O.S. 245 **Beowulf:** facsimile of British Museum MS. Cotton Vitellius £6·00
A. xv, with a transliteration and notes by J. Zupitza, a new
reproduction of the manuscript with an introductory note by
Norman Davis. 1959 *(for 1958), reprinted* 1967.

246 **The Parlement of the Thre Ages,** ed. M. Y. Offord. 1959, £2·40
reprinted 1967.

247 **Facsimile of MS. Bodley 34:** St. Katherine, St. Margaret, £3·75
St. Juliana, Hali Meiðhad, Sawles Warde, with an introduction by N. R. Ker. 1960 *(for* 1959).

248 **Þe Liflade ant te Passiun of Seinte Iuliene,** ed. S. R. T. O. £2·40
d'Ardenne. 1961 *(for* 1960).

249 **The English Text of the Ancrene Riwle:** Ancrene Wisse, £3·00
Corpus Christi College Cambridge MS. 402, ed. J. R. R.
Tolkien, with introduction by N. R. Ker. 1962 *(for* 1960).

250 **Laȝamon's Brut,** Vol. I, Text (lines 1–8020), ed. G. L. £6·00
Brook and R. F. Leslie. 1963 *(for* 1961).

251 **The Owl and the Nightingale:** facsimile of Jesus College £3·00
Oxford MS. 29 and British Museum MS. Cotton Caligula
A. ix, with an introduction by N. R. Ker. 1963 *(for* 1962).

252 **The English Text of the Ancrene Riwle,** British Museum MS. £3·00
Cotton Titus D. xviii, ed. F. M. Mack, and the Lanhydrock
Fragment, Bodleian MS. Eng. th. c. 70, ed. A. Zettersten. 1963
(for 1962).

253 **The Bodley Version of Mandeville's Travels,** ed. M. C. £3·00
Seymour. 1963.

254 **Ywain and Gawain,** ed. Albert B. Friedman and Norman £3·00
T. Harrington. 1964 *(for* 1963).

255 **Facsimile of British Museum MS. Harley 2253,** with an £6·00
introduction by N. R. Ker. 1965 *(for* 1964).

256 **Sir Eglamour of Artois,** ed. Frances E. Richardson. 1965. £3·00

257 **The Praise of Folie by Sir Thomas Chaloner,** ed. Clarence H. £3·00
Miller. 1965.

258 **The Orcherd of Syon,** Vol. I, Text, ed. Phyllis Hodgson and £6·00
Gabriel M. Liegey. 1966.

259 **Homilies of Ælfric, A Supplementary Collection,** Vol. I, £6·00
ed. J. C. Pope. 1967.

260 **Homilies of Ælfric, A Supplementary Collection,** Vol. II, £6·00
ed. J. C. Pope. 1968.

261 **Lybeaus Desconus,** ed. M. Mills. 1969. £3·00

262 **The Macro Plays:** The Castle of Perseverance, Wisdom, £3·00
Mankind, ed. Mark Eccles. 1969.

263 **The History of Reynard the Fox translated from the Dutch** £3·00
Original by William Caxton, ed. N. F. Blake. 1970.

264 **The Epistle of Othea translated from the French text of** £3·00
Christine de Pisan by Stephen Scrope, ed. C. F. Bühler. 1970.

265 **The Cyrurgie of Guy de Chauliac,** Vol. I, Text, ed. Margaret S. £6·00
Ogden. 1971.

266 **Wulfstan's Canons of Edgar,** ed. R. G. Fowler. 1972. £1·80

267 **The English Text of the Ancrene Riwle,** British Museum MS. £4·25
Cotton Cleopatra C. vi, ed. E. J. Dobson. 1972.

O.S. 268 **Of Arthour and of Merlin,** Vol. I, Text, ed. O. D. Macrae- £3·00
Gibson. 1973.

269 **The Metrical Version of Mandeville's Travels,** ed. M. C. £3·00
Seymour. 1973.

270 **Fifteenth Century Translations of Alain Chartier's Le Traite** £3·00
de l'Esperance and Le Quadrilogue Invectif, Vol. I, Text, ed.
Margaret S. Blayney. (1974.)

271 **The Minor Poems of Stephen Hawes,** ed. Florence Gluck and £2·50
Alice B. Morgan. (1974.)

SUPPLEMENTARY SERIES

S.S. 1 **Non-Cycle Plays and Fragments,** ed. Norman Davis with an £3·60
appendix on the Shrewsbury Music by F. Ll. Harrison. 1970.

2 **The Book of the Knight of the Tower translated by William** £3·25
Caxton, ed. M. Y. Offord. 1971.

3 **The Chester Mystery Cycle,** Vol. I, Text, ed. R. M. Lumiansky £5·50
and David Mills. (1974.)

FORTHCOMING VOLUMES

O.S. 272 **Thomas Norton's The Ordinal of Alchemy,** ed. John Reidy. £3·00
(1975.)

273 **The Cely Letters, 1472–1488,** ed. Alison Hanham. (1975.) £4·50

274 **The English Text of the Ancrene Riwle,** Magdalene College
Cambridge MS Pepys 2498, ed. A. Zettersten. (1976.)

275 **Dives and Pauper,** Text Vol. I, ed. Priscilla H. Barnum (1976.)

LIST 2

ORIGINAL SERIES 1864–1938

O.S. 1 **Early English Alliterative Poems** . . . from MS. Cotton Nero A. x, £3·20
ed. R. Morris. 1864, *revised* 1869, *reprinted* 1965.

2 **Arthur, ed. F. J. Furnivall.** 1864, *reprinted* 1965. 60p

3 **William Lauder Ane conpendious and breue tractate concernyng ye** £1·10
Office and Dewtie of Kyngis, ed. F. Hall. 1864, *reprinted* 1965.
Also available reprinted as one volume with O.S. 41 £2·75
William Lauder The Minor Poems, ed. F. J. Furnivall. 1870, *reprinted*
Kraus 1973.

4 **Sir Gawayne and the Green Knight,** ed. R. Morris. 1864. Superseded
by O.S. 210.

5 **Alexander Hume of the Orthographie and Congruitie of the Britan** £1·10
Tongue, ed. H. B. Wheatley. 1865, *reprinted* 1965.

6 **The Romans of Lancelot of the Laik,** re-ed. W. W. Skeat. 1865, *re-* £2·50
printed 1965.

7 **The Story of Genesis and Exodus,** ed. R. Morris. 1865, *reprinted* £4·50
Kraus 1973.

8 **Morte Arthure** [alliterative version from Thornton MS.], ed. E. Brock. £1·50
1865, *reprinted* 1967.

9 **Francis Thynne Animadversions uppon Chaucer's Workes** . . . 1598, £3·25
ed. G. H. Kingsley. 1865, *revised* F. J. Furnivall 1875, *reprinted* 1965.

10, 112 **Merlin,** ed. H. B. Wheatley, Vol. I 1865, Vol. IV with essays £10·75
by J. S. S. Glennie and W. E. Mead 1899; *reprinted as one volume*
Kraus 1973. (See O.S. 21, 36 for other parts.)

11, 19, 35, 37 **The Works of Sir David Lyndesay,** Vol. I 1865; Vol. II £9·00
1866 The Monarch and other Poems, ed. J. Small; Vol. III 1868 The
Historie of . . . Squyer William Meldrum etc., ed. F. Hall; Vol. IV
Ane Satyre of the Thrie Estaits and Minor Poems, ed. F. Hall.
Reprinted as one volume Kraus 1973. (See O.S. 47 for last part.)

12 **Adam of Cobsam The Wright's Chaste Wife,** ed. F. J. Furnivall. 1865, 60p
reprinted 1965. (See also O.S. 84.)

13 **Seinte Marherete,** ed. O. Cockayne. 1866. Superseded by O.S. 193.

14 **King Horn, Floriz and Blauncheflur, The Assumption of our Lady,** £3·00
ed. J. R. Lumby. 1866, *revised* G. H. McKnight 1901, *reprinted* 1962.

15 **Political, Religious and Love Poems,** from Lambeth MS. 306 and £3·75
other sources, ed. F. J. Furnivall. 1866, *reprinted* 1962.

16 **The Book of Quinte Essence** . . . Sloane MS. 73 *c.* 1460-70, ed. F. J. 60p
Furnivall. 1866, *reprinted* 1965.

17 **William Langland Parallel Extracts from 45 MSS. of Piers Plowman,** 55p
ed. W. W. Skeat. 1866, *reprinted* Kraus 1973.

18 **Hali Meidenhad,** ed. O. Cockayne. 1866, *revised* F. J. Furnivall 1922 £2·00
(*for* 1920), *reprinted* Kraus 1973.

19 **Sir David Lyndesay The Monarch and other Poems,** Vol. II. See
above, O.S. 11.

20 **Richard Rolle de Hampole English Prose Treatises,** ed. G. G. Perry. £1·10
1866, *reprinted* Kraus 1973.

21, 36 **Merlin,** ed. H. B. Wheatley. Vol. II 1866, Vol. III 1869; *reprinted* £10·00
as one volume Kraus 1973

22 **The Romans of Partenay or of Lusignen,** ed. W. W. Skeat. 1866, £5·50
reprinted Kraus 1973.

O.S. 49   An Old English Miscellany : a Bestiary, Kentish Sermons, Proverbs of £5·75 Alfred and Religious Poems of the 13th Century, ed. R. Morris. 1872, *reprinted* Kraus 1973.

50   King Alfred's West-Saxon Version of Gregory's Pastoral Care, ed. H. £4·00 Sweet. Vol. II 1871, reprinted with corrections by N. R. Ker 1958, *reprinted* Kraus 1973. (See O.S. 45 for Vol. I.)

51   þe Liflade of St. Juliana, ed. O. Cockayne and E. Brock. 1872, re- £2·25 *printed* 1957. (See O.S. 248 for more recent edition.)

52   Palladius On Husbandrie, ed. B. Lodge. Vol. I 1872, *reprinted* Kraus £3·75 1973. (See O.S. 72 for Vol. II.)

53   Old English Homilies of the 12th Century etc., ed. R. Morris. Vol. II £5·00 1873, *reprinted* Kraus 1973. (See O.S. 29, 34 for Vol. 1.)

54   William Langland The Vision of Piers Plowman, ed. W. W. Skeat. £3·25 Vol. III Text C 1873, *reprinted* 1959. (See O.S. 28, 38, 67, and 81 for other parts.)

55, 70   Generydes, a romance, ed. W. A. Wright. Vol. I 1873, Vol. II £4·25 1878; *reprinted as one volume* Kraus 1973.

56   The Gest Hystoriale of the Destruction of Troy. Vol. II. See above, O.S. 39.

57   Cursor Mundi, ed. R. Morris. Vol. I Text ll. 1–4954, 1874, *reprinted* £2·40 1961. (See O.S. 59, 62, 66, 68, 99, and 101 for other parts.)

58, 63, 73   The Blickling Homilies, ed. R. Morris. Vol. I 1874, Vol. II £4·25 1876, Vol. III 1880; *reprinted as one volume* 1967.

59   Cursor Mundi, ed. R. Morris. Vol. II ll. 4955–12558, 1875, *reprinted* £3·00 1966. (See O.S. 57, 62, 66, 68, 99, and 101 for other parts.)

60   Meditations on the Supper of our Lord, and the Hours of the Passion, £1·25 translated by Robert Manning of Brunne, ed. J. M. Cowper. 1875, *reprinted* Kraus 1973.

61   The Romance and Prophecies of Thomas of Erceldoune, ed. J. A. H. £2·30 Murray. 1875, *reprinted* Kraus 1973.

62   Cursor Mundi, ed. R. Morris. Vol. III ll. 12559–19300, 1876, *reprinted* £2·40 1966. (See O.S. 57, 59, 66, 68, 99, and 101 for other parts.)

63   The Blickling Homilies, Vol. II. See above, O.S. 58.

64   Francis Thynne's Emblemes and Epigrames, ed. F. J. Furnivall. 1876, £2·20 *reprinted* Kraus 1973.

65   Be Domes Dæge, De Die Judicii: an Old English version of the Latin £1·80 poem ascribed to Bede, ed. J. R. Lumby. 1876, *reprinted* 1964.

66   Cursor Mundi, ed. R. Morris. Vol. IV ll. 19301–23836, 1877, *reprinted* £2·40 1966. (See O.S. 57, 59, 62, 68, 99, and 101 for other parts.)

67   William Langland The Vision of Piers Plowman, ed. W. W. Skeat. £8·50 Vol. IV. 1 Notes, 1877, *reprinted* Kraus 1973. (See O.S. 28, 38, 54, and 81 for other parts.)

68   Cursor Mundi, ed. R. Morris. Vol. V ll. 23827–end, 1878, *reprinted* £2·40 1966. (See O.S. 57, 59, 62, 66, 99, and 101 for other parts.)

69   Adam Davy's 5 Dreams about Edward II etc. from Bodleian MS. Laud £2·20 Misc. 622, ed. F. J. Furnivall. 1878, *reprinted* Kraus 1973.

70   Generydes, a romance, Vol. II. See above, O.S. 55.

71   The Lay Folks Mass Book, ed. T. F. Simmons. 1879, *reprinted* 1968. £5·40

72   Palladius On Husbandrie, ed. B. Lodge and S. J. Herrtage. Vol. II £2·50 1879. (See O.S. 52 for Vol. I.) *Also available reprinted as one volume with* O.S. 52.

73   The Blickling Homilies, Vol. III. See above, O.S. 58.

74   The English Works of Wyclif hitherto unprinted, ed. F. D. Matthew. £10·50 1880, *reprinted* Kraus 1973.

75   Catholicon Anglicum, an English–Latin Wordbook 1483, ed. S. J. H. £8·00 Herrtage and H. B. Wheatley. 1881, *reprinted* Kraus 1973.

O.S. 76, 82 **Ælfric's Lives of Saints,** ed. W. W. Skeat. Vol. I. i 1881, Vol. I. ii   £3·60
1885; *reprinted as one volume* 1966. (See O.S. 94 and 114 for other parts.)

77   **Beowulf,** autotypes of Cotton MS. Vitellius A. xv. 1882. Superseded by O.S. 245.

78   **The Fifty Earliest English Wills** . . . **1387–1439,** ed. F. J. Furnivall.   £3·00
1882, *reprinted* 1964.

79   **King Alfred's Orosius,** ed. H. Sweet. Vol. I Old English Text and Latin Original (*all published*) 1883, *reprinting* Kraus 1974.

80   **The Life of Saint Katherine,** from Royal MS. 17 A. xxvii etc., ed.   £4·25
E. Einenkel. 1884, *reprinted* Kraus 1973.

81   **William Langland The Vision of Piers Plowman,** ed. W. W. Skeat.   £9·50
Vol. IV. 2 General Preface and indexes. 1884, *reprinted* Kraus 1973. (See O.S. 28, 38, 54, and 67 for other parts.)

82   **Ælfric's Lives of Saints,** Vol. I. ii. See above, O.S. 76.

83   **The Oldest English Texts,** ed. H. Sweet. 1885, *reprinted* 1966.   £6·50

84   [Adam of Cobsam] **Additional Analogs to The Wright's Chaste Wife,**   £1·00
ed. W. A. Clouston. 1886, *reprinted* Kraus 1973. (See also O.S. 12.)

85   **The Three Kings of Cologne,** ed. C. Horstmann. 1886, *reprinted* Kraus   £5·75
1973.

86   **The Lives of Women Saints** etc., ed. C. Horstmann. 1886, *reprinted*   £4·25
Kraus 1973.

87   **The Early South-English Legendary,** from Bodleian MS. Laud Misc.   £9·50
108, ed. C. Horstmann. 1887, *reprinted* Kraus 1973.

88   **Henry Bradshaw The Life of Saint Werburge of Chester,** ed. C. Horst-   £4·50
mann. 1887, *reprinted* Kraus 1973.

89   **Vices and Virtues** [from British Museum MS. Stowe 240], ed. F.   £2·40
Holthausen. Vol. I Text and translation. 1888, *reprinted* 1967. (See O.S. 159 for Vol. II.)

90   **The Rule of S.** Benet, Latin and Anglo-Saxon interlinear version, ed.   £3·25
H. Logeman. 1888, *reprinted* Kraus 1973.

91   **Two Fifteenth-Century Cookery-Books,** ed. T. Austin. 1888, *reprinted*   £2·50
1964.

92   **Eadwine's Canterbury Psalter,** ed. F. Harsley. Vol. II Text and notes   £4·75
(*all published*) 1889, *reprinted* Kraus 1973.

93   **Defensor's Liber Scintillarum,** ed. E. W. Rhodes. 1889, *reprinted*   £4·50
Kraus 1973.

94, 114   **Ælfric's Lives of Saints,** ed. W. W. Skeat. Vol. II. i 1890, Vol. II.   £3·60
ii 1900; *reprinted as one volume* 1966. (See O.S. 76, 82 for other parts.)

95   **The Old English Version of Bede's Ecclesiastical History of the English**   £3·20
People, ed. T. Miller. Vol. I. i 1890, *reprinted* 1959.

96   **The Old English Version of Bede's Ecclesiastical History of the English**   £3·20
People, ed. T. Miller. Vol. I. ii 1891, *reprinted* 1959. (See O.S. 110, 111 for other parts.)

97   **The Earliest Complete English Prose Psalter,** ed. K. D. Bülbring.   £3·55
Vol. I (*all published*) 1891, *reprinted* Kraus 1973.

98   **The Minor Poems of the Vernon MS.,** ed. C. Horstmann. Vol. I 1892,   £7·50
reprinted Kraus 1973. (See O.S. 117 for Vol. II.)

99   **Cursor Mundi,** ed. R. Morris. Vol. VI Preface etc. 1892, *reprinted*   £2·10
1962. (See O.S. 57, 59, 62, 66, 68, and 101 for other parts.)

100   **John Capgrave The Life of St. Katharine of Alexandria,** ed. C. Horst-   £8·50
mann, forewords by F. J. Furnivall. 1893, *reprinted* Kraus 1973.

101   **Cursor Mundi,** ed. R. Morris. Vol. VII Essay on manuscripts and   £2·10
dialect by H. Hupe. 1893, *reprinted* 1962. (See O.S. 57, 59, 62, 66, 68, and 99 for other parts.)

102   **Lanfrank's Science of Cirurgie,** ed. R. von Fleischhacker. Vol. I Text   £6·25
(*all published*) 1894, *reprinted* Kraus 1973.

O.S. 131   The **Brut,** or the Chronicles of England . . . from Bodleian MS. Rawl.   £3·25
B. 171, ed. F. W. D. Brie. Vol. I 1906, *reprinted* 1960. (See O.S. 136
for Vol. II.)

132   The **Works of John Metham,** ed. H. Craig. 1916 (*for* 1906), *reprinted*   £3·60
Kraus 1973.

133, 144   The **English Register of Oseney Abbey** . . . *c.* 1460, ed. A. Clark.   £4·80
Vol. I 1907, Vol. II 1913 (*for* 1912); *reprinted as one volume* Kraus
1971.

134, 135   The **Coventry Leet Book,** ed. M. D. Harris. Vol. I 1907, Vol. II   £9·50
1908; *reprinted as one volume* Kraus 1971. (See O.S. 138, 146 for
other parts.)

136   The **Brut,** or the Chronicles of England, ed. F. W. D. Brie. Vol. II   £5·25
1908, *reprinted* Kraus 1971. (See O.S. 131 for Vol. I.)

137   **Twelfth Century Homilies in MS. Bodley 343,** ed. A. O. Belfour.   £1·65
Vol. I Text and translation (*all published*) 1909, *reprinted* 1962.

138, 146   The **Coventry Leet Book,** ed. M. D. Harris. Vol. III 1909, Vol.   £6·60
IV 1913; *reprinted as one volume* Kraus 1971. (See O.S. 134, 135 for
other parts.)

139   **John Arderne Treatises of Fistula in Ano** etc., ed. D'Arcy Power.   £2·65
1910, *reprinted* 1968.

140   **John Capgrave's Lives of St. Augustine and St. Gilbert of Sempring-**   £3·25
ham and a sermon, ed. J. J. Munro. 1910, *reprinted* Kraus 1971.

141   The **Middle English Poem Erthe upon Erthe,** printed from 24 manu-   £1·80
scripts, ed. H. M. R. Murray. 1911, *reprinted* 1964.

142   The **English Register of Godstow Nunnery,** Vol. III. See above, O.S.
130.

143   The **Prose Life of Alexander** from the Thornton MS., ed. J. S. West-   £1·85
lake. 1913 (*for* 1911), *reprinted* Kraus 1971.

144   The **English Register of Oseney Abbey,** Vol. II. See above, O.S. 133.

145   The **Northern Passion,** ed. F. A. Foster. Vol. I 1913 (*for* 1912),   £4·00
reprinted Kraus 1971. (See O.S. 147, 183 for other parts.)

146   The **Coventry Leet Book,** Vol. IV. See above, O.S. 138.

147   The **Northern Passion,** ed. F. A. Foster. Vol. II 1916 (*for* 1913),   £3·60
reprinted Kraus 1971. (See O.S. 145, 183 for other parts.)

148   A **Fifteenth-Century Courtesy Book,** ed. R. W. Chambers, and **Two**   £1·80
Fifteenth-Century Franciscan Rules, ed. W. W. Seton. 1914, *re-*
printed 1963.

149   **Lincoln Diocese Documents, 1450–1544,** ed. A. Clark. 1914, *re-*   £6·00
printed Kraus 1971.

150   The **Old English Versions of the enlarged Rule of Chrodegang,** the   £2·25
Capitula of Theodulf and the Epitome of Benedict of Aniane, ed.
A. S. Napier. 1916 (*for* 1914), *reprinted* Kraus 1971.

151   The **Lanterne of Liȝt,** ed. L. M. Swinburn. 1917 (*for* 1915), *reprinted*   £3·35
Kraus 1971.

152   **Early English Homilies from the Twelfth-Century MS. Vespasian D.**   £2·50
xiv, ed. R. D.-N. Warner. 1917 (*for* 1915), *reprinted* Kraus 1971.

153   **Mandeville's Travels** . . . from MS. Cotton Titus C. xvi, ed. P.   £4·00
Hamelius. Vol. I Text 1919 (*for* 1916), *reprinted* Kraus 1973.

154   **Mandeville's Travels** . . . from MS. Cotton Titus C. xvi, ed. P.   £2·40
Hamelius. Vol. II Introduction and notes. 1923 (*for* 1916), *reprinted*
1961.

155   The **Wheatley Manuscript :** Middle English verse and prose in British   £2·50
Museum MS. Additional 39574, ed. M. Day. 1921 (*for* 1917), *re-*
printed Kraus 1971.

156   The **Donet by Reginald Pecock,** ed. E. V. Hitchcock. 1921 (*for* 1918),   £4·75
reprinted Kraus 1971.

O.S. 207   The Liber de Diversis Medicinis in the Thornton Manuscript, ed.   £2·50
M. S. Ogden. 1938 (*for* 1936), *revised reprint* 1969.

208   The Parker Chronicle and Laws (Corpus Christi College, Cambridge   £9·50
MS. 173); a facsimile, ed. R. Flower and H. Smith. 1941 (*for* 1937),
reprinted 1973.

209   Middle English Sermons, from British Museum MS. Royal 18 B.   £4·50
xxiii, ed. W. O. Ross. 1940 (*for* 1938), *reprinted* 1960.

EXTRA SERIES 1867–1920

E.S. 1   The Romance of William of Palerne, ed. W. W. Skeat. 1867, *reprinted*   £6·50
Kraus 1973.

2   On Early English Pronunciation, by A. J. Ellis. Part I. 1867, *reprinted*   £3·60
Kraus 1973. (See E.S. 7, 14, 23, and 56 for other parts.)

3   Caxton's Book of Curtesye, with two manuscript copies of the treatise,   £1·30
ed. F. J. Furnivall. 1868, *reprinted* Kraus 1973.

4   The Lay of Havelok the Dane, ed. W. W. Skeat. 1868, *reprinted* Kraus   £3·75
1973.

5   Chaucer's Translation of Boethius's ' De Consolatione Philosophiæ', ed.   £2·40
R. Morris. 1868, *reprinted* 1969.

6   The Romance of the Cheuelere Assigne, re-ed. H. H. Gibbs. 1868,   £1·10
reprinted Kraus 1973.

7   On Early English Pronunciation, by A. J. Ellis. Part II. 1869, *reprinted*   £3·60
Kraus 1973. (See E.S. 2, 14, 23, and 56 for other parts.)

8   Queene Elizabethes Achademy etc., ed. F. J. Furnivall, with essays on   £3·25
early Italian and German Books of Courtesy by W. M. Rossetti and
E. Oswald. 1869, *reprinted* Kraus 1973.

9   The Fraternitye of Vacabondes by John Awdeley, Harman's Caveat,   £2·40
Haben's Sermon etc., ed. E. Viles and F. J. Furnivall. 1869, *reprinted*
Kraus 1973.

10   Andrew Borde's Introduction of Knowledge and Dyetary of Helth, with   £6·50
Barnes's Defence of the Berde, ed. F. J. Furnivall. 1870, *reprinted*
Kraus 1973.

11, 55   The Bruce by John Barbour, ed. W. W. Skeat. Vol. I 1870, Vol. IV   £3·75
1889; *reprinted as one volume* 1968. (See E.S. 21, 29, for other parts.)

12, 32   England in the Reign of King Henry VIII, Vol. I Dialogue between   £7·00
Cardinal Pole and Thomas Lupset, ed. J. M. Cowper (1871), Vol. II
Starkey's Life and Letters, ed. S. J. Herrtage (1878); *reprinted as one
volume* Kraus 1973.

13   Simon Fish A Supplicacyon for the Beggers, re-ed. F. J. Furnivall,   £2·20
A Supplycacion to . . . Henry VIII, A Supplication of the Poore
Commons and The Decaye of England by the great multitude of shepe,
ed. J. M. Cowper. 1871, *reprinted* Kraus 1973.

14   On Early English Pronunciation, by A. J. Ellis. Part III. 1871, *re-*   £6·50
printed Kraus 1973. (See E.S. 2, 7, 23, and 56 for other parts.)

15   The Select Works of Robert Crowley, ed. J. M. Cowper. 1872, *re-*   £3·75
printed Kraus 1973.

16   Geoffrey Chaucer A Treatise on the Astrolabe, ed. W. W. Skeat. 1872,   £2·40
reprinted 1968.

17, 18   The Complaynt of Scotlande, re-ed. J. A. H. Murray. Vol. I 1872,   £5·50
Vol. II 1873; *reprinted as one volume* Kraus 1973.

19   The Myroure of oure Ladye, ed. J. H. Blunt. 1873, *reprinted* Kraus   £7·50
1973.

20, 24   The History of the Holy Grail by Henry Lovelich, ed. F. J. Furnivall.   £8·00
Vol. I 1874, Vol. II 1875; *reprinted as one volume* Kraus 1973. (See
E.S. 28, 30, and 95 for other parts.)

E.S. 21, 29   **The Bruce by John Barbour,** ed. W. W. Skeat. Vol. II 1874, Vol.   £5·40
III 1877; *reprinted as one volume* 1968. (See E.S. 11, 55 for other part.)

22   **Henry Brinklow's Complaynt of Roderyck Mors,** The Lamentacyon of a   £2·75
Christen agaynst the Cytye of London by Roderigo Mors, ed. J. M.
Cowper. 1874, *reprinted* Kraus 1973.

23   **On Early English Pronunciation,** by A. J. Ellis. Part IV. 1874, *re-*   £7·75
printed Kraus 1973. (See E.S. 2, 7, 14, and 56 for other parts.)

24   The History of the Holy Grail by Henry Lovelich, Vol. II. See above,
E.S. 20.

25, 26   **The Romance of Guy of Warwick,** the second or 15th-century   £4·50
version, ed. J. Zupitza. Vol. I 1875, Vol. II 1876; reprinted as one
volume 1966.

27   **John Fisher The English Works,** ed. J. E. B. Mayor. Vol. I (*all pub-*   £7·75
lished) 1876, *reprinted* Kraus 1973.

28, 30, 95   **The History of the Holy Grail by Henry Lovelich,** ed. F. J.   £6·75
Furnivall. Vol. III 1877; Vol. IV 1878; Vol. V The Legend of the Holy
Grail, its Sources, Character and Development by D. Kempe 1905;
reprinted as one volume Kraus 1973. (See E.S. 20, 24 for other parts.)

29   The Bruce by John Barbour, Vol. III. See above, E.S. 21.

30   The History of the Holy Grail by Henry Lovelich, Vol. IV. See above,
E.S. 28.

31   **The Alliterative Romance of Alexander and Dindimus,** re-ed. W. W.   £2·20
Skeat. 1878, *reprinted* Kraus 1973.

32   England in the Reign of King Henry VIII, Vol. II. See above, E.S. 12.

33   **The Early English Versions of the Gesta Romanorum,** ed. S. J. H.   £6·00
Herrtage. 1879, *reprinted* 1962.

34   The English Charlemagne Romances I: **Sir Ferumbras,** ed. S. J. H.   £3·20
Herrtage. 1879, *reprinted* 1966.

35   The English Charlemagne Romances II: **The Sege of Melayne, The**   £3·60
Romance of Duke Rowland and Sir Otuell of Spayne, ed. S. J. H.
Herrtage. 1880, *reprinted* Kraus 1973.

36, 37   The English Charlemagne Romances III and IV: **The Lyf of**   £3·20
Charles the Grete, translated by William Caxton, ed. S. J. H. Herrtage.
Vol. I 1880, Vol. II 1881; *reprinted as one volume* 1967.

38   The English Charlemagne Romances V: **The Romance of the Sowdone**   £3·00
of Babylone, re-ed. E. Hausknecht. 1881, *reprinted* 1969.

39   The English Charlemagne Romances VI: **The Taill of Rauf Coilyear,**   £2·50
with the fragments of Roland and Vernagu and Otuel, re-ed. S. J. H.
Herrtage. 1882, *reprinted* 1969.

40, 41   The English Charlemagne Romances VII and VIII: **The Boke of**   £10·75
Duke Huon of Burdeux translated by Lord Berners, ed. S. L. Lee. Vol. I
1882, Vol. II 1883; *reprinted as one volume* Kraus 1973. (See E.S. 43,
50 for other parts.)

42, 49, 59   **The Romance of Guy of Warwick,** from the Auchinleck MS.   £6·50
and the Caius MS., ed. J. Zupitza. Vol. I 1883, Vol. II 1887, Vol. III
1891; *reprinted as one volume* 1966.

43, 50   The English Charlemagne Romances IX and XII: **The Boke of**   £4·25
Duke Huon of Burdeux translated by Lord Berners, ed. S. L. Lee.
Vol. III 1884, Vol. IV 1887; *reprinted as one volume* Kraus 1973.

44   The English Charlemagne Romances X: **The Foure Sonnes of Aymon,**   £5·50
translated by William Caxton, ed. O. Richardson. Vol. I 1884, *re-*
printed Kraus 1973.

45   The English Charlemagne Romances XI: **The Foure Sonnes of Aymon,**   £6·50
translated by William Caxton, ed. O. Richardson. Vol. II 1885, *re-*
printed Kraus 1973.

46, 48, 65   **The Romance of Sir Beues of Hamtoun,** ed. E. Kölbing. Vol. I   £8·00
1885, Vol. II 1886, Vol. III 1894; *reprinted as one volume* Kraus 1973.

Furnivall (1899), Vol. II ed. F. J. Furnivall (1901), Vol. III introduction, notes, glossary, etc. by K. B. Locock (1904); *reprinted as one volume* Kraus 1973.

E.S. 78 **Thomas Robinson The Life and Death of Mary Magdalene**, ed. H. O. Sommer. 1899. £1·80

79 **Dialogues in French and English by William Caxton**, ed. H. Bradley. 1900, *reprinted* Kraus 1973. £1·60

80 **Lydgate's Two Nightingale Poems**, ed. O. Glauning. 1900, *reprinted* Kraus 1973. £2·20

80A Selections from Barbour's Bruce (Books I–X), ed. W. W. Skeat, 1900, *reprinted* Kraus 1973. £9·00

81 **The English Works of John Gower**, ed. G. C. Macaulay. Vol. I *Confessio Amantis* Prologue–Bk. V. 1970. 1900, *reprinted* 1969. £3·60

82 **The English Works of John Gower**, ed. G. C. Macaulay. Vol. II *Confessio Amantis* V. 1971–VIII, *In Praise of Peace*. 1901, *reprinted* 1969. £3·60

83 **The Pilgrimage of the Life of Man**, Vol. II. See above, E.S. 77.

84 **Lydgate's Reson and Sensuallyte**, ed. E. Sieper. Vol. I Manuscripts, Text, and Glossary. 1901, *reprinted* 1965. (See E.S. 89 for Part II.) £3·00

85 **The Poems of Alexander Scott**, ed. A. K. Donald. 1902, *reprinted* Kraus 1973. £2·10

86 **The Poems of William of Shoreham**, ed. M. Konrath. Vol. I (*all published*) 1902, *reprinted* Kraus 1973. £4·40

87 **Two Coventry Corpus Christi Plays**, re-ed. H. Craig. 1902; *second edition* 1957, *reprinted* 1967. £1·80

88 **Le Morte Arthur**, a romance in stanzas, re-ed. J. D. Bruce. 1903, *reprinted* Kraus 1973. £3·00

89 **Lydgate's Reson and Sensuallyte**, ed. E. Sieper. Vol. II Studies and Notes. 1903, *reprinted* 1965. (See E.S. 84 for Part I.) £2·10

90 **English Fragments from Latin Medieval Service-Books**, ed. H. Littlehales. 1903, *reprinted* Kraus 1973. 55p

91 **The Macro Plays**, ed. F. J. Furnivall and A. W. Pollard. 1904. Superseded by O.S. 262.

92 **The Pilgrimage of the Life of Man**, Vol. III. See above, E.S. 77.

93 **Henry Lovelich's Merlin**, ed. E. A. Kock. Vol. I 1904, *reprinted* Kraus 1973. (See E.S. 112 and O.S. 185 for other parts.) £7·25

94 **Respublica**, ed. L. A. Magnus. 1905. Superseded by O.S. 226.

95 **The History of the Holy Grail by Henry Lovelich**, Vol. V. See above, E.S. 28.

96 **Mirk's Festial**, ed. T. Erbe. Vol. I (*all published*) 1905, *reprinted* Kraus 1973. £6·50

97 **Lydgate's Troy Book**, ed. H. Bergen. Vol. I Prologue, Books I and II, 1906, *reprinted* Kraus 1973. (See E.S. 103, 106, and 126 for other parts.) £7·00

98 **John Skelton Magnyfycence**, ed. R. L. Ramsay. 1908 (*for* 1906), *reprinted* 1958. £3·25

99 **The Romance of Emaré**, ed. E. Rickert. 1908 (*for* 1906), *reprinted* 1958. £1·80

100 **The Middle English Harrowing of Hell and Gospel of Nicodemus**, ed. W. H. Hulme. 1908 (*for* 1907), *reprinted* 1961. £3·00

101 **Songs, Carols and other Miscellaneous Poems from Balliol MS. 354**, Richard Hill's Commonplace-book, ed. R. Dyboski. 1908 (*for* 1907), *reprinted* Kraus 1973. £4·25

102 **The Promptorium Parvulorum**: the First English–Latin Dictionary, ed. A. L. Mayhew. 1908, *reprinted* Kraus 1973. £9·50

E.S. 103, 106 **Lydgate's Troy Book,** ed. H. Bergen. Vol. II, Book III, 1908; £8·00
Vol. III, Books IV and V, 1910; *reprinted as one volume* Kraus 1973.
(See E.S. 97, 126 for other parts.)

104 **The Non-Cycle Mystery Plays,** ed. O. Waterhouse. 1909. Superseded by S.S. 1.

105 **The Tale of Beryn,** with a Prologue of the Merry Adventure of the £4·25
Pardoner with a Tapster at Canterbury, ed. F. J. Furnivall and W. G.
Stone. 1909, *reprinted* Kraus 1973.

106 **Lydgate's Troy Book,** Vol. III. See above, E.S. 103.

107 **John Lydgate The Minor Poems,** ed. H. N. MacCracken. Vol. 1 £4·25
Religious Poems. 1911 (*for* 1910), *reprinted* 1961. (See O.S. 192 for
Vol. II.)

108 **Lydgate's Siege of Thebes,** ed. A. Erdmann. Vol. I Text. 1911. £3·00
reprinted 1960. (See E.S. 125 for Vol. II.)

109 **The Middle English Versions of Partonope of Blois,** ed. A. T. Bödtker. £8·25
1912 (*for* 1911), *reprinted* Kraus 1973.

110 **Caxton's Mirrour of the World,** ed. O. H. Prior. 1913 (*for* 1912), £3·00
reprinted 1966.

111 **Raoul Le Fevre The History of Jason,** translated by William Caxton, £3·60
ed. J. Munro. 1913 (*for* 1912), *reprinted* Kraus 1973.

112 **Henry Lovelich's Merlin,** ed. E. A. Kock. Vol. II 1913, *reprinted* £2·60
1961. (See E.S. 93 and O.S. 185 for other parts.)

113 **Poems by Sir John Salusbury and Robert Chester,** ed. Carleton Brown. £2·80
1914 (*for* 1913), *reprinted* Kraus 1973.

114 **The Gild of St. Mary, Lichfield:** Ordinances and other documents, £1·50
ed. F. J. Furnivall. 1920 (*for* 1914), *reprinted* Kraus 1973.

115 **The Chester Plays,** ed. Dr. Matthews. Vol. II 1916 (*for* 1914), *re-* £2·20
printed 1967.

116 **The Pauline Epistles** in MS. Parker 32, Corpus Christi College, £6·50
Cambridge, ed. M. J. Powell. 1916 (*for* 1915), *reprinted* Kraus 1973.

117 **The Life of Fisher,** ed. R. Bayne. 1921 (*for* 1915), *reprinted* Kraus £2·60
1973.

118 **The Earliest Arithmetics in English,** ed. R. Steele. 1922 (*for* 1916), £1·90
reprinted Kraus 1973.

119 **The Owl and the Nightingale,** ed. J. H. G. Grattan and G. F. H. £2·20
Sykes. 1935 (*for* 1915), *reprinted* Kraus 1973.

120 **Ludus Coventriæ,** or The Plaie called Corpus Christi, Cotton MS. £3·60
Vespasian D. viii, ed. K. S. Block. 1922 (*for* 1917), *reprinted* 1961.

121 **Lydgate's Fall of Princes,** ed. H. Bergen. Vol. I 1924 (*for* 1918), £3·75
reprinted 1967.

122 **Lydgate's Fall of Princes,** ed. H. Bergen. Vol. II 1924 (*for* 1918), £3·75
reprinted 1967.

123 **Lydgate's Fall of Princes,** ed. H. Bergen. Vol. III 1924 (*for* 1919), £3·75
reprinted 1967.

124 **Lydgate's Fall of Princes,** ed. H. Bergen. Vol. IV 1927 (*for* 1919), £5·40
reprinted 1967.

125 **Lydgate's Siege of Thebes,** ed. A. Erdmann and E. Ekwall. Vol. II £4·00
Introduction, Notes, Glossary etc. 1930 (*for* 1920), *reprinted* Kraus
1973.

126 **Lydgate's Troy Book,** ed. H. Bergen. Vol. IV 1935 (*for* 1920), *re-* £9·75
printed Kraus 1973. (See E.S. 97, 103, and 106 for other parts.)

University Press, Oxford, England

DATE DUE

APR 04 2001			